A Place *for* Meaning

ART, FAITH, AND MUSEUM CULTURE

(front cover)

FOR SALE, BANGLAMPHU DISTRICT, BANGKOK, THAILAND

Jesse Kalisher

American, 2004, printed 2007; chromogenic print. Gift of Helen and Jesse Kalisher in memory of Ilse Kalisher. © 2004 Jesse Kalisher, 2007.9. (detail)

A Place *for* Meaning

ART, FAITH, AND MUSEUM CULTURE

Learning from the *Five Faiths Project* at the Ackland Art Museum

AMANDA MILLAY HUGHES

CAROLYN H. WOOD

Ackland Art Museum

The University of North Carolina at Chapel Hill

Publication of *A Place for Meaning: Art, Faith, and Museum Culture* was made possible by a generous grant from the Henry Luce Foundation with additional support from the William Hayes Ackland Trust.

A Place for Meaning: Art, Faith, and Museum Culture
Learning from the Five Faiths Project at the Ackland Art Museum
Ackland Art Museum
The University of North Carolina at Chapel Hill

Library of Congress Control Number: 2009905542
ISBN: 9780974365633

Published in the United States by:
Ackland Art Museum
The University of North Carolina at Chapel Hill
Campus Box 3400
Chapel Hill, North Carolina 27599-3400

Designed by:
Rivers Agency
Chapel Hill, North Carolina
www.riversagency.com

Printed in the United States by:
Correction Enterprises
Raleigh, North Carolina

Distributed by:
The University of North Carolina Press
116 Boundary Street
Chapel Hill, North Carolina 27514-3803
www.uncpress.edu

This is one of my favorite experiences, to think about what it would look like if museums got serious about the question: *What is the most important role that we can play in the world?*

– RAY WILLIAMS

CONTENTS

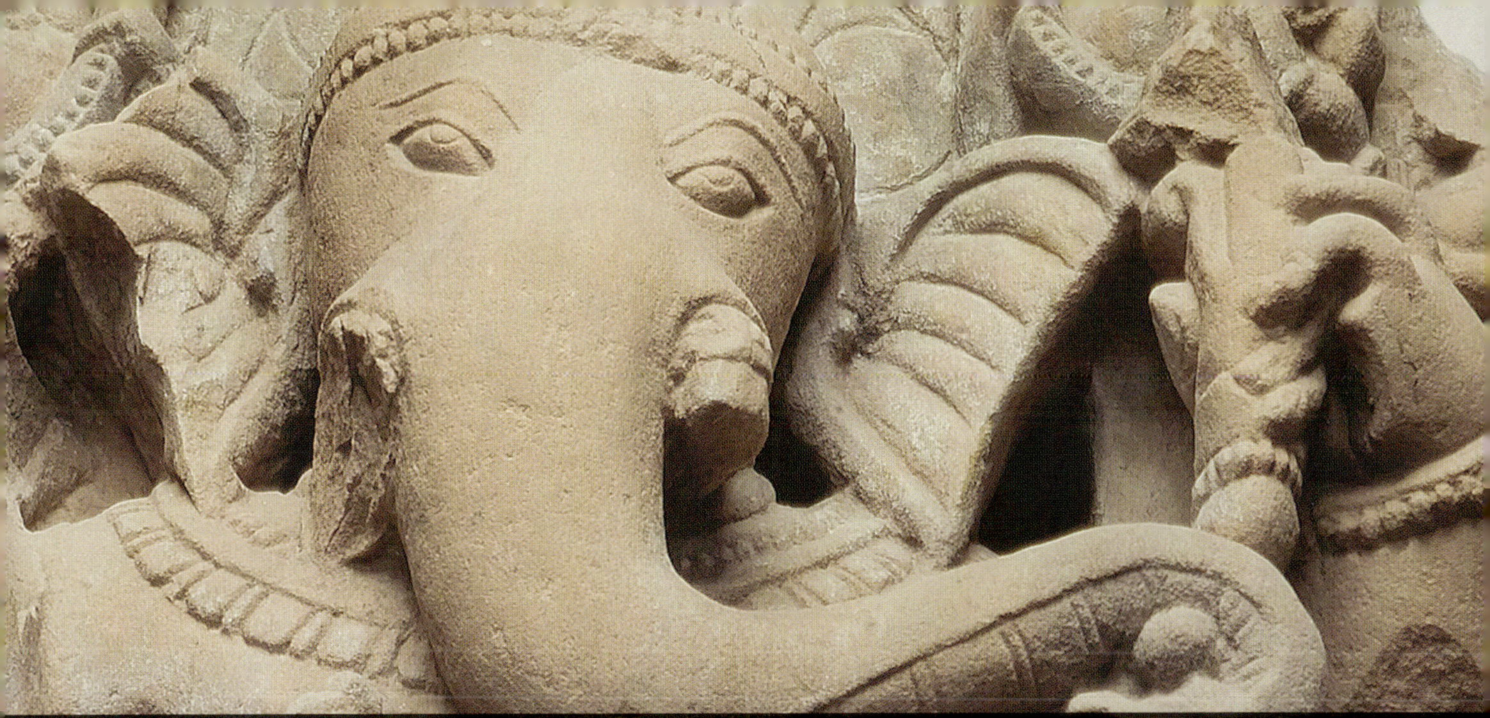

CAN THE MUSEUM BE A PLACE FOR MEANING?

... a place where art, faith, and the rigors of museum culture mesh to produce new opportunities to engage difference, build appreciation, and sustain relationships?

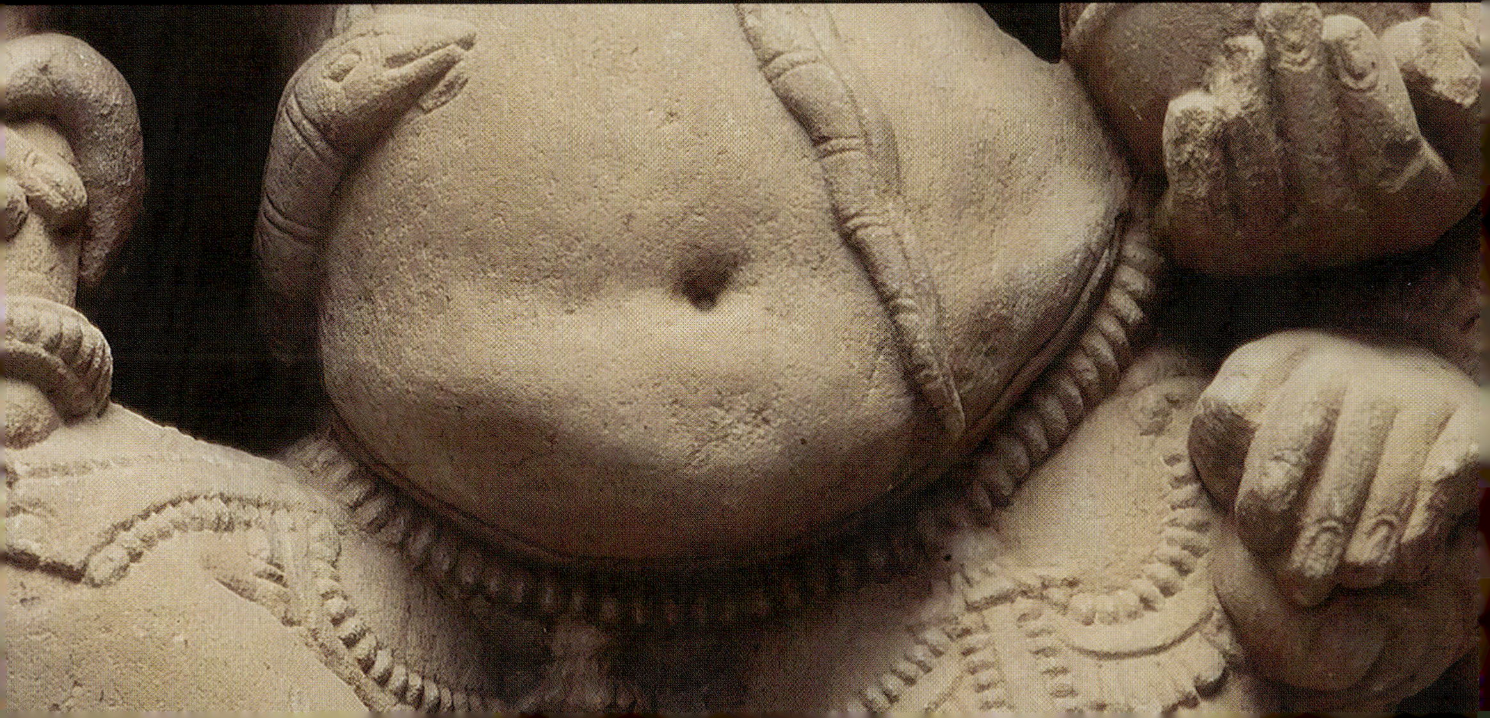

GANESHA

Unknown

Central Indian, 11th-12th century; sandstone. Gift of Clara T. and Gilbert J. Yager in honor of Dr. Charles Morrow and his wife, Mary Morrow, for their many contributions to the University and to the Ackland Art Museum during his term as Provost. 85.2.1. (detail)

This medieval stele of the Hindu diety Ganesha is carved in relief from sandstone. It is the amiable Ganesha who devotees invoke before an important undertaking and petition to remove barriers in life. Just as earthly elephants are capable of knocking down trees, the powerful Ganesha clears obstacles from one's path and assures safe passage into the future. Here the six-armed elephant-headed God is depicted in a lively pose, dancing and holding a goad, axe, pineapple, and a bowl of sweet balls (ladoos). He has daintily selected morsels from the bowl with his trunk and one of his right hands. Believers enjoy his very human, sensual nature and offer him sweets on festival days. Accompanying Ganesha (at the sculpture's lower left) is a tiny mouse which, despite its small size, serves occasionally as his steed.

FOREWORD

> The University of North Carolina at Chapel Hill serves "all the people of the state, and indeed the nation, as a center for scholarship and creative endeavor. The University exists to teach students at all levels in an environment of research, free inquiry and personal responsibility; to expand the body of knowledge; to improve the condition of human life through service and publication; and to enrich the culture."

Three months after my arrival on the campus of The University of North Carolina at Chapel Hill in 2006, the Museum presented and published *Fashioning the Divine: South Asian Sculpture at the Ackland Art Museum.* The exhibition and catalogue represented the culmination of more than five years of collaboration among UNC-Chapel Hill scholars, students, nationally recognized experts in the field of Asian art, local community members, and our own staff. The exhibition suggested the landscapes and traditions from which these objects emerged as well as presenting some of flavor of the many local communities who practice Hinduism and Buddhism in and around the Research Triangle area of North Carolina. The gallery included incense and saffron, photographs, object installations that suggested original context, and temple diagrams. It was a lush and ornate presentation, suggesting to visitors the diversity and the beauty of the world in South Asia, and the world in North Carolina. The catalogue published new research developed in a multi-year initiative bringing together scholars and graduate students in art history to study these twenty-six objects, many of which are included in this publication.

The *Five Faiths Project* was more than ten years old when I arrived and *Fashioning the Divine* opened to the public. Many of the lessons of the *Project* were visible in this exhibition and still fresh in people's minds. Collaboration, inclusivity, diversity, fairness, and parallel practice were frequently referred to in exhibition and interpretation planning meetings. Members of the Ackland staff demonstrated a curatorial hospitality rooted in what I now understand to be a direct outgrowth of the *Five Faiths Project.*

In the winter of 2009, Carolyn Wood and Amanda Hughes presented this book (in manuscript form) for my review. For the past several years, a little at a time, Carolyn and

Amanda worked on their book. Funded by two generous grants from the Henry Luce Foundation, they designed, organized, and facilitated a series of three colloquies with experts from across the campus and the nation. At the end of the series, the second grant allowed them time to complete this manuscript. Like the *Five Faiths Project* itself, the book was a bit of a mystery to me. When I finally had the chance to read it (having afforded them the privacy authors seem to appreciate), the manuscript gave me a deeper appreciation of the broad implications of the *Project*. The text offers an overview, a summary of the Ackland's initial investment, as well as the chance to listen in as more than thirty individuals, over the course of three years, gave their attention to the *Project* and the questions and conclusions emerging from it. Working from more than sixty-five hours of transcribed conversations, email exchanges, informal conversations, and formal presentations, the authors have compiled and created an important contribution to the field of museum interpretation and community outreach. By the end of the book, I found myself wishing I had participated in these remarkable sessions.

The development of the Ackland's collection and curatorial practices mirrors the development of the Research Triangle and the state of North Carolina. Since the Museum's founding in the late 1950s, we have diversified, a little at a time. What was once a collection firmly rooted in the Judeo-Christian tradition of European and American art, today, is increasingly diverse and international. The collection is strong in works of art from China, Japan, Thailand, as well as Africa. Works by artists from the Latin American countries of Mexico and Brazil have entered the collection. Like so many changes in our communities, the process of assimilating new groups and ideas into the hitherto mainstream is often an *ad hoc* process. But, the Ackland's tackling of the *Five Faiths Project* and the incorporation of all that the Museum learned from this *Project* represented maturity, clarity of purpose, and social responsibility to our evolving populations. By recognizing and acting on the importance of bringing art, people, and values together for greater understanding, the Ackland acted out its mission statement and invested in the future of the region and the nation.

From my perspective, the recommendations in this book offer a useful framework for more than just the interpretation of faith-based art in an art museum. New ideas about the inclusion of multiple voices, the "authority" of the curator, and an ongoing commitment to accuracy, balance, and fairness are applicable across collecting institutions, and represent important insights into the changing ways that people access information and construct meaning in the 21st century.

I want to thank Carolyn Wood and Amanda Hughes for their dedication to this *Project* and, as they say in this text, their commitment to hospitality that will inform our work for years to come. Without their dedication, and the thoughtful facilitation of this long-standing work, the knowledge born out of this Project would not have been published. I commend them for their skillfulness and the many ways in which this text demonstrates the core values of the *Project.* Similarly, I extend my thanks to the Henry Luce Foundation for funding this contribution to resources on best practices in museum interpretation.

Finally, I affirm, with the authors, the Colloquy participants, and all the community partners that yes, indeed, the Ackland Art Museum (together with museums across the nation) is a place for meaning and I thank each one for their contribution to our shared endeavor.

Emily Kass
Director of the Ackland Art Museum
April 2009

PREFACE

In the mid-1990s, Ray Williams discerned through his work as Ackland curator of education that the rapidly changing demographics of North Carolina were visible in the growing presence of school children practicing faith traditions new to the state, as well as an increasing number of children who appeared to be unaware of any faith tradition. As a native Tar Heel, he recognized tensions these demographic shifts provoked, and he understood the challenges these dynamics presented to public school teachers required by a state-mandated curriculum to teach about cultures with which they were often unfamiliar.

Williams' vision was to ground a world religions project in the Ackland's collection – which included Hindu, Buddhist, and Christian art – to promote understanding of emerging as well as established faith communities while developing resources to support K-12 schoolteachers in their fulfillment of the North Carolina Standard Course of Study. In 1995, we began to plan and develop an array of short-term exhibitions and long-term installations, acquisitions, and academic and community-based programs that over time embedded what became the *Five Faiths Project* throughout the whole Museum.

The *Project* gradually crystallized around three premises. First: works of art originally used in worship, when placed in the museum setting, can become powerful tools for promoting conversation and learning about diverse faith traditions and cultural practices. Second, as an art museum at a public, secular university, the Ackland would be a safe place to conduct potentially difficult conversations provided that the dialogue centered on works of art. In this dialogue, we could report, but we would not endorse the truth claims that inspired creation of the objects at hand. Finally, we would "*revoice*" the Museum, both its programs and publications, by engaging the multiple perspectives of scholars, museum professionals, educators, and most significantly, faith practitioners from our own North Carolina communities.

To augment the traditions already represented in the Ackland's collection, we increased the presence of Judaism and Islam through acquisitions and loans. To demonstrate the living vitality of faith cultures visible in objects made hundreds of years ago and to illuminate the evolution of visual language, it was essential that we exhibit and collect work by contemporary artists who created objects for use in worship or otherwise addressed cultures of faith. Museum collections and exhibitions, along with stories and photographs from faith practitioners in North Carolina, generated a core of curricular support materials and lesson plans tested in K-12 classrooms across this state and elsewhere while generating new public programming and engagement initiatives in Chapel Hill.

From its inception, the *Five Faiths Project* animated UNC-Chapel Hill's art museum as a laboratory to test ideas and create knowledge about works of art. As the Ackland was amplifying its national presence by circulating exhibitions and publications, so, too, with the *Five Faiths Project* we were seeking to design a model for community engagement that could be adapted and nurtured in museums elsewhere in the country. Yet questions proliferated, including those concerning the legal framework in which religious concepts could be investigated and acknowledged in secular settings, the best practices for studying cultures of faith in public schools, and what constituted appropriate language for comparing and differentiating among faith practices approached through religious works of art.

In this endeavor, we were fortunate to find a patron in the Henry Luce Foundation and a mentor in Michael Gilligan, its president. With reassuring support from the Luce Foundation and with Michael's guidance, we convened over the course of three years a think tank of scholars, faith community leaders, museum colleagues, educators, and others. Our goals included examining the obstacles and benefits of using works of art to introduce the practices and beliefs of faith communities; outlining best practices for engaging local faith communities as partners in interpreting sacred objects; and deepening knowledge about religious objects in the Ackland collection.

This book chronicles the proceedings and products of the resulting Luce Colloquies. Several papers prepared by the participants are included. The case studies and appendices offer guidance for nurturing respectful dialogue regarding religious objects. We hope that by communicating some of the processes tested and lessons learned along the way, we will encourage others to join in advancing our work of sharing, understanding, and celebrating the human and divine spirits manifest in works of art.

Gerald D. Bolas
January 12, 2009

The Ackland Art Museum gratefully acknowledges the following organizations, foundations, trusts, and individuals for their support of the *Five Faiths Project*:

The Henry Luce Foundation, Inc.
MetLife Foundation, Museum and Community Connections Grant
National Endowment for the Arts
North Carolina Humanities Council
The Randleigh Foundation Trust
Samuel H. Kress Foundation
Z. Smith Reynolds Foundation, Inc.
The William Hayes Ackland Trust
Members and Friends of the Ackland Art Museum

FIVE FAITHS
PROJECT CHRONOLOGY

1995	Initial planning and outreach
1997 – 1999	*Visions of Faith: Photographs by Wendy Ewald and Children* exhibition and catalogue *Voices of Faith* Louise Omoto Kessel with 40 volunteers public performances and audio recordings
2000	*Mass and Masterpiece: Celebrating the Eucharist in the Renaissance and Baroque* exhibition and brochure
2001	Five Faiths Curricular Resources for public school educators
2001 – 2003	*Buddhist Art and Ritual from Nepal and Tibet* exhibition and brochure
2002	*Word and Worship: Approaching Islam through Art* exhibition Five Faiths Colloquy (Year I) – Sacred Ground and Common Ground
2003	*Spectans Specula: Reflecting on Princely and Priestly Perfections* exhibition and brochure Five Faiths Colloquy (Year II) – Considering the Lives of Sacred Images
2004	*Seeking and Certainty: Conversations on art, faith, and our changing cultural landscape*
2004	Five Faiths Colloquy (Year III) – A Place for Meaning: Art, Faith, and Museum Culture
2004	*Five Artists, Five Faiths: Spirituality in Contemporary Art* exhibition and catalogue
2006	*Five Voices Five Faiths: an interfaith primer* (Cowley Books, Boston, MA) Amanda Millay Hughes, editor and contributing author, with Yaakov Ariel, Amy Nelson, Anantanand Rambachan, and Pat Phelan
2009	*A Place for Meaning: Art, Faith, and Museum Culture. Learning from the Five Faiths Project at the Ackland Art Museum*

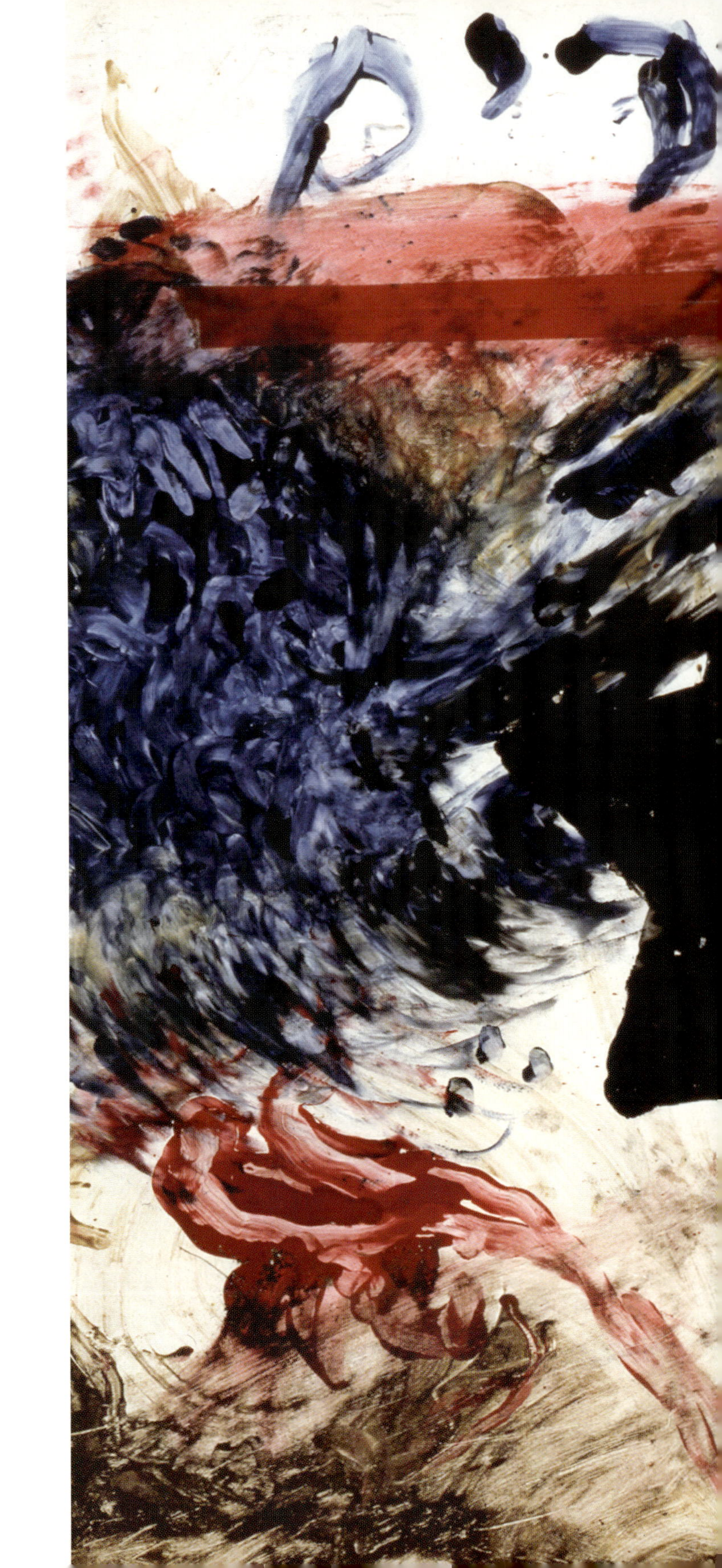

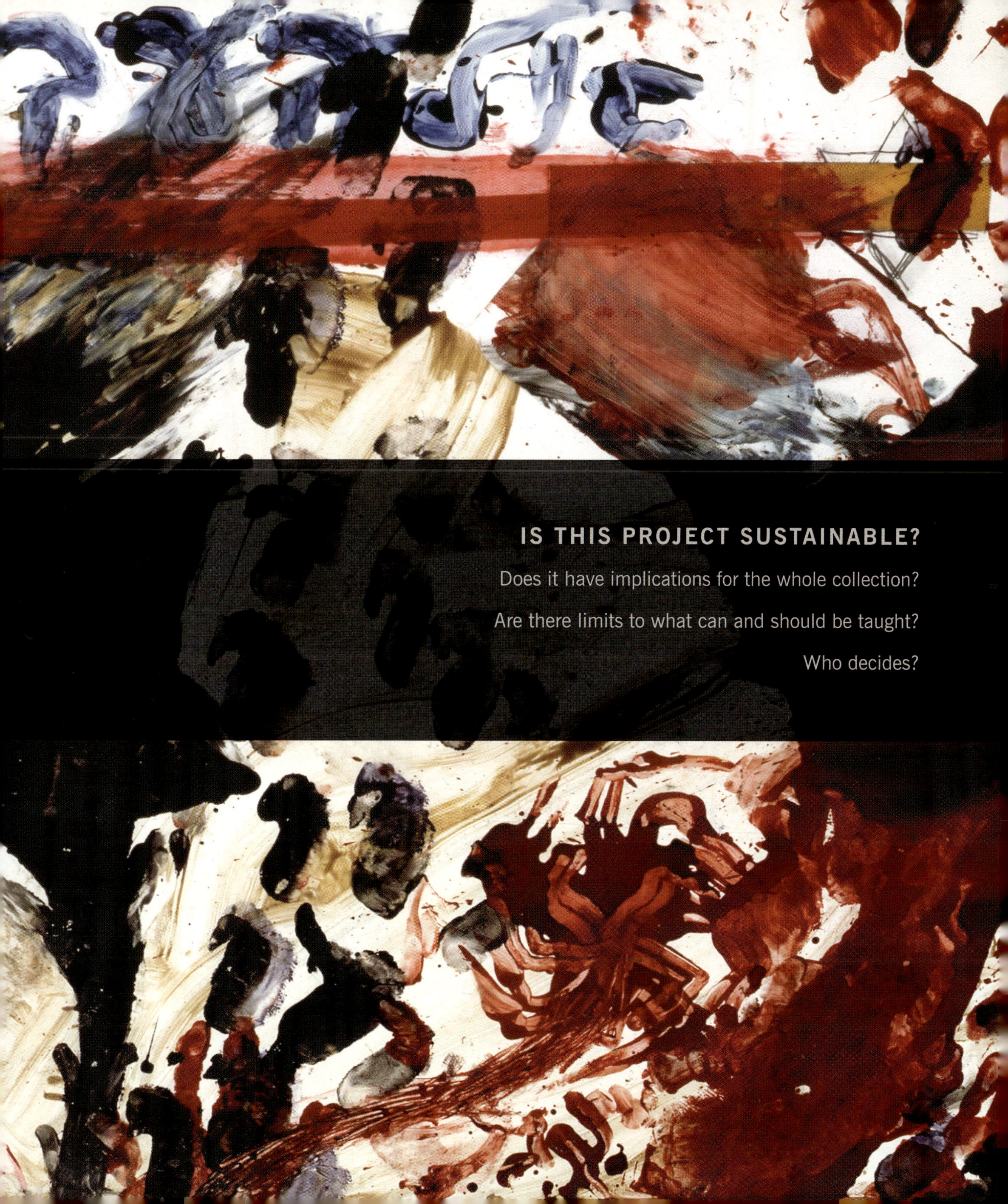

IS THIS PROJECT SUSTAINABLE?

Does it have implications for the whole collection?

Are there limits to what can and should be taught?

Who decides?

TO THE HEBREWS
Moshe Gershuni
Israeli, born 1936: 1984;
mixed media on paper.

Ackland Fund, 97.2.
(detail)

Introduction

> Museums are quintessentially places that have the potency to change what people may know, or think, or feel, to affect what attitudes they may adopt or display, to influence what values they form.[i]

> Art understood as expression differs from art understood as instruction. It invites conversation across personal and cultural borders, and can make alien ideas attractive. It is not clear, however, how far the arts can take us into understanding without, at some point, a direct address also to differences over theological beliefs and moral values.[ii]

In the early 1990s, the Ackland adopted a new mission statement that declares the Museum's intent to "animate, inspire, and transform people's lives with works of art." The idea that a museum might animate and inspire is not new. For generations, individuals and families, school groups and university students have visited museums as one way to enhance their understanding of the world around them. However, the idea that a museum has the potential to transform lives and thereby whole communities is newer and was reinforced by the Education Task Force of the American Association of Museums. Their published report, *Excellence and Equity: Education and the Public Dimension of Museums (1992)*, offered new guidelines and tips for approaching this transformational work and, with them, the assurance that transformation was a worthy mission.[1]

It was with this in mind that the Ackland embarked on a multiyear, multifaceted initiative to attract new audiences, reinterpret our collection, create new installations, exhibitions, and public programs, inform gallery teaching, and serve the broader community. What began as a project rooted in the K-12 education program at the Museum, eventually garnered support from major funding organizations and foundations, the attention of the local news media, and support from the community. Something about this project had what Stephen Weil called "the potency" to transform.

The *Five Faiths Project* is founded on the conviction that original works of art can be powerful tools for promoting conversation and learning about diverse faith traditions and cultural practices. Using works from the Ackland's permanent collection and relationships with university scholars and other friends and advisors, the Museum has been exploring the beliefs and practices of Hinduism, Judaism, Buddhism, Christianity, and Islam[2] with local and national audiences. We chose these five faiths for two pragmatic reasons: all have vibrant communities within our area, and the Ackland has, or could readily acquire, works of art from these traditions that meet the aesthetic needs of our collection plan and the expository needs of the *Project.*

The Research Triangle (Raleigh, Durham, and Chapel Hill) in North Carolina has experienced remarkable growth in the last twenty years. A region once defined by a white majority and an African American minority, North Carolina today is home to a wide range of immigrant communities. These chang-

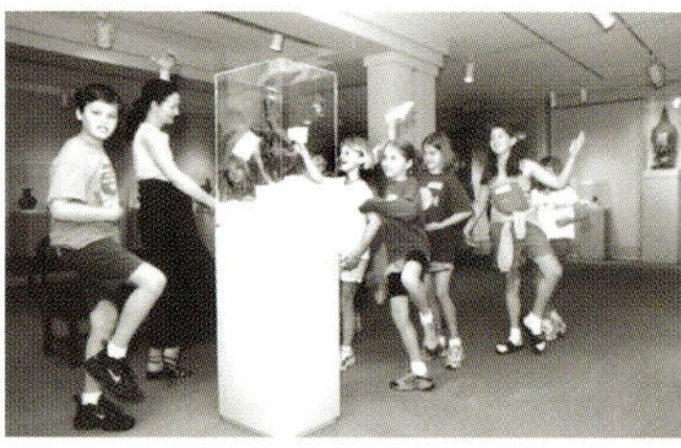

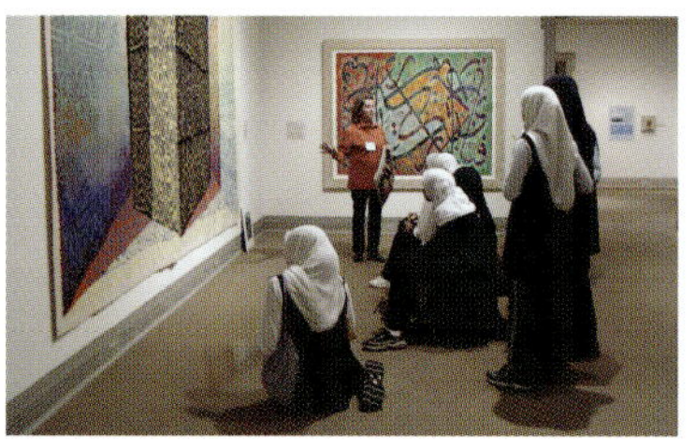

Public school students in front of the Ackland's *Mosque Lintel with Calligraphy.*

Kinesthetic learning is one way that students engage with works of art.

Students from Al Imam School, Islamic Center of Raleigh, visit the Ackland.

1 *Excellence and Equity: Education and the Public Dimension of Museums* is available online at *www.aam-us.org/sp/exc-eq.cfm*

2 Where possible, the Ackland lists the traditions included in the *Five Faiths Project* in order of historical appearance.

ing demographics have had a profound impact on state infrastructures: public schools and universities, hospitals, industries, and state-funded cultural institutions.

The Ackland saw an opportunity to bring together in the museum setting curators, educators, representatives of local faith communities, faith leaders, and the broader public to envision and embrace the benefits of pluralism. Over the course of the *Project*, the Ackland included the perspectives of people with clear faith affiliations – members of local and recognizable communities – as well as people with no apparent faith affiliation. Similarly, we approached scholars with expertise in the five traditions as well as scholars who expressed interest in the goals of the *Project* without academic credentials or familiarity with art, art history, or the historical or contemporary practices of these traditions. Often, simple enthusiasm for the idea that the *Five Faiths Project* might establish a place where the scholarship and practices of art and faith might come together peaceably and to the advantage of all was the entry point. As an art museum affiliated with a leading research university, the Ackland was well positioned to use our galleries as laboratories or at least as organizing tools for exploring the premise of the *Project*. Over the first few years, the *Project* grew from a temporary education outreach program to a more systematic approach to the Ackland's collection and to the Museum's interpretation of it.[3]

The Ackland's collection consists of more than 15,000 works of art, including North Carolina's premier collections of Asian art and works of art on paper. The collection easily supported discussion of Hinduism, Buddhism, and Christianity, but lacked objects from the Jewish and Islamic traditions. To include all five outlined traditions, new loans and acquisitions were essential. In 1996-97, as one of the initial activities of the *Project*, Ray Williams, then head of the education department of the Ackland, and Gerald D. (Jerry) Bolas, then director, dedicated substantial time and resources to identify what kinds of objects would promote the richest discussions of faith practices and beliefs, while meet-

---

3 With hindsight, perhaps a more systematic approach to the inclusion of our general audience members and a more aggressive outreach to people with no faith affiliation would have offered us another layer of insight and changed the course of the project. Similarly, the *Project* focused its initial activities almost exclusively on emerging communities. As we look ahead to the future of the *Project*, a more broadly conceived advisory council would be essential and membership in that council should not fall into as simple a qualification as "faith" or "no faith," "scholar" or "faith leader" might suggest. In retrospect, we understand that most of the people who were involved in the *Project* – including ourselves – defy such limited titles.

ing the aesthetic standards of the Museum. By upholding these aesthetic standards, the Ackland was able to fend off criticism that we might in some way diminish the Collection. The Museum never purchased objects solely for their functional value, but rather sought and found art objects of the highest quality possible within a limited budget.

Objects under consideration for the *Five Faiths Project* received the same careful scrutiny by the acquisitions committee as any other objects entering the collection. However, the acquisition process was accorded an additional range of expertise: faith leaders and religious studies scholars suggested the potential of certain types of objects as well-suited for teaching and learning, as well as objects from differing subtraditions that might encourage the exploration of the nuanced diversity within each tradition.

The original premise that works of art encouraged productive conversation and learning about diverse faiths proved true. Conversations with local faith communities generated new ideas for exhibitions, and outreach to scholars suggested the power of personal narratives and traditional stories to illuminate fundamental principles. The fields of ethnographic and documentary studies supported both a long-term approach to building relationships with and gathering stories from local congregations as well as the importance of documenting these relationships and stories with text, audio recordings, and images. With funding from the Williams Hayes Ackland Trust, Z. Smith Reynolds Foundation, Randleigh Foundation Trust, the National Endowment for the Arts, and the North Carolina Humanities Council, the Ackland undertook two community-based projects in 1997: *Visions of Faith: Photographs by Wendy Ewald and Children* and *Voices of Faith: Stories with Louise Omoto Kessel and Friends of the Ackland.*

Outreach to local faith communities brought more than

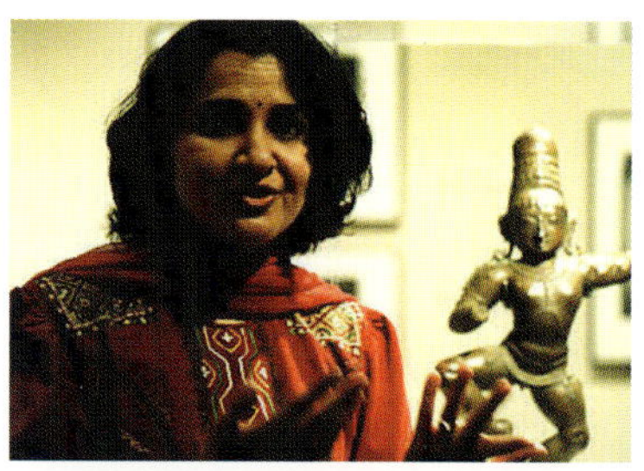

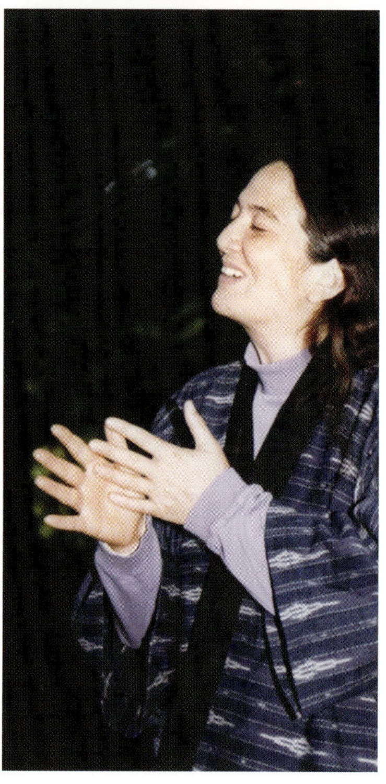

Surekha Pendyal was one of more than 40 volunteers who worked with Louise Omoto Kessel to create *Voices of Faith.*

Louise Omoto Kessel.

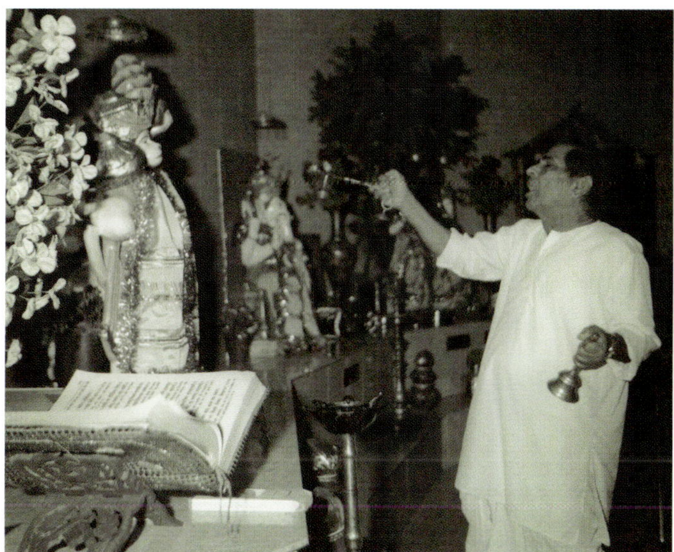

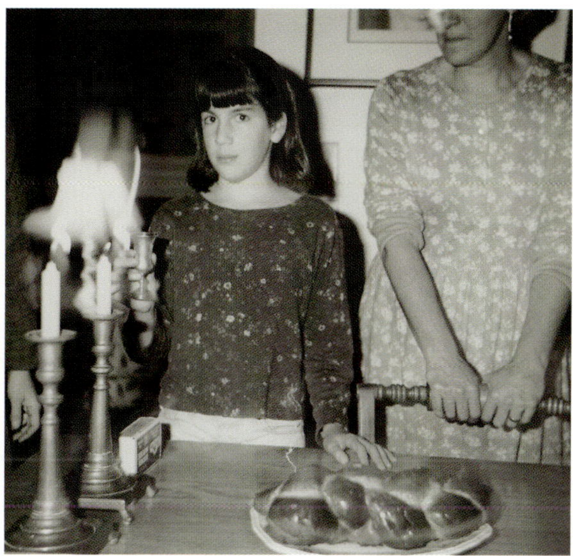

Visions of Faith presented photographs taken by children from local faith communities. Each image offered a new perspective on the local expressions of these traditions as well as insight into works in the Ackland Collection.

forty new volunteers to the Museum. Working with storyteller Louise Omoto Kessel, these volunteers learned how to tell faith-based stories and share them in performances in the Museum and other public venues. Outreach by Ackland educators engaged forty-six children between the ages of eight and thirteen from the Hindu Bhavan in Morrisville; Beth El Hebrew School in Durham; the Greensboro Buddhist Center; the Immaculate Conception Catholic Church in Durham; and Al-Iman School in Raleigh. The children worked with artist and documentary photographer Wendy Ewald to think about what they wanted their classmates to understand about their religion, as well as what could be learned from ritual objects, community activities, and family life.[4] Photography workshops began with these

4 For more information on Ewald's work with children see *www.wendyewald.com* and *I Wanna Take Me A Picture: Teaching Photography and Writing to Children* (Beacon Press, Boston MA, 2002)

children in 1997 and resulted in the exhibition *Visions of Faith*, which displayed the new documentary photographs together with ritual objects from the Ackland's collection, and accompanying catalogue in 1999.[5] The opening reception for the exhibition brought the most diverse audience the Ackland had ever experienced. Parents and grandparents arrived with their children to see the photographs. Regard for the perspectives of children engaged visitors to look closely not only at the images from their own communities, but to view all the images carefully. Christian families looked at pictures of Hindu dancers and Jewish families looked at images of a Buddhist ritual and festival.

Both of these projects brought new audiences to the Museum and fueled the next activity of the *Project*, the creation of curricular resources to meet the needs of teachers and students in North Carolina.

Working with LearnNC, the Ackland created *Krishna in Context*, a website now dated but still in use. The site was constructed to demonstrate our approach to objects with sacred content: one object interpreted from a variety of perspectives. The Ackland developed introductory texts for all five traditions and had them vetted by educators, scholars, and faith leaders; local designer Jennie Malcolm worked with Ackland staff to create posters featuring works from our collection, quotations from sacred texts, and strategies for interpreting the objects; and the Ackland recorded thirty stories told by participants in *Voices of Faith*. The materials were distributed at no charge to 135 North Carolina teachers and resource centers. All are available online at *www.ackland.org/fivefaiths*.

In *Visions of Faith*, the images produced by the young photographers gave audiences the opportunity to glimpse both public and private expressions of religious devotion and practice. Over the life of the *Project*, select images have been used in permanent gallery installations to suggest how our objects may have been used in their original contexts.

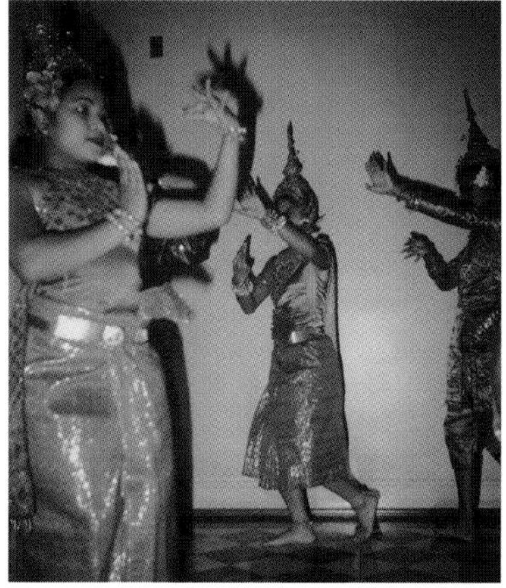

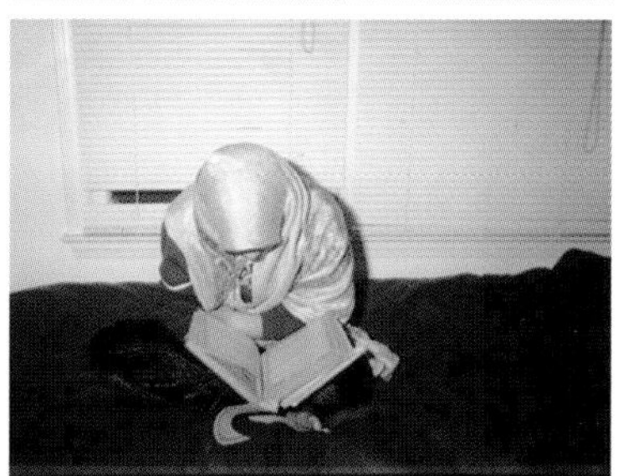

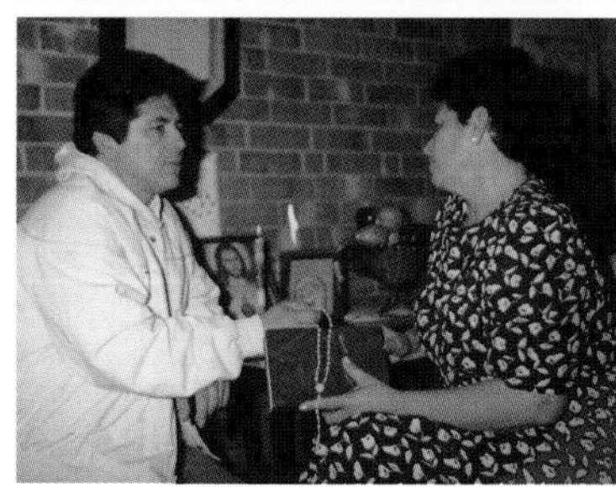

5 To order *Visions of Faith*, visit *www.ackland.org/art/public/* or call the Ackland at 919.966.5736

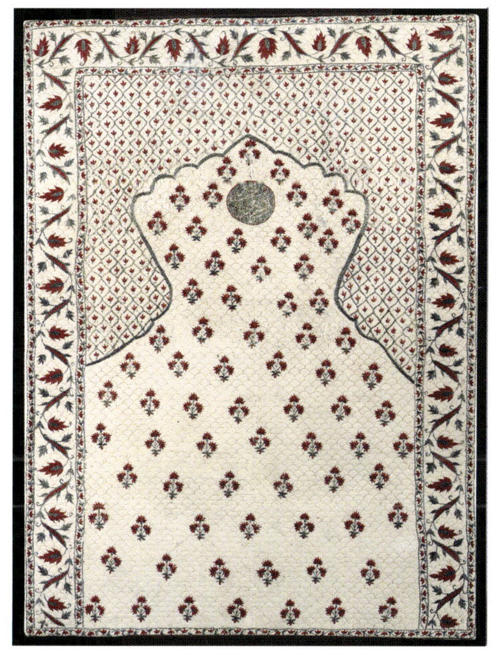

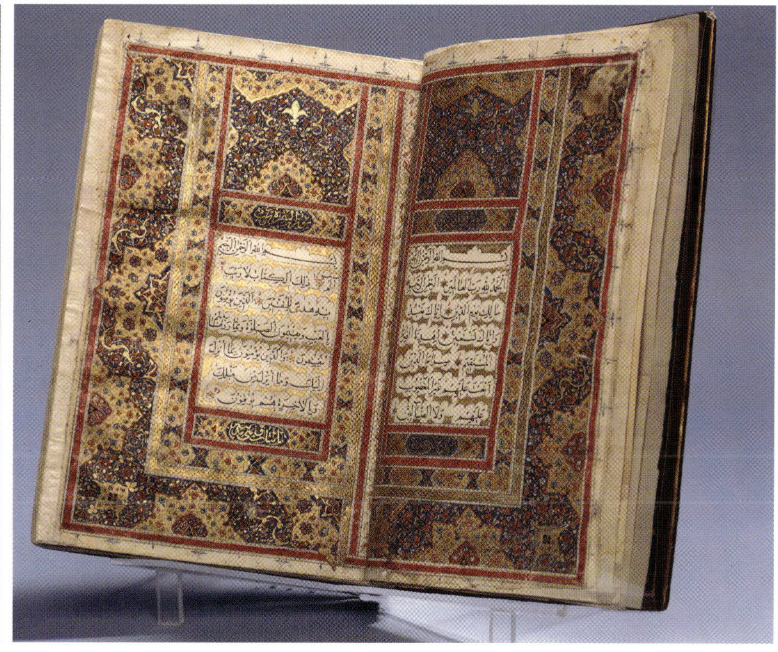

PRAYER MAT
Unknown
North Indian, Mughal, 18th century; silk embroidery on quilted cotton. Ackland Fund, selected by The Ackland Associates, 96.5.

COPY OF THE QUR'AN
Unknown
Persian, Qajar Dynasty, 19th century: 1828; ink, opaque watercolor and gold on paper; lacquer binding. Ackland Fund, selected by The Ackland Associates, 96.4.1.

Concurrent with these projects, the Ackland installed its new acquisitions, including a copy of the Qur'an and an Islamic prayer mat, a Kiddush cup and a Hannukiah. These new additions, along with interpretive materials, gave visitors to the Museum the opportunity to see and learn about these five traditions whether in the context of a school tour or as a solitary visitor. Each of these objects, and the additional objects acquired or borrowed over the life of the *Project*, offered a new window on the traditions and the many practices and beliefs that accompany them. The *Project's* success quickly manifested in a number of ways: overall attendance grew significantly between 1996 and 2001, from 31,000 visitors each year to 65,000, requests for Five Faiths tours and teacher training increased, and Ackland staff members were invited to conduct workshops on the *Project* and its implications for museums and

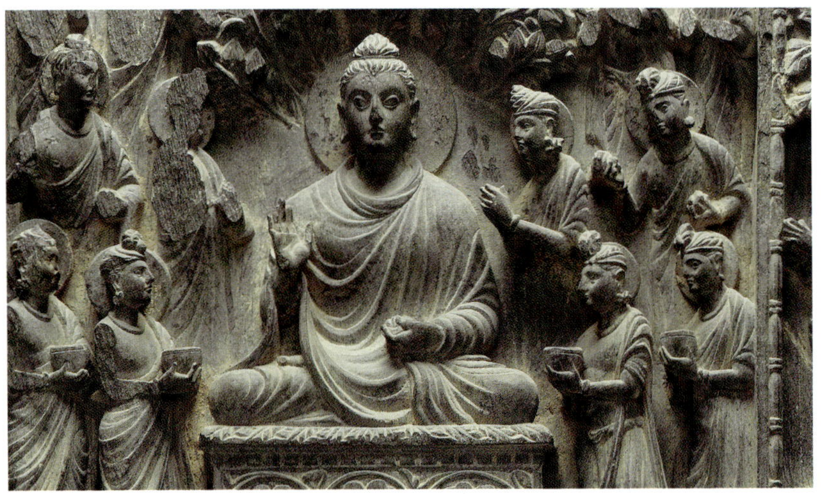

THE OFFERING OF THE FOUR BOWLS TO BUDDHA
Unknown
Gandhara region, 2nd century CE; schist. Gift of Clara T. and Gilbert J. Yager and Ackland Fund, 90.35. (detail)

public schools.[6]

As requests increased, the museum formalized its training of volunteer gallery teachers. From occasional and casual conversations about the Ackland's faith-based objects, museum educators developed a sequential program of lectures, off-site visits to places of worship, and assigned readings. What may not have been evident then, but is now, were all the ways in which teachers and their students began to see the Ackland as a new kind of resource for information about the beliefs and practices of these five faiths. The authority of the Museum and the University made the Ackland a trusted ally in the efforts of local teachers to meet specific objectives of the

6 Ray Williams and other Ackland educators have conducted workshops on the *Five Faiths Project* for museum staff and gallery teachers at more than twenty art museums across the country, including the National Gallery, Washington, D.C., the Museum of Fine Arts, Boston, the Toledo Museum of Art, the Getty Museum, the Museum of Fine Arts, Houston, and others. In addition, the *Project* received an award from the American Association of Museums for Educational Resources. While there are undoubtedly many other contributing factors to this growth, the Ackland's community outreach for the *Five Faiths Project* played a significant role.

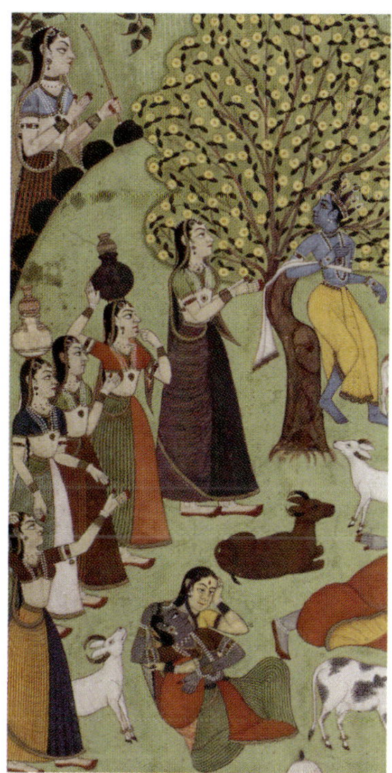

KRISHNA AND THE GOPI GIRLS
Unknown
20th century; opaque watercolor and gold. Gift of Clara T. and Gilbert J. Yager, 87.2. (detail)

Over time, the leadership and others involved with of the Hindu Bhavan in Morrisville, North Carolina, like members of so many faith communities, became invaluable resources for understanding traditional narratives as part of contemporary practice. In this image, Krishna is seen with women who tend the goats. According to the narratives, the Gopi Girls are examples of unyielding devotion to Krishna.

North Carolina Standard Course of Study.[7]

This prompted new questions and concerns, and a deepening sense of responsibility. Educators and leadership within the Museum found themselves confronting complex questions. Among them, is this *Project* sustainable? Does it have implications for the whole collection? Are there limits to what can and *should* be taught about contemporary faith experience with objects from an historical collection? How might museum installations overcome the inherent limitations of a single object to convey the richness and diversity within each faith over time and across cultures? To address these and other concerns, the Ackland realized its need to draw upon more of the resources of the University, other museum professionals, and national faith leaders to examine the original premise of the *Project* and assist in realizing its promise.

At the same time, an opportunity arose to present the Ackland's altarpiece, *Madonna and Child with Saints* attributed to Jacopo del Sellaio, in an installation suggesting its original worship context.[8] For the first time, the Ackland had an opportunity to test the limits and potential of a work of art in con-

7 The North Carolina Standard Course of Study can be viewed online at *www.dpi.state.nc.us/curriculum/*. In every state in which there is a uniform course of study, there is a requirement that students learn about world religions. Research at the Ackland showed that the resources available to teachers to meet these objectives were few and that important consideration of the plurality of belief systems evident in our public schools was emerging in classrooms and courtrooms all across America. The *Five Faiths Project* developed resources to be used as supplemental material in classrooms across North Carolina and beyond. To learn more about the Ackland's outreach and service to public school teachers, visit *www.ackland.org/education/fivefaiths/ff_index.html.* Sample materials designed to assist teachers in approaching objects are included in the Tools for Teaching and Learning chapter of this text.

8 The Samuel H. Kress Foundation's *Old Masters in Context* program provided funding to research and present the altarpiece within the broader context of historical Catholic practice. See Chapter I, Case Study 1: *Mass and Masterpiece* for more information on this process and the resulting exhibition.

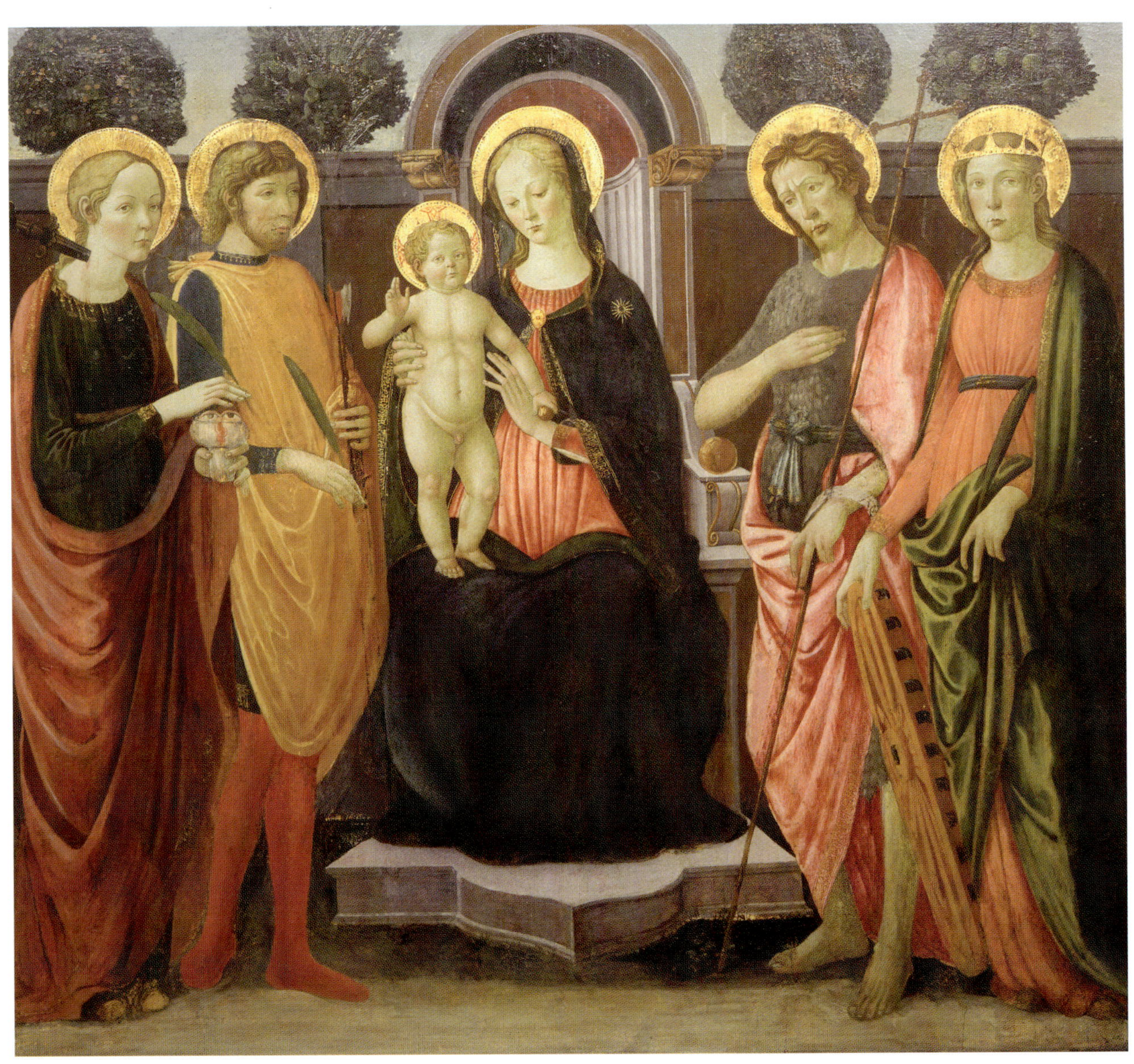

THE MADONNA AND CHILD WITH SAINTS
Attributed to Jacopo del Sellaio, Italian, Florence, ca. 1441-1493; tempera and gold on wood. The William A. Whitaker Foundation Art Fund, 63.18.1. (detail)

text as a strategy to promote understanding of an active faith tradition in North Carolina. At the time, and still today, Catholicism in North Carolina is a minority faith faced with many of the same strains that other minority traditions experience. Misunderstandings of core doctrine – among other long standing and deeply held prejudices regarding Catholics and Catholic practice, including the role of immigrant communities in enlarging the local Catholic presence – alerted the Ackland to the complexity of what we, somewhat naively, were striving to accomplish with the Five Faiths *Project*.[9]

In response, the Ackland applied for and received funding from the Henry Luce Foundation to engage thirty participants to consider various aspects of the *Project* over the course of three annual colloquies. In year one, emphasis was given to the limits and potential of visual communication and verbal representation in the context of exhibitions and installations of art with sacred content. In year two, topics included the reductive nature of traditional museum labels and the impact of multiple voices and contextual materials as tools for deepening understanding and appreciation of works of art with complex histories and biographies. In the final year, the implications and benefits of exhibitions that include traditional *and* contemporary works of art to deepen conversations about "then and now, there and here" produced new strategies for taking the best aspects of the *Five Faiths Project* and using them to establish the art museum as a place for meaning – a place where art, faith, and the rigors of museum culture mesh to produce new opportunities to engage difference, build appreciation, and sustain relationships.

Each Colloquy included prepared talks addressing specific issues, extended conversations in small and large groups, art-based activities that tested and problematized our emerging conclusions, and a considerable amount of informal conversation and subsequent correspondence that suggested that the *Five Faiths Project* had implications for museums (with and without multicultural collections) across the country. With additional funding from the Henry Luce Foundation, this book is our attempt to extract from the experience of community-based projects, exhibitions, public programs, and stimulating conversations with colloquy participants some principles, applications, and caveats for museum professionals and funders. We also recognize that the book may interest mu-

---

9 See Chapter I, Case Study 1: *Mass and Masterpiece* for a more thorough discussion of these complexities.

seum visitors as they consider how objects are selected, interpreted, and presented in galleries around the world. We hope readers will draw on this foundational work to create new museum-based projects that ask and answer new questions based on changing cultural and societal circumstances.

Over the years and under the auspices of the *Five Faiths Project*, the Ackland has launched a variety of ventures not referenced in this text. It is impossible to name all the collaborative partners. We are indebted to all the storytellers, young photographers, and their parents who joined the *Project* early and gave us a window on their unique experiences. Also worthy of thanks are the artists who contributed to exhibitions and programs, as well as the many museum interns and work-study students whose efforts amplified and refined both the tangible products of the *Project* and our thinking. Many communities of faith showed us remarkable hospitality and shared critical insights. Our colleagues in the Museum also sharpened our thinking with exacting questions and, in some cases, with memorable resistance. The Ackland is also grateful to the volunteer gallery teachers who were willing to learn new ways of presenting objects in our collection, and the entire education staff who worked tirelessly to develop, improve, and refine lesson plans and interpretive materials for formal and informal learning in the galleries.

We owe a special thanks to Ray Williams and Jerry Bolas who entrusted us with what had been their *Project* and encouraged us to take it in new directions as we imagined them. Finally, we are grateful to Peter Iver Kaufman. With his visionary assistance, what began as a community outreach program became a more analytical consideration of the intersection of art, faith, and museum culture in contemporary society.

We are deeply indebted to all the individuals who shared

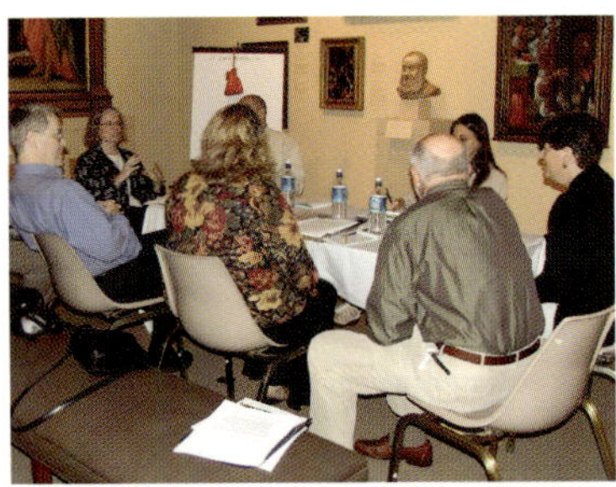

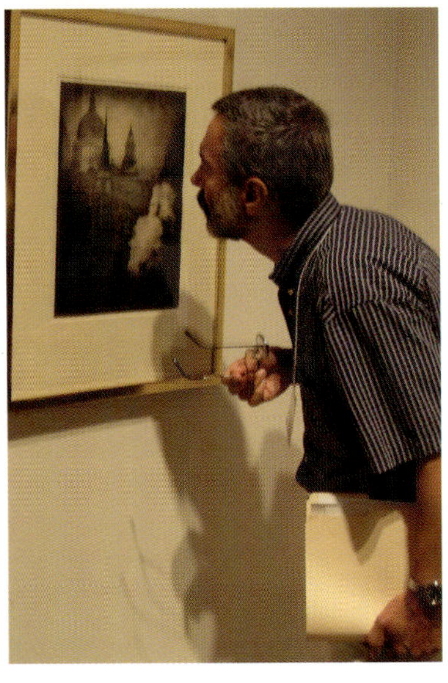

Small-group discussions allowed participants from different backgrounds and with different experiences to work together on the implications of presentations and other large group discussions.

Every small-group had a designated note-taker to ensure that final materials reflected these conversations as well as the large group sessions.

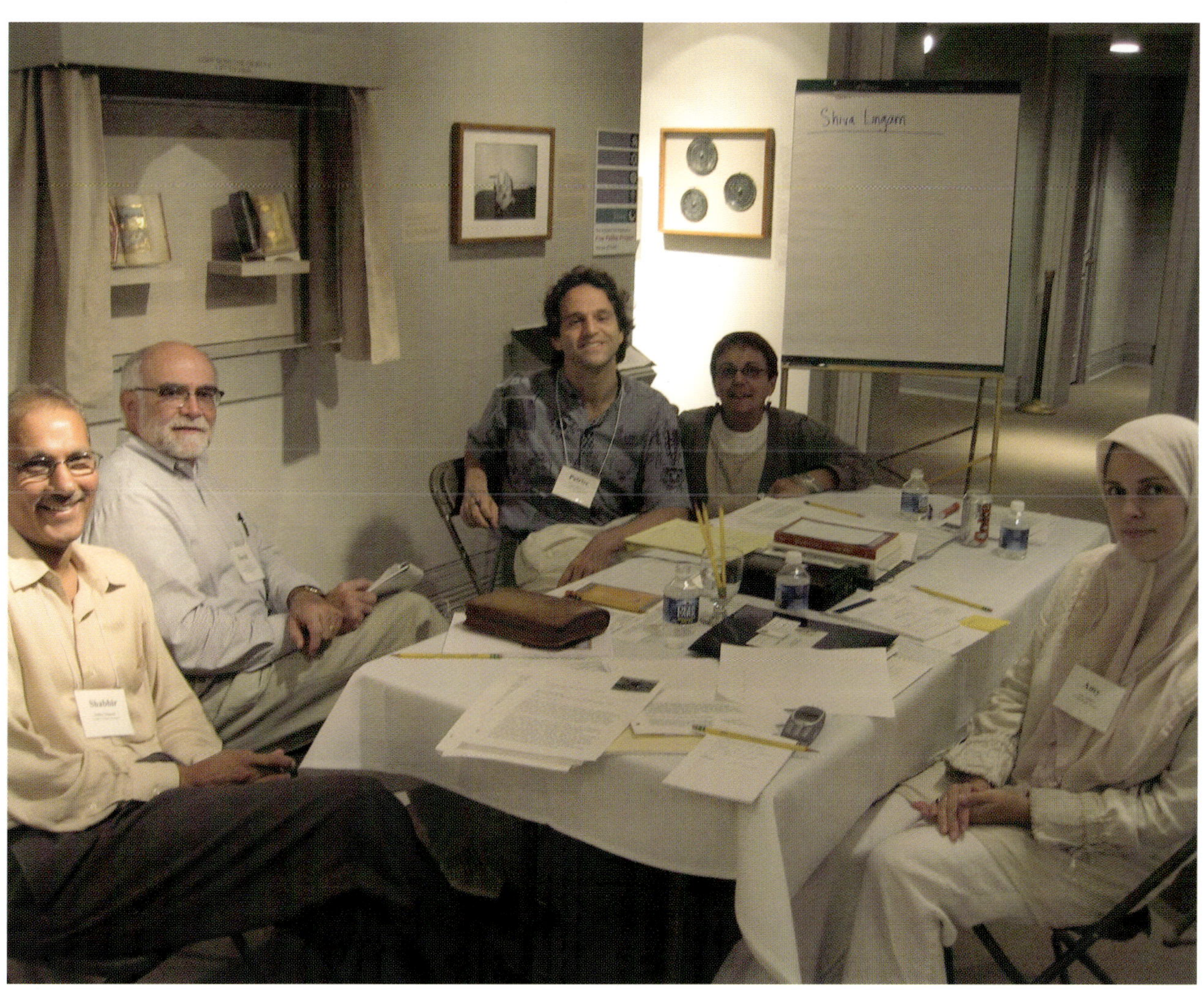

Because the groups met in the galleries, participants were able to use installations, objects, and labels as examples during small-group sessions.

their expertise, their insights, and their questions with us during the Colloquies:[10]

10 All titles and affiliations are correct at the time of this book's first publication and may not reflect the status and affiliation of all the participants at the time of the Colloquies. Not all participants attended all three years.

Yaakov Ariel

Department of Religious Studies, The University of North Carolina at Chapel Hill

Mark Bozzuti-Jones

Priest for Pastoral Care and Nurture, Trinity Wall Street, New York, New York

Patrice Brodeur

Department of Religious Studies, University of Montreal, Canada

David Carr

Retired, School of Information and Library Science, The University of North Carolina at Chapel Hill

Richard H. Davis

Religion Program, Bard College, Annandale-on-Hudson, New York

Terry Dempsey, S.J.

Director, Museum of Contemporary Religious Art, Saint Louis University

Mimi Gardner Gates

Former Director, Seattle Art Museum

Michael Gilligan

President, Henry Luce Foundation, Inc., New York, New York

Charles C. Haynes

Senior Scholar, Freedom Forum World Center, First Amendment Center, Washington, D.C.

Heather Kane

Department of Sociology, University of North Carolina at Chapel Hill

Eugene Korn

Former Director of Interfaith Affairs, Anti-Defamation League

Vivian B. Mann

Morris & Eva Feld Chair in Judaica, The Jewish Museum, New York, New York

Shabbir Mansuri

Director, The Institute on Religion and Civic Values, Los Angeles, California

Sharon Mars

Assistant Director of Spiritual Life at Wexner Heritage Village, Columbus, Ohio

Amy Nelson

On-air broadcaster, WUNC-Radio, and Islamic faith practitioner

Charles D. Orzech

Department of Religious Studies, The University of North Carolina at Greensboro

Josho Pat Phelan

Taitaku, Chapel Hill Zen Center, Chapel Hill, North Carolina

David N. Power, OMI

Professor Emeritus, The Catholic University of America, Washington, D.C.

Anantanand Rambachan

Religion Department, St. Olaf College, Northfield, Minnesota

Lynn Szwaja

Director of Theology, Henry Luce Foundation, Inc., New York, New York

Ruth Slavin

Curator for Education, The University of Michigan Museum of Art, Ann Arbor, Michigan

Thomas A. Tweed

Department of Religious Studies, University of Texas at Austin

Meera S. Viswanathan

Dean of the Faculty and Sheikh Salman bin Hamad Al-Khalifa Distinguished Chair in the Theory and Practice of Knowledge, The King's Academy, Madaba-Manja, Jordan

Ray Williams

Director of Education, Harvard Art Museums, Harvard University, Cambridge, Massachusetts

Christopher C. Wilson

Department of Art, The George Washington University, Washington, DC

Barbara Diane Wudel

The Divinity School, Wake Forest University, Winston-Salem, North Carolina

Ackland Staff:

Carolyn Allmendinger, *Director of Academic Programs*

Leslie Balkany, *Educator*

Gerald D. Bolas, *Former Ackland Director*

Beth Shaw McGuire, *Educator*

Barbara Matilsky, *Former Ackland Curator of Exhibitions*

We also wish to thank Emily Kass, current director of the Ackland, for giving us the time and space to complete this work among our other duties. Colloquy participants Jerry Bolas, Ray Williams, Charles Orzech, Charles Haynes, and Lynn Szwaja read a draft of this book and offered several important corrections and additions. Ulrike Guthrie and Suzanne Rucker provided invaluable editorial assistance. Ackland intern Lauren Sanford patiently gathered images for this publication.

Our deepest gratitude goes to Michael Gilligan, president, and Lynn Szwaja, program director for theology of the Henry Luce Foundation, for their commitment, their wise counsel, and their remarkable belief in the potential of the *Five Faiths Project* to inform museum practices across the country.

Amanda Millay Hughes *Carolyn H. Wood*

HOW TO READ THIS BOOK

A Place for Meaning introduces the Colloquy findings through three summary chapters that present aspects of the conversations and conclusions of each annual gathering. At the end of each of the first two chapters, two or three of the papers presented are included along with abstracts of other presentations. A complete transcript of the opening panel discussion follows the third chapter. Each chapter includes at least one case study to demonstrate how the Ackland applied the suggestions and conclusions within the context of museum exhibitions, programs, installations, and publications.

In the conclusion, the authors present their final recommendations to curators, educators, and directors. Appendices offer museum educators tools for training volunteer gallery teachers and examples of published materials in which these principles were applied. These materials were developed for use in training volunteer gallery teachers, public school educators, and as resources for visitors who wished to learn more about the *Project.*

Extensive illustrations serve to demonstrate the Ackland's core value for the presentation of works of art and our belief in the power of images as effective vehicles of communication. Certain objects proved to be highly evocative for the *Project.* Some of these objects appear in multiple locations within this text.

We have done our best to represent accurately the tenor of the colloquy conversations and to present ideas in the order in which they emerged from Colloquy I through Colloquy III. Working from verbatim transcripts, we have edited for clarity.

---

i *Making Museums Matter*, Stephen E. Weil, Smithsonian Institution Press, 2002.

ii Dan Pals, Colloquy I, Keynote address.

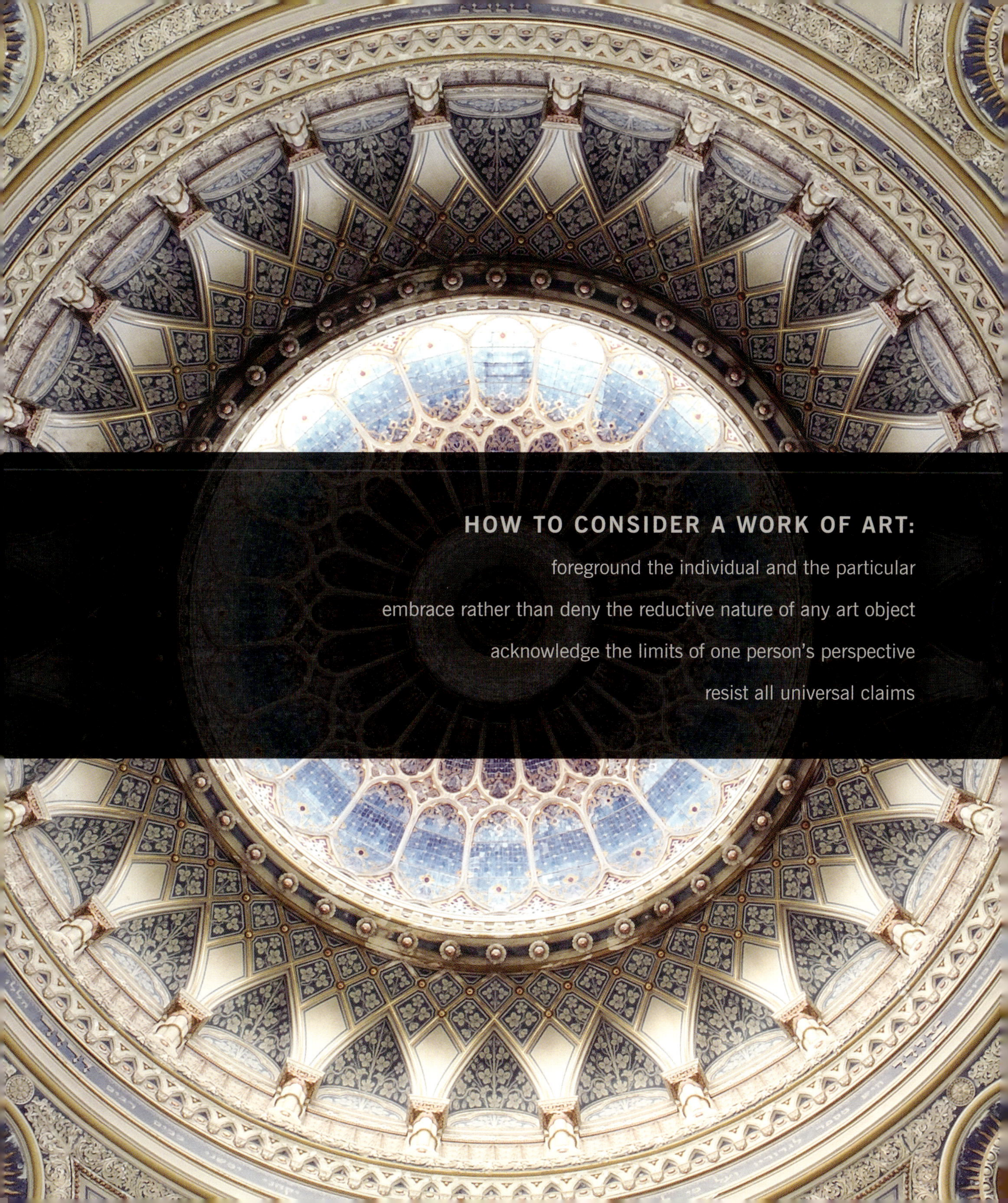

HOW TO CONSIDER A WORK OF ART:

foreground the individual and the particular

embrace rather than deny the reductive nature of any art object

acknowledge the limits of one person's perspective

resist all universal claims

**DOME #30705,
NEW SYNAGOGUE,
SZEGED, HUNGARY**
David Stephenson
American, born 1955: 2000,
printed 2004; c-print.
Ackland Fund, 2006.17.1.
(detail)

Colloquy I

SACRED GROUND AND COMMON GROUND

In the catalogue for *Visions of Faith*, Ray Williams opens his essay like this:

> The story begins with children: visitors to the art museum who want to know "Why are there so many paintings of that lady in the blue dress?" "What did they use *that* for?" "Why are that man's ear lobes so long?" The museum is a natural environment for such questions, and although the answers move us into discussions of religious belief and practice, the conversation feels safe. Nobody is in danger of being converted to another faith, and some very significant learning can begin with the questions these objects evoke.

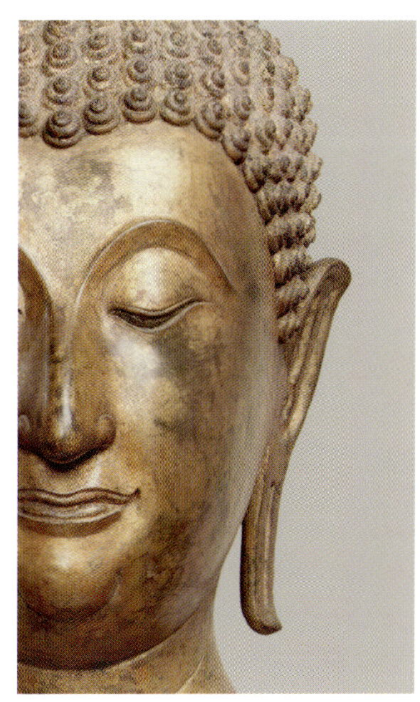

HEAD OF THE BUDDHA
Unknown
Thai, 13-15th century: gilt bronze.
Ackland Fund, 91.2. (detail)

The first five years of the *Five Faiths Project* focused on the needs of children, particularly public-school children in North Carolina. Certainly adults were engaged through the *Stories of Faith* and other programs, both as volunteers and as audiences. For the most part, however, the *Project*'s exhibitions, curricular resource materials, and stories were intended to support the

North Carolina Standard Course of Study. Their goal, as Williams put it, was to "foster interfaith dialogue and understanding."[1]

But as the *Project* grew and engaged more and more of the Museum's staff and resources, questions emerged concerning our institutional responsibilities. As a publicly funded museum, could the Ackland afford to be so strongly identified with a project that might be construed to promote religious devotion? Similarly, as a university art museum, could we continue to present introductory materials that were reductive in nature without represesenting the complexities, nuances, and changes over time within these traditions? Finally, as an art museum, was the *Five Faiths Project* leading us away from our primary mission to acquire, preserve, and interpret works of art?

The Colloquies gave us the opportunity to reflect on the very nature of the *Project* and critically assess its costs, benefits, fundamental premise, and future.

To prepare for the first Colloquy, we gave the participants – religious studies scholars, faith leaders, and museum professionals – two fundamental issues that had emerged from the Ackland's considerations of our work to date:

1 the inherent problem of appropriate (and appropriating) language in efforts to teach about and understand the five faith traditions
2 the potential and the limitations of works of art as communicators of faith-based ideas, beliefs, and narratives in a pluralistic and predominantly secular American culture

We also reminded the participants of the original premise of our proposed undertaking: "The *Five Faiths Project* is founded on the conviction that centering conversations about faith traditions on works of art originally used in worship promotes objective and thoughtful consideration of those traditions, while also inhibiting unproductive ideological debates that impede tolerant understanding and learning." We did not send them exhibition catalogues, curricular resource materials, or any other materials developed by the *Project*. Our intent was to ensure that they focused on the questions raised by the

1 *Stories of Faith* presented a series of programs at the Ackland, area community colleges, and area worship centers. The performances were funded by a grant from the North Carolina Humanities Council. Over time, the entire enterprise with the storytellers and Kessel became known as *Voices of Faith*.

premise itself and not the strengths or weaknesses of our application of that premise.

We talked with all the participants in advance of the first meeting. These conversations helped us frame some of our initial questions, including:

- How do museums craft an environment conducive to teaching and learning about diverse religious traditions in the galleries?
- How might museums establish framing principles or values?
- By what means do museums communicate what they consider appropriate responses to objects?
- What happens when museums expand their definitions of "appropriate" to allow for feelings of empathy and reverence toward sacred objects?

After these initial conversations, we invited several participants to prepare and present short responses to the fundamental issues. Charles Haynes discussed First Amendment issues. Meera Viswanathan examined several constraints and considerations related to the use of language in the exhibition of sacred objects. Charles Orzech presented some of the implications of understanding the museum as a "contact zone" for diverse communities. While every presentation and discussion informed the next presentation and subsequent discussions, for the sake of brevity and clarity for readers, we have edited more than sixty hours of presentations and discussions among thirty-five participants over three years into a series of focused presentations that most clearly define a path for the *Five Faiths Project* and the Museum as a cultural institution.

The authors are grateful for the work of all the participants. Museum educators in particular, who may appear to be underrepresented in this manuscript, were remarkably adept teachers in every session. Their examples of the power of narratives, the potential of objects to engage, their candor about their struggles with curators and directors (some of whom were in the room with them) gave the outsiders to museum culture a powerful taste of the tensions that flow through the offices of a museum. Similarly, the three museum directors, Mimi Gates, Terry Dempsey, S.J., and Jerry Bolas, provided important context for the participants by explaining their concerns about museum identity, funding restrictions, and donor concerns. Curators and scholars shared their expertise, taking notable risks in working outside their comfort zones as they listened to faith practitioners challenge their presentation and interpretation of beliefs and practices.

The faith leaders brought a remarkable sensitivity to the nuances of lived practice in light of tradition. All the participants engaged in every activity and every conversation with a generosity and kindness we could never have anticipated or required.

The first Colloquy attempted to define two territories navigated by the *Five Faiths Project*: the sacred ground of five distinct faith traditions and the common ground of the art museum. The *Project* asserted that museums could be "safe" places for inquiry and learning about world faiths. While no one challenged this premise, as the *Project* expanded, the dividing line between sacred ground and common ground seemed to blur. Throughout the Colloquies there were discussions of the term "faith" as well as a basic assumption of the benefit of pluralism.[2] The Ackland invited into the conversations Charles Haynes, senior scholar for the First Amendment Center at the Freedom Forum World Center, in the hope that he would give us a civic framework in which to define the boundary between endorsement and empathy when presenting works with sacred content in the museum context. According to Supreme Court Justice Sandra Day O'Connor, "The typical museum setting, though not neutralizing the religious content of a religious painting, negates any message of endorsement of that content," and therefore is protected under religious liberty clauses, but we were concerned that the Ackland, by actively drawing attention to religious content, may have become an atypical museum setting.[3]

Haynes articulated several key points to bear in mind when museums present material loosely defined as having "sacred content."

---

2 A discussion of the use of the word "faith" begins on page 38 and is noted later, on page 76.

3 Lynch, Mayor of Pawtucket, et al. v. Donnelly et al. Supreme Court of the United States, 465 U.S. 668.March 5, 1984: Pawtucket's display of its creche, I believe, does not communicate a message that the government intends to endorse the Christian beliefs represented by the creche. Although the religious and indeed sectarian significance of the creche, as the District Court found, is not neutralized by the setting, the overall holiday setting changes what viewers may fairly understand to be the purpose of the display as a typical museum setting, though not neutralizing the religious content of a religious painting, negates any message of endorsement of that content. The display celebrates a public holiday, and no one contends that declaration of that holiday is understood to be an endorsement of religion. The holiday itself has very strong secular components and traditions. Government celebration of the holiday, which is extremely common, generally is not understood to endorse the religious content of the holiday, just as government celebration of Thanksgiving is not so understood. The creche is a traditional symbol of the holiday that is very commonly displayed along with purely secular symbols, as it was in Pawtucket.
www.law.cornell.edu/supct/html/historics/USSC_CR_0465_0668_ZC.html

1. Because the museum setting has authority, what a museum includes and excludes – the works collected and what is said about them – is tacitly accepted by all visitors as being significant.
2. To say nothing about the religious significance of an object (how it embodies a set of religious beliefs or how it is used in religious practice, for example) is not a neutral position. It privileges the curatorial perspective (aesthetic value and/or cultural value) over any other.
3. Museums must include multiple perspectives in order to be neutral and fair (the ultimate challenge of First Amendment liberties) in the presentation of sacred objects and images.
4. The *Project* must respect people of faith and no faith, people of all faiths and none.

He assured us that it was possible to establish the museum as common ground. Nevertheless, colloquy participants continued to raise important questions about how all of this should be accomplished in the museum setting. Eugene Korn said, "I think there is an inherent tension between neutrality and the authenticity of religious art. Art does not seek to be neutral and it doesn't seek to be safe." So, he asked, "How do you retain authenticity? This is the serious question that every museum should wrestle with."

It was interesting to note that, in small-group discussions, faith leaders and religious studies scholars could more easily articulate a direction for museums, while museum directors and curators were cautious and offered more conditional recommendations. Museum educators were often the first to embrace directives, seeing opportunities for application in their gallery teaching.

Among the directives and cautionary notes that emerged from these conversations in Year One were:

1. Museums must directly acknowledge that some works of art are expressions, even assertions, of deeply held religious convictions.

   In some cases, best practices in museum culture support acknowledging these religious convictions. For example, the Ackland's *Shiva Linga* has

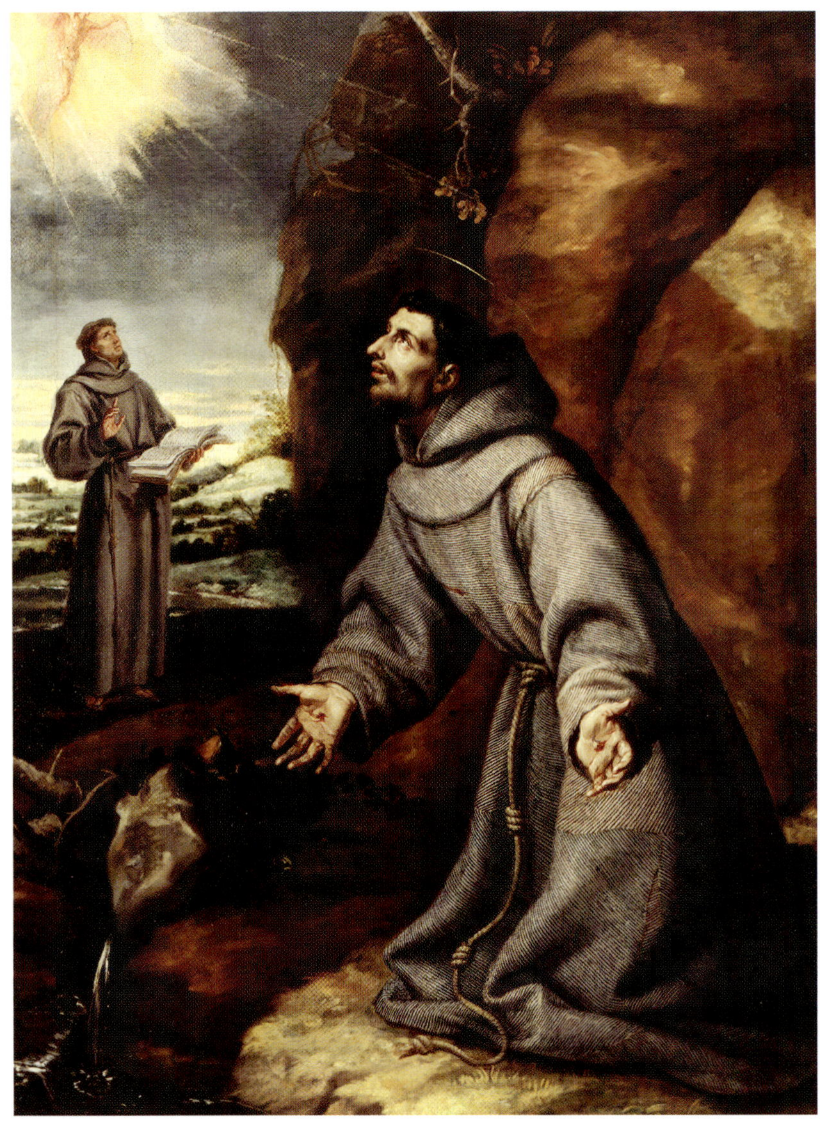

This label, written before the Five Faiths Colloquy series holds several examples of the "problem" of language.

For example: The story comes from a particular narrative of St. Francis' life and yet is uncited; the use of Christ instead of Jesus; the miracle story of Francis' stigmatization is recounted as simple fact.

This label makes several assumptions that became important in our discussions:

This painting depicts an episode in the life of St. Francis of Assisi (1181 -1226). In 1224, Francis was praying on Monte La Verna in the Appennine mountains when he had the vision of a seraph with six wings carrying the image of a man crucified. After the vision he found that his body was marked with wounds in the hands, feet and side, corresponding to the wounds that Christ had received. These "stigmata" (the Latin word for marks made by a brand) remained with him for the rest of his life.

The figure in the distance is one of Francis' early followers, Brother Leo, who witnessed the miracle. The book he holds probably refers to the biography of St. Francis that he would later write in collaboration with two of the saint's other companions.

ST. FRANCIS RECEIVING THE STIGMATA
Vicente Carducho
Spanish, born in Italy, 1576/78-1638: c. 1610-1630; oil on canvas. The William A. Whitaker Foundation Art Fund, 95.3.

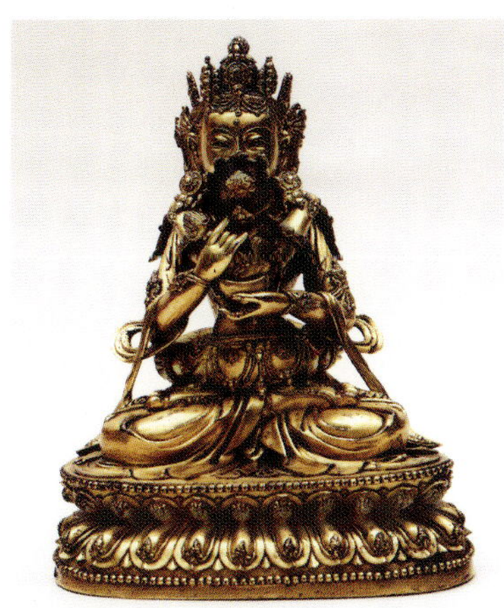

WHITE CHAKRASAMVARA AND VAJRAVARAHI
Unknown
Sino-Tibetan, 15th century: Early Ming Dynasty; gilt bronze. The William A. Whitaker Foundation Art Fund, 2004.9.

remnants of ritual *kumkum* on it.[4] To say nothing about the religious significance of the kumkum and how it suggests the object's use in the ritual practice of caring for a Hindu deity leads to false understandings and denies visitors a fuller experience of the object.

In some cases, withholding information is dishonest and dangerous if the goal is to build understanding. If the goal is limited to the appreciation of aesthetic quality, one need say very little about an object like the Ackland's *Chakrasamvara.* For outsiders to Tibetan Buddhism, however, it leads to a gross misunderstanding of the profound philosophical concept that the coupling represents. As one museum visitor asked, "Why is that big god having sex with that little god?" For Pat Phelan in one Colloquy discussion, the issue was larger. She wondered why the Museum let the *Chakhrasamvara* stand for Buddhism when it represented only a very small aspect of it. Of course, the Ackland never intended the object to stand for Buddhism as a whole. Nevertheless, once one establishes that objects have a potential to increase understanding, then visitors may expect to approach every object with that goal in mind.

2 Any work of art with religious content is a frag-

4 *Kumkum* is a red-orange powder made from saffron and turmeric used for social and religious marking in Hindu practice.

ment taken out of the larger context of beliefs and practices in particular places and times. In the case of some objects, there may be multiple contexts and changing practices. Therefore, museums have an obligation to present at least some of that context in order to create and sustain a more informed critical dialogue.

Again, using the *Shiva Linga* as an example, in its original context, the linga would never appear in isolation. It would have lived or resided in the center of a temple, and been completed by a yoni. Its presentation would have included regular ritual practices of circumambulation and offering. Without that information the conversation about the object remains fragmentary. Without context, the object may be understood as nothing more than a skillfully carved stone.

"I still can't go into a museum, I must confess, and look at a murti[5] *without thinking of it as sacred, without bringing a feeling of reverence to it because I have still not acclimatized myself to seeing a sacred murti in a non-sacred space. These are objects of living worship traditions ..."*

ANANTANAND RAMBACHAN

5 In Hinduism, *murti* refers to any image in which the divine is expressed, represented, or manifested.

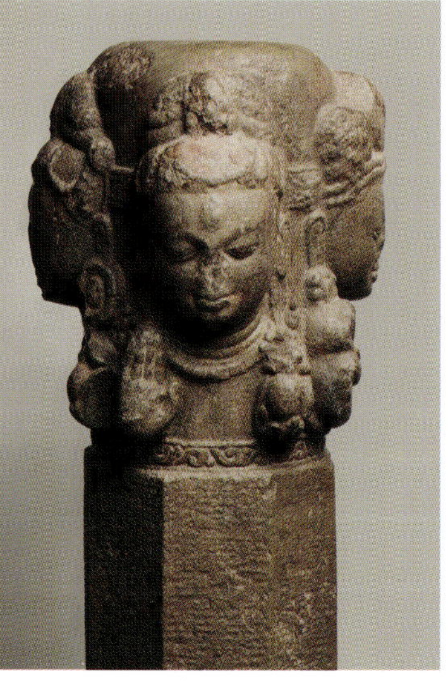

CHAKRASAMVARA AND VAJRAVARAHI
Deepak Joshi
Nepali, born 1963: 2000-2002; ground pigment with animal glue binder on linen. Ackland Fund, 2002.30.

SHIVA LINGA, 12TH CENTURY
Nepali, Transitional Period (879/80-1200), 12th century; green schist. Gift of Gilbert J. and Clara T. Yager in honor of our advisor Dr. Sherman Lee, 95.4.2. (detail)

VISHNU/SHIVA
Unknown Indian
Tamil Nadu, Kaveri delta region, 11th century; granite. Ackland Fund, 82.6.1.

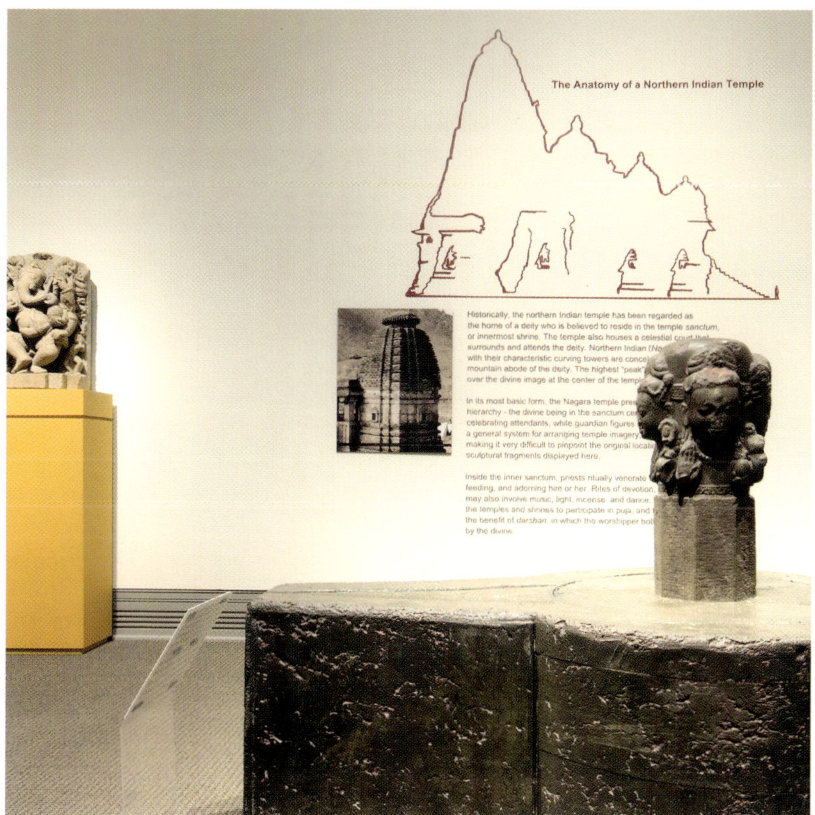

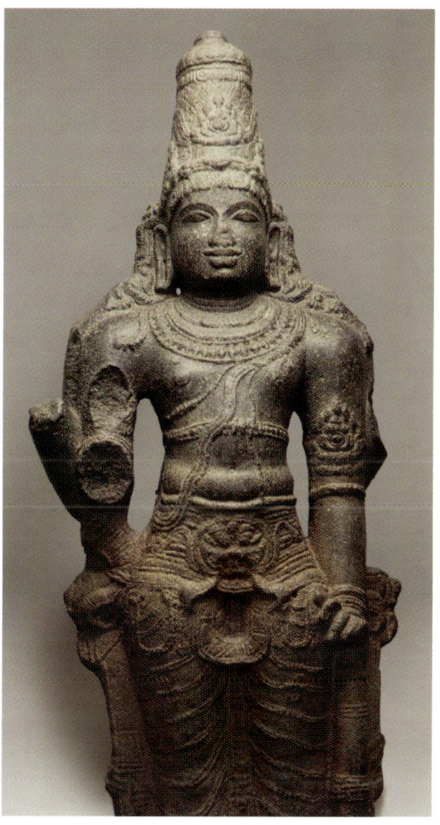

Shiva Linga with recreated yoni in *Fashioning the Divine: South Asian Sculpture at the Ackland Art Museum* (21 January – 25 March 2007).

The recreated base suggested how the Linga may have appeared in its original context. The yoni changed the way in which the object could be approached by visitors and offered subtle insight into the challenging circumstance of all the objects on display.

3 However, museums should not try to contextualize every object or apply the same contextual treatment to all objects.

Neither the staff of a museum, nor all of its objects, can sustain this level of explanation. It may be nothing more than a deeply held bias among museum professionals, but the bias is clear: museum visitors grow weary of too much information if it becomes predictable or distracts from appreciation of the object itself; and, first and perhaps foremost, visitors come to see the art, not to read about it. However, by selecting key objects through which curators and educators may suggest context for others, museums indirectly teach visitors approaches to objects in every gallery. For example, if a label introduces the notion of "ritual practice" and directs visitors to other objects in the gallery, visitors may extrapolate and apply the new information. If one label tells a sacred story about a central figure within the tradition, visitors are emboldened to recognize the figure in other objects.

"I think there is an inherent tension between neutrality or safeness and authenticity of religious art. That is, religious art is usually inspired and expresses a certain passion for the religious experience of that particular adherent or religion. It doesn't seek to be neutral ... there is nothing neutral about religious art."
EUGENE KORN

4 When museums overtly draw attention to religious context there is always a risk that some visitors may respond religiously.

Whenever museums attempt to recreate ritual context for sacred objects, they run the risk of encouraging insiders to perform the ritual (or at least aspects of it). The context also empowers outsiders to react. Outsiders to the tradition may participate (which may or may not be appropriate from an insider perspective), reject, or negatively assess the beliefs that surround the object (deciding, for example, that it is too strange or unfamiliar, or even sacrilegious when approached from the perspective of their own or another tradition).

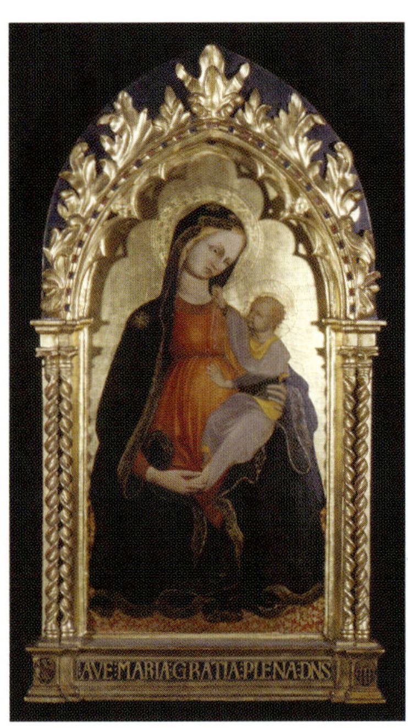

THE VIRGIN AND CHILD
Master of 1419
Italian, Florence, active early 15th century: c. 1415. Ackland Fund, 80.34.1.

The problem arises not only with insiders and outsiders, but also with the broad diversity within each tradition. For example, Protestants

"I think that if there were a picture of Mary and people were so moved that they prayed in front of it, this would be a great success for the museum. It is the kind of situation that many artists hope for: that their pictures will mean so much to people."
YAAKOV ARIEL

"... several of us found it disturbing that the Museum had a consecrated sand mandala and feared it was going to become a religious attraction in the Museum. So the Museum suppressed the information about the consecration. My reaction was 'ouch,' but also understanding the problem. When you start to invite people from the community in and use or present objects in an actual setting, they become ritual objects again."
CHARLES ORZECH

"But what is the problem with that?"
RAY WILLIAMS

"Creating sacred spaces and creating objects that are actually worshipped in a museum setting raises questions about violating conscience for museum visitors. I think it also raises questions about violating the integrity of the faith being represented; even if 100 percent of the people of that faith in the local area voted yes, we like this, they don't speak for the whole tradition."
CHARLES HAYNES

may find images of saints and their attributes unfamiliar and "dangerous." In particular, images expressing devotion to Mary have long been subject to internal contestation in the Christian traditions.

At the Ackland, there were long-standing concerns about visitors taking off their shoes and circumambulating the *Shiva Linga.* Some of the faith leaders were as uncomfortable as the museum directors with the possibility of reenactment as well as interpretative strategies that might encourage participation in ritual practices in front of museum objects. Many of the colloquy participants asked whether by placing the *Shiva Linga* in a central location in the gallery, and reminding visitors to walk around it and look at all sides, the museum was encouraging, or even compelling, a devotional attitude for outsiders and insiders alike.

In the end, the problems associated with any one object were of less concern than finding principles that might be employed with many objects and across the traditions. Colloquy participants recommended that museums provide choices for visitors – options for ways of approaching art with sacred content (or none) – and present multiple, even opposing, perspectives simultaneously. By doing so, the presence of this kind of contestation would reflect the reality of a pluralistic society.

The challenge rests in considering which perspectives to present. If museums agree that there is some obligation to select opposing perspectives, then they must reflect on the authority to choose, who assists in this decision-making, and how

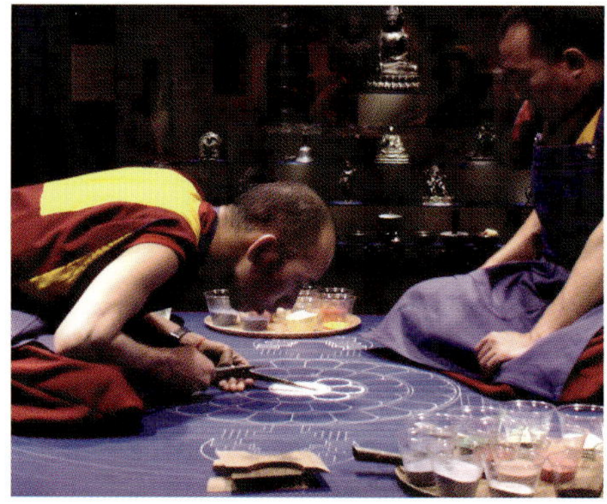

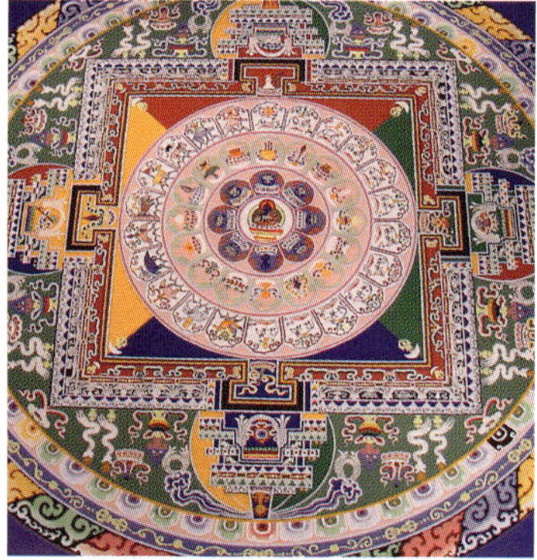

Buddhist monks from the Namgyal Monastery in Ithaca, New York creating a Medicine Buddha Sand Mandala at the Ackland Art Museum in 2001.

Finished Medicine Buddha Sand Mandala.

To learn more, visit: www.ackland.org/art/exhibitions/buddhistart/

they will make their final choices and the logic behind them as transparent as possible.[6] One possible (and simple) solution suggested by the colloquy participants was to provide clear attributions for every label text and to name the curator for every exhibition and gallery installation. In other words, every text that accompanies a work of art should have the author's name and affiliation. Introductory texts in every gallery should include the name and title of the curator (*as in* Timothy Riggs, curator of collections) and labels that suggest the use of the object in context might be approved by and attributed to the faith leader(s) who helped with the labels' production (*as in* Josho Pat Phelan, Taitaku, Chapel Hill Zen Center).

Participants concluded that an institutional commitment to attribution would allow the Museum to be more direct and assertive in labels as well as other interpretive materials. Reliable scholarship cites all its sources, pointing the reader to the path of research. As museums present the perspectives of curators, scholars, and insiders to a tradition, and attribute those

6 Transparency became an important theme of the Colloquies. See authors conclusions, pages 181-187.

"I was standing in front of a painting analyzing the composition, when a ten-year-old boy came up and pointed: 'Jesus, Mary, Joseph, Jesus.' It was such an instructive experience. I was analyzing diagonals, but for this child, the painting was an image of faith. No matter how many labels we write, and how much we try to engineer an experience, we must always allow for the visitor coming with his or her own experience and responding from it."
VIVIAN MANN

perspectives clearly, the institutions progress toward fairness and perhaps toward a kind of institutional neutrality, while enhancing visitor experience.

Neutrality is a word that participants struggled with from its first suggestion in Charles Haynes' presentation. Are museums capable of neutrality when so much of museum practice challenges neutral responses? Museums make value-based judgments in selecting works, in presenting them within certain constructs of meaning, and in organizing them within galleries. Most of the discussions rejected the use of the word neutral and focused on the word "fair" as more attainable within a museum context. Fair, in the context of these discussions, came to mean balanced, accurate, and transparent. All three of these words – balanced, accurate, and transparent – seemed to prompt the thoughtfulness that would allow for an increased openness to multiple perspectives within the museum's established practices.

Of course, labels alone do not create context. The extended program offerings that surround the exhibition of objects also create context. From musical performances that suggest the sounds of worship to academic discussions of the fundamental differences between historical trends and streams within each tradition, programs can offer other layers of interpretation and investigation. The label is the most limited of all opportunities for context, and yet it is the most heavily relied upon.

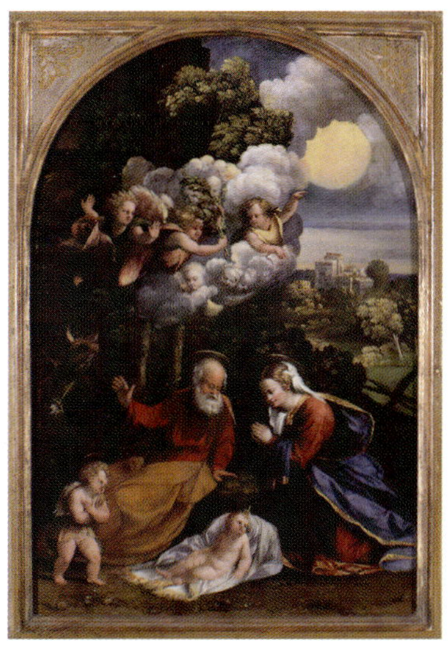

THE HOLY FAMILY WITH THE INFANT ST. JOHN THE BAPTIST
Battista Luteri, called Battista Dossi
Italian, active 1517-1548: c. 1530; oil on wood panel.
Ackland Fund, 85.22.1.

In her presentation, Viswanathan accepted that "the museum is a natural place for the exhibition of sacred objects." However, she emphasized that even with clear attribution and extensive programming, exhibiting these objects will not be easy, but a "dangerous, messy business." As a case in point, Viswanathan described the experience of visiting the Los Angeles County Museum of Art (LACMA) with her mother:

> We immigrated to this country when I was five. This is in the early 1960s and I remember one of the most embarrassing things. We would go to the museum quite regularly. They have a marvelous collection of South Asian sculpture and painting, and before you enter the galleries with the major sculptures of Shiva and Vishnu, there is a large bronze Nandi, a statue of a bull, ritually associated with Shiva. I should add the Nandi in south Indian temples normally sits in the courtyard before the temple and it is a very auspicious, important object. At the museum, this was one of the few objects that was not encased in glass. I remember every visit to the museum [being] punctuated by my mother pushing us forward, touching the Nandi, and praying.
>
> For me, of course, the LACMA was my first Hindu temple in America.
>
> And the museum guard would say, "Ma'am, please don't touch the statues," and my mother, each time, would say, "Oh, no, I won't" and then we would do the same thing the next time. To this day, my mother still does this. No one can persuade her that this is a desacralized object in a museum.

No one could convince her mother that the museum had fully translated the object from one set of meanings into another. According to Viswanathan, museum curators are translators in the original sense. In Europe during the Middle Ages, the word *translatio* referred to the transferring of a saint's relics from one place to another. "That is what art museums do: translate sacred relics."

This being so, Viswanathan went on to ask, how might museums thoughtfully explain the translations of objects from ritual to museum settings, from being valued for their ritual meaning to being valued for their aesthetic quality? She advised against simple explanations and cavalier approaches that assume a secularized world in which all museum visitors hold religion at arm's length and disregard the sacred quality of the object. Viswanathan suggested that the language we use in labels is often at fault.

She questioned the ways in which museums manage simple things like capitalization, often without thinking about consistency across faiths: God or god? And what of the titles: Lord Ganesha and the Virgin Mary, or Ganesha and Mary? The Holy Bible and the Holy Qur'an, or the Bible and the Qur'an? "We often talk about Hindu mythology,"

Viswanathan noted, "but what if we say biblical mythology?"[7]

As part of her presentation, she introduced the work of Jan Assman, who, in an article, "Translating Gods," describes three kinds of translation.[8] The first, "mutual translation" occurs when cultures intersect and bleed into one another. "It is a kind of globalization," Viswanathan explained, "in which we pick up terminology from different traditions without knowing

7 The continued use of B.C. and A.D. rather than BCE and CE is another case in point.

8 Jan Assman, "Translating Gods: Religion as a Factor of Cultural (Un)Translatability," in Sanford Budick and William I Ser, eds., *The Translatability of Cultures: Figurations of the Space Between* (Stanford, 1996).

GANESHA
Unknown
Central Indian, 11th-12th century; sandstone. Gift of Clara T. and Gilbert J. Yager in honor of Dr. Charles Morrow and his wife, Mary Morrow, for their many contributions to the University and to The Ackland Art Museum during his term as Provost, 85.2.1.

THE SORROWING VIRGIN
Follower of Jose de Mora
Spanish, 1642-1724: after 1700; wood and fabric with polychrome, silver leaf, glass, and ivory. Ackland Fund, 75.11.1.

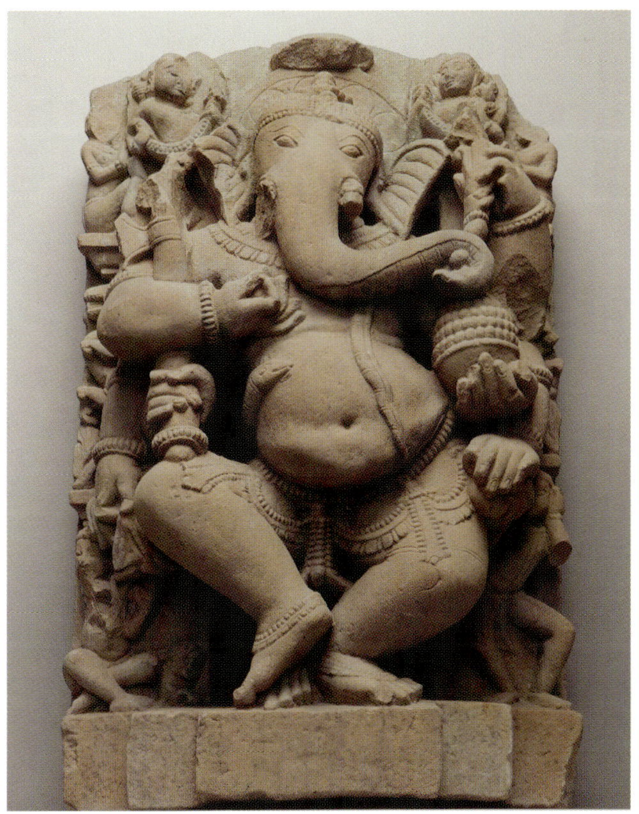

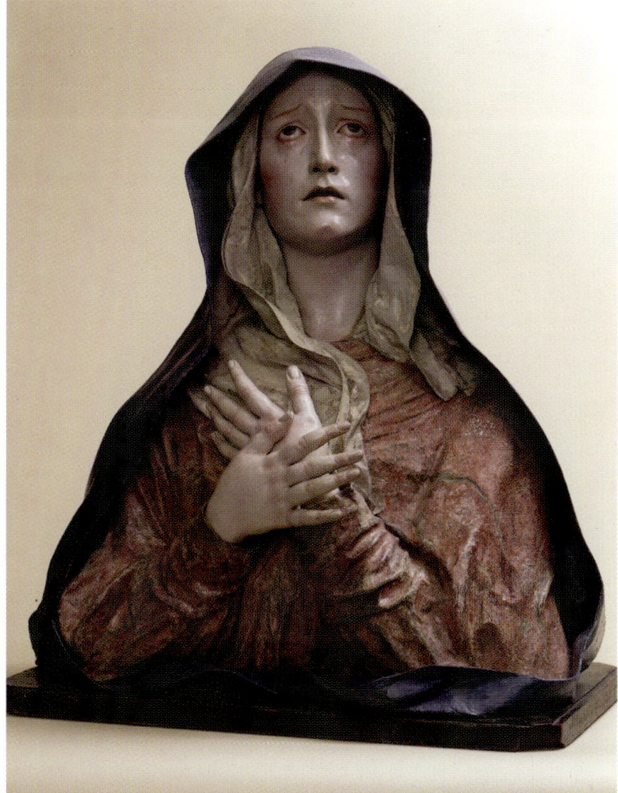

exactly what the terms mean." The example she gave was "Zen" and the many ways the word and idea of Zen have infiltrated popular culture. The second translation, one most often used in museums, is an assimilatory or "competitive translation" in which a dominant culture assimilates others. "Museum curators," she asserted, "tend to interpret things from other traditions using terminology and categories of experience that come from our dominant, Judeo-Christian tradition. Thus, interpretations become a different form of what we already know."[9] Even if the museum attributes that perspective to the curator, the assumptions behind the perspective may remain hidden.

A prime example of Viswanathan's point is found in the name of the *Five Faiths Project*. Faith is a word that emerges directly from a "Judeo-Christian" and Western world-view. By calling the project *Five Faiths*, the Museum suggests that all five traditions can be understood as "faiths," that all can (and perhaps will) be understood within the framework of Christianity in which the creeds and canons assert belief and faith in God as essential components. Colloquy participants wrestled with this. Should the Ackland rename the project the *Five Belief Systems* or the *Five Practices*? There was no agreement and the group let it go, but the discussion did alert everyone to the difficulty of finding language that is fair and accurate. The discussion helped the Ackland to add consideration of the subtext – our own unintended messages – that sits behind titles and within labels.

The third type of translation, which Viswanathan endorsed, is "syncretistic translation." It is different from the first and second because it involves translation into a third language, or engages a third language as a mediator between the original two. Assman's essay offered as an example the ways Christianity adopted Greek as a middle ground between Arabic and Latin. The third language becomes a place to put shared agreements among contesting voices.

Museums are left to find this third language, one that is neither wholly faith-based – that is, rooted in a single religious perspective – nor wholly art historical or curatorial. It is a negotiated third, in which conflicting perspectives agree to invest meaning. Viswanathan

---

9 The authors resist the use of "Judeo-Christian" and "Abrahamic Traditions" as descriptive labels as often as possible because both imply a kind of cohesion across Judaism and Christianity in the first, and Judaism, Christianity, and Islam in the latter. While often convenient, these terms undermine appreciation of the unique truth claims of each tradition and suggest agreements that may or may not exist. In this case, we have included the term in order to use a direct quote from transcripts of Viswanathan's presentation.

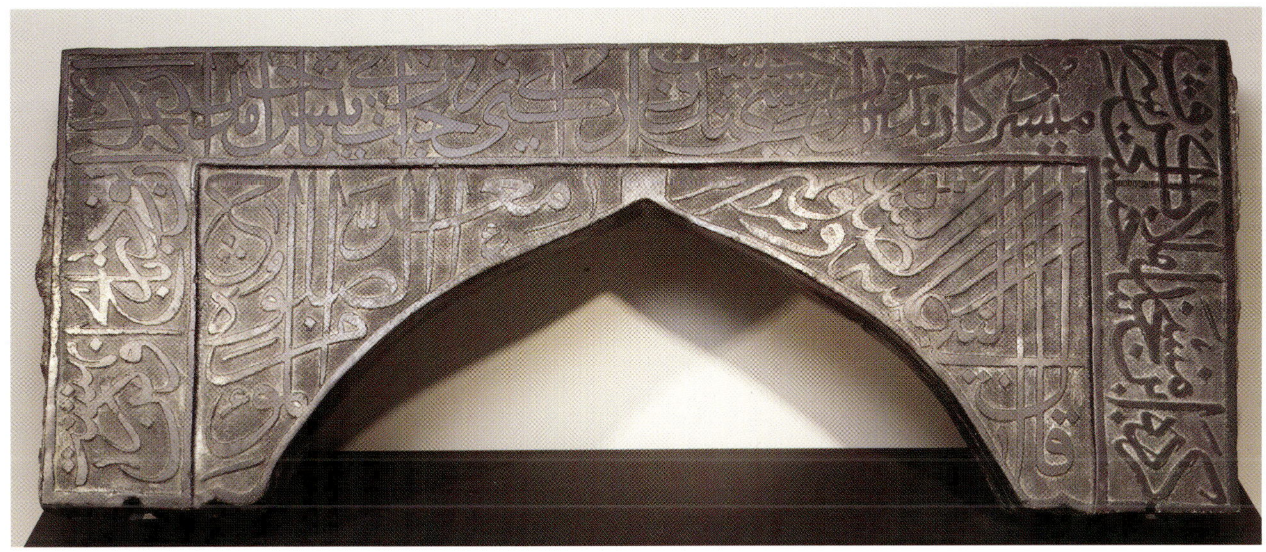

MOSQUE LINTEL WITH CALLIGRAPHY
Unknown
South Indian, Golconda, Andhra Pradesh, 1570; black basalt.
Ackland Fund, 97.14.2.

encouraged the Museum to consider how to create this new language, a language in which, because of its fundamental agreement to be neither this perspective nor that perspective alone, the Museum might establish a "parity of esteem."[10]

If museums are successful, the new language could create common ground in which galleries and exhibitions become safe and productive areas for negotiating understanding. However, it will be impossible to create a new language until museums acknowledge the limitations and biases of the language

"All these objects have been taken out of the context in which power, spiritual power, might flow. The fountains in museums are dry, but we have the responsibility to inform our visitors that water once flowed through them."

GERALD BOLAS

10 *Parity of esteem* is a phrase used in political philosophy to explain a theory to overcome inter-communal conflict. Promoters of the theory argue that *parity of esteem* "offers a language for negotiation of a post-conflict equilibrium." This negotiation begins with the communities recognizing the stalemate of their position. Rather than trying to out-do each other, the communities should attempt to negotiate a peaceful coexistence in a shared physical space, despite their cultural differences. *Parity of esteem* accepts various nationalist traditions within one state. Today, *parity of esteem* is a core concept to the peace process in Northern Ireland. See: Tom Hennessey and Robin Wilson, 1997, *With all Due Respect: Pluralism and Parity of Esteem.*

they already speak.

This is precisely the point Charles Orzech made when he reflected on the history of museums and the European culture from which they emerged. He noted how many of our conversations were rooted in the premises and presumptions of the museum culture. Before he shifted our conversational perspective from that of museum insiders – "what can museums do to meet their obligations to their diverse communities" – to that of museum outsiders and to the implications of engaging outsiders fully in museum practice, Orzech introduced three metaphors to help colloquy participants understand the museum culture they were seeking to change: Museums as Collections; Museums as Narratives; Museums as Contact Zones.

Orzech reminded museum insiders of the hidden framework of our enterprise, noting that all cultural institutions "ex-

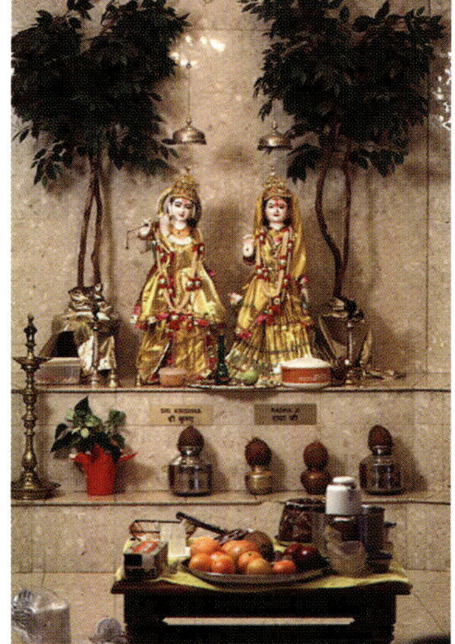

At the Hindu Bhavan in Morrisville, N.C., the altar is prepared for *puja*.

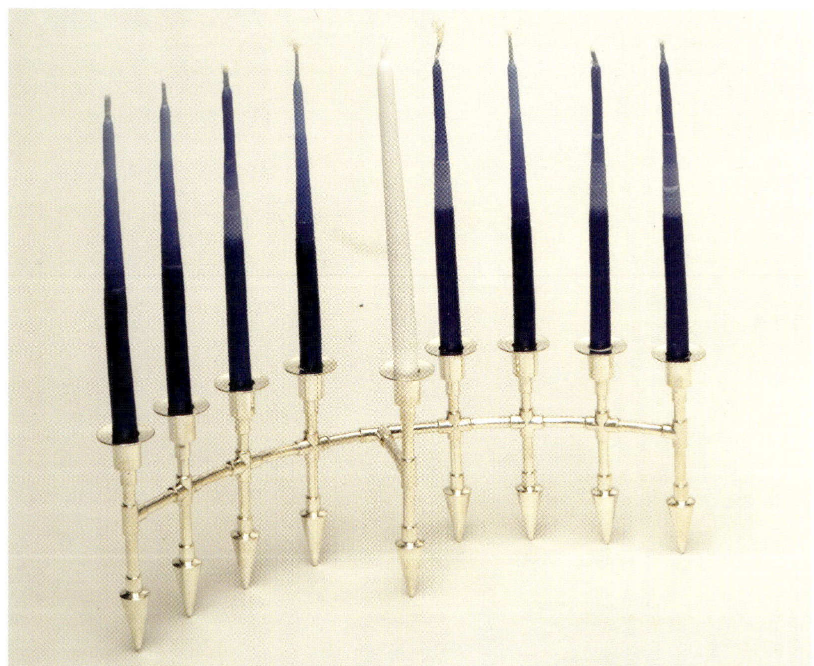

To suggest the use of the Hannukiah, the Ackland included candles in its installation during Hanukka. The Jewish "Festival of Lights," celebrates the legendary rededication of the holy temple in Jerusalem in 165 BCE after its desecration. To remember this event, a candle is lit on each night of the holiday and placed in a special candleholder called a hanukkiah. Hanukkiahs, such as this one in the Ackland, have room for nine candles: one for each night of the festival and an extra one used to kindle the others.

HANUKKIAH
John Cogswell
American, 1999; silver. Ackland Fund, 2000.2.

"Expressing the fact that an object represents a living tradition lies in the tenses that you use in your labels and your text panels. If you say, 'This was used by Jews,' or 'This is being used by Jews of this tradition,' it's a world of difference."
VIVIAN MANN

"I think you are right that we want museums to get out of the way, museums are in the way all the time, but that doesn't mean you are going to actually set out votive candles so people can light them and have a prayer."
CHARLES HAYNES

"I firmly believe that meaningful dialogue and rich, multisensory experience – smells and bells – are central to museums. If we are to be vibrant centers of learning and community, there is a need for change, for experimentation and taking risks by museum professionals, the need to transcend the traditional museum response of 'this is the way it is done.'"
MIMI GATES

"What we need is a kind of poly-vocality with all of the messiness that comes with it. That is what the civic arena requires. The museum is safe in a certain sense, but there is also a sense of danger because of the potential for conflict. What we're doing is surfacing conflict and being honest about it."
THOMAS TWEED

periment with various sequences of remembering," are "structured on a sort of taxonomy," hold "unacknowledged narratives," but typically are browsed by visitors "just as we browse a magazine." By doing this, Orzech articulated just how profound a challenge the *Five Faiths Project* raised for museum culture. He argued that museums unconsciously hearken back to the etymological roots of the word "museum" as "home for the Muses" or as "scholar's study" (definitions suggested by the Oxford English Dictionary), when in fact today museums constitute a place where cultural contact is inevitable, although rarely addressed. As Orzech put it, if the *Five Faiths Project* hoped "to turn the Museum to the purposes of cultural encounter and understanding," then this social/cultural interaction must move to the foreground, and the institution must be prepared to set museum objects "free" for use by their communities, to grant these communities space, and therefore to give voice to their stories in the museum. This means allowing religious communities to have a say in the display and use of objects in the collection.

Outsiders to museum culture found this assertion liberating; insiders were deeply troubled. Vivian Mann, speaking as a museum professional, objected:

> We are, above all, custodians of works of art. One just can't be cavalier about who's going to come in and conduct a service using our artifacts, or ask, "Can I have that thing I donated to the museum forty years ago for my grandson's bar mitzvah in Spokane, Washington?" No. We would have to send a guard, we would have to send the curator, and we would have to be there right next to the boy as he read the Torah. It's impossible. You cannot allow these kinds of things if you are concerned with the work of art as an object which should be preserved, and that is a very important consideration for museum people.

Participants appreciated her candor – and the reminder that museums are protectors, institutions charged with preservation. But Orzech offered three suggestions to help museums balance the requirements of curatorial obligation with the enthusiasms of new participants in the curatorial enterprise.

1 Take great care to foreground historical and contemporary religious interaction. In doing so, we push to the background everything that encourages use of the museum as a catalogue to be browsed randomly in social isolation.
2 Encourage religious communities to take a role in the display and interpretation of objects in the museum setting.
3 Provide "thick" descriptive and illustrative material for key objects in the collection, being especially careful to unpack the metaphoric worlds of certain objects and their role in religious practice and cultural interaction.

If there is a bridge between the sacred ground of religious traditions and the common ground of a museum setting, Orzech said, "it is built with *many* voices." One possibility would be museum/community partnerships with a combination of gallery talks, community speakers, *and* museum sponsored participatory visits to religious centers, all backed up by *ongoing* consultation between museum professionals and local religious communities.[11]

No matter how forward thinking, Orzech's advocacy for many voices in constructing meaning and interpreting sacred objects in museums created a dilemma for museum curators, as Mann's response to his presentation indicates. If curators and educators invite many voices, how will the museum present them? What happens when you are compelled to disregard some of their suggestions? When museums decide to foreground "poly-vocality" (with all its messiness and contradictions), will visitors be able to make

11 Orzech referenced Clifford's extensive discussion of the advantages and the pitfalls of such discussions in "Museums as Contact Zones," in *Routes*, pp. 188 – 219. Gallery talks that feature community speakers often involve contesting views and cultural tension. Even where no scholarly or museum viewpoint is presented alongside that of a representative of the community it is still difficult to overcome the sense that the museum's context and the values it represents (this is first of all great art!) are definitive.

sense of it all?

On the other hand, if curators, directors, and educators continue to insist on constructing meaning and meaningful order out of the disorder of so many voices, will these many voices become so homogenized that individual perspectives are subsumed into a curatorial whole? By whole, the curators were quick to clarify, they meant a seamless, overarching narrative through which the museum (that is, the curator) attempts to design the visitor's experience of *our* objects.

In response to the issue of poly-vocality, Shabbir Mansuri asked an interesting question: Whose voices are reliable? In his view, a voice of faith should not represent a religion in the museum setting. He recommended that the "presentation of a religion should come from those who have studied it, that is, scholars." His comment surprised faith leaders and religious studies scholars alike.

Patrice Brodeur countered by asking, "Are scholars immune from their own biases? Where does the objective presentation of a tradition reside?"

Mansuri answered, "If I want to know what a religious community is all about, I go to a scholar rather than to a person who is praying."

Orzech questioned Mansuri's use of "religious community" as though it were timeless and universal. He asked, "Is there really such a thing as the tradition – a generic core?"

To this, Haynes suggested, "... perhaps there is a generic core with local and contemporary variations. That is to say, perhaps there are shared points of contact across all the differences, past and present."

Orzech, agreed, but concluded that those points of contact are only possible if museums pay attention to "the current lived situation of religious groups." He said, "It is a terrible trap for museums to present faith groups as having been existent in the past [as represented through historical objects], and yet to deny, through neglect, their contemporary presence. It is the objects, which in most museums are from the past, that blind museums to the potential of contemporary communities."

Vivian Mann suggested that museums might avoid the trap by changing tense in labels and text panels, by substituting "This object was used by Jews" with "This object is being used by Jews of this particular tradition."

Participants also considered the ways in which museums might overcome the presumption that there are definitive approaches to the works. In other words, are there ways that we might open up a conversation within the labels themselves? An opportunity to test this came up in Colloquy III with responses among faith leaders and scholars to photographs by Pamela Singh depicting aspects of Tantric Hinduism. The Ackland curators loved Singh's photographs and, in fact, the Museum purchased one for the permanent collection. However, Dr. G. D. Sharma, priest at the Hindu Bhavan in Morrisville, North Carolina, and a long-time collaborative partner in the *Five Faiths Project*, described the photographs as encouraging a kind of "devil worship." When Rambachan and Viswanathan examined the photographs, they defined Tantric Hinduism as rigorous and challenging, but noted that it was unrelated to mainstream Hinduism and therefore, in their view, marginal. How might we present these and other differing perspectives into a label? And if we do, what kind of basic introduction to the faith must we supply to make the debate understandable?

In the end, discussions about whose voice best represents faith traditions, which language best articulates the beliefs embodied in religious objects, and what museum practice best

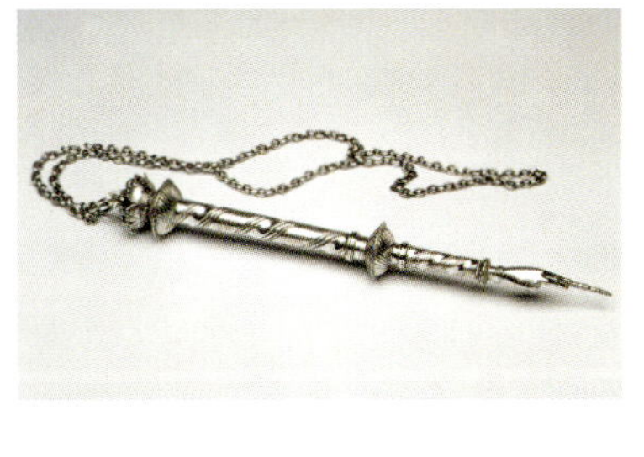

TORAH POINTER
Unknown
Netherlands or Northern Germany, late 17th-early 18th century; silver: cast, chased, and engraved. The Jewish Museum, New York. Gift of Dr. Harry G. Friedman. F 3518

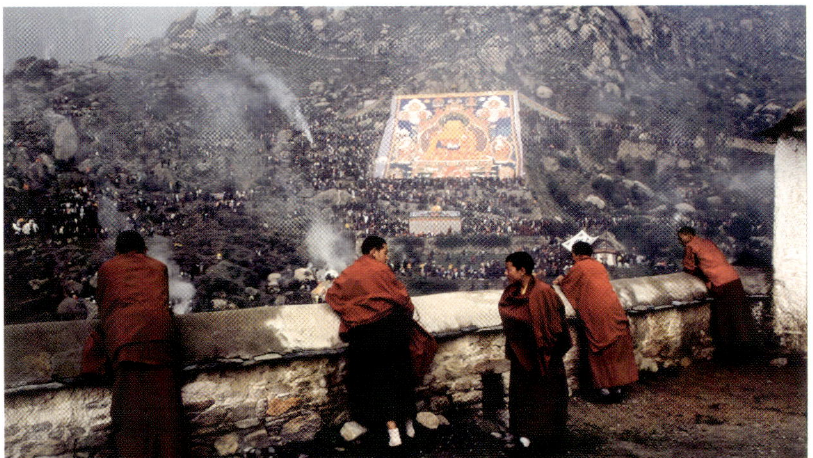

GRAND SILK TANGKA
Steve McCurry
American, born 1950: Drepung Monastery, Tibet, 2001; cibachrome. Ackland Fund, 2003.23. (detail)

TANTRIC SELF PORTRAIT IN JAIPUR #1
Pamela Singh
Indian, born 1962: 2000-2001; mixed-media photograph. © 2000-2001 Pamela Singh/ Sepia International. Ackland Fund, 2005.1.

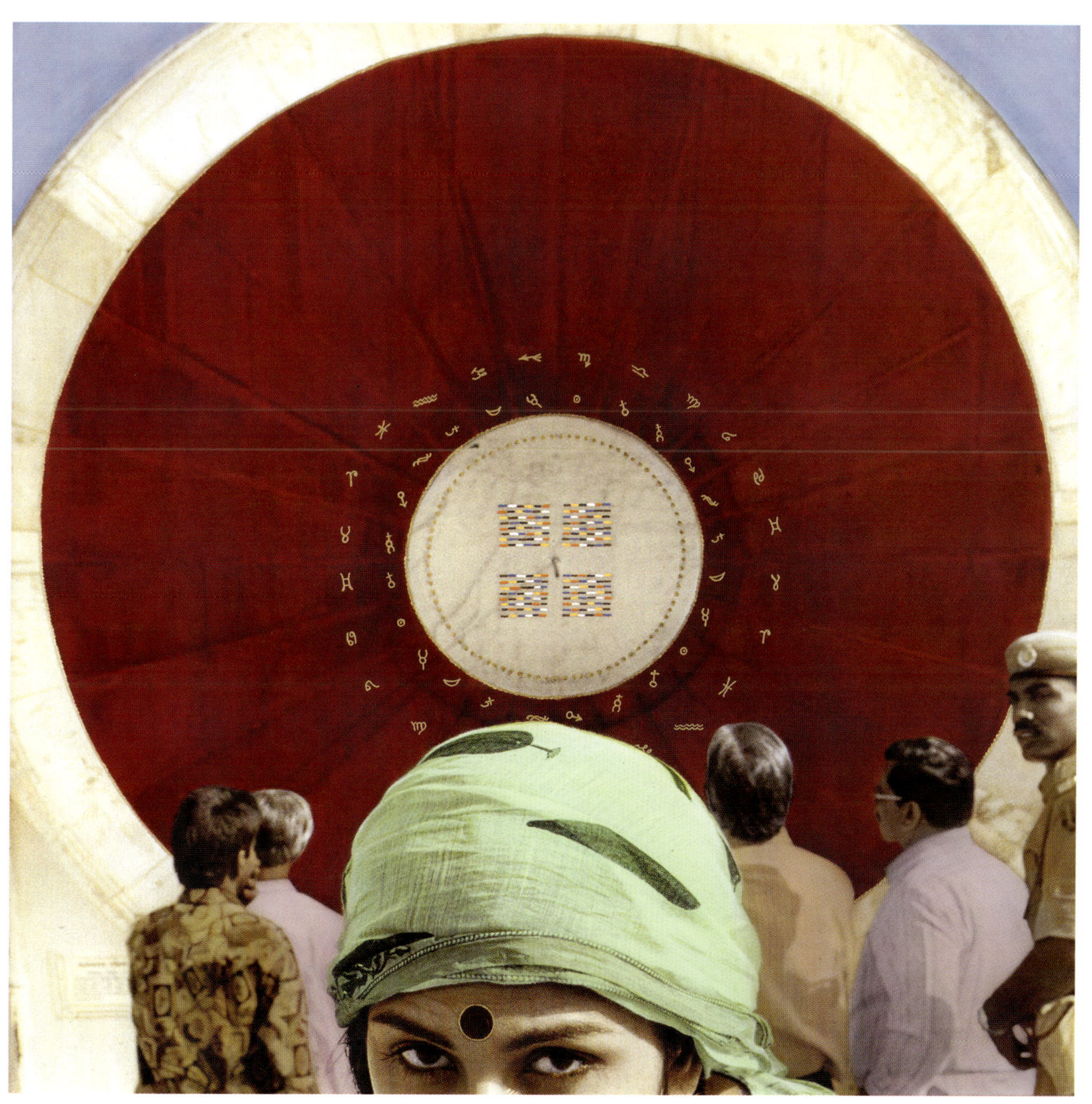

honors objects as works of art *and* subjects of religious veneration led to a general conclusion agreed to by all. Openness and transparency hold the most promise for museums who wish to use their multi-cultural collections to engage diverse audiences and increase understanding about them. Therefore, museums should:

1. Foreground the individual and the particular as represented in the object,
2. embrace rather than deny the reductive nature of an art object (and of a person's perspective, for that matter), and
3. resist all universal claims.

The more explicit museums can be in their interpretive materials, the more they stand to realize the potential of objects to promote the appreciation and understanding that is central to their mission. Relatively small changes to museum practice are important steps toward the transparency participants wanted. For example, identify who is speaking and from what perspective; which sacred texts are being used as sources; the essential features of an object (what it is, where it was made, how it was used, and by whom); and to which cultural tradition the object belongs.

In the same vein of transparency, important questions emerged concerning the hidden goals and "secret practices" of museums. Why would the museum be less than explicit about exhibition goals or curatorial practices? Are museums promoting commonality by downplaying contradictions and conflict? Are museums neglecting the present in favor of the past? How might museums be attentive to possible political, cultural, and religious messages that ostensibly objective labels present? Whose understanding of an object or a faith tradition does the museum present? And whose does the museum ignore?

The discussions and conclusions of the first Colloquy encouraged several recommendations for change in the Ackland's practice within the scope of the *Five Faiths Project.* These included: taking care to identify the authors of labels and other interpretive texts, with the goal of phasing out the Museum's use of the omniscient voice; establishing a museum-wide policy, consistent across faith traditions, for the use of capitalization and omission of honorifics; and convening community advisory groups with whom to consult on the interpretation and presentation of objects with sacred content.

In reviewing the transcripts, it became clear that the discussions followed the diverse interests of the participants, leading us to broad consideration of First Amendment rights, language and its biases, the abiding principles of the museum culture, the role faith communities should (or should not) play in the interpretation of objects, etc. In the end, however, these conversations came back to consideration of the objects themselves and the practical implications of their translation from the ritual to the secular setting. This focus on sacred objects and on the circumstances of their museum environment suggested to us the theme for the second Colloquy: *Considering the Lives of Sacred Images.*

Religious Liberty in the Museum

A Civic Framework for Understanding the Sacred in a Neutral Space

Submitted by
Charles Haynes
First Amendment Center, Freedom Forum World Center

> Congress shall make no law respecting an establishment of religion, or prohibiting the free exercise thereof ...
>
> *Religious liberty clauses of the First Amendment to the U.S. Constitution*

More than 200 years after their enactment, the first sixteen words of the Bill of Rights undergird the boldest and most successful experiment in religious freedom in history. The two clauses are essentially one provision for protecting freedom of conscience by prohibiting state sponsorship of religion and state interference with religious liberty.

What do the religious liberty clauses of the First Amendment have to do with how sacred objects and images are treated in museums? In strictly legal terms, the First Amendment speaks to what the government may or may not do. This means that the First Amendment applies directly to public museums, exhibits in private museums funded with government money, and museum education programs involving public school children. The fact that religious objects and subjects are frequently treated in all of these settings rarely implicates the First Amendment.

The Supreme Court has indicated (*in dicta*) that displays of religious art in public museums are not a violation of the Establishment clause because, in Justice Sandra Day O'Connor's words, "a typical museum setting, though not neutralizing the religious content of a religious painting, negates any message of endorsement of the content." Moreover, courts have rejected Free Exercise claims against museum displays that offend someone's religious faith.

Court decisions, however, are only the starting point for addressing religious liberty in museums. Beyond what is legal (a question easily answered in most cases), it is important for museums to ask: What is the right thing to do? Or, to put it another way: How can the religious liberty principles of the First Amendment provide a civic framework for negotiating the relationship between religion and museums, especially when museums undertake the sensitive task of educating the public about the meaning and purpose of sacred objects?

To answer this question, we need to take a close look at what the religious liberty principles of "no establishment" and "free exercise" might mean in a museum setting. Here are some key topics to consider:

- *If the Establishment clause requires neutrality by government towards religion (neutral among religions and between religion and non-religion), how should this principle be applied in a museum?* Confusion about the meaning of "neutrality" may cause some public museums to avoid including religious perspectives or educating the public fully about sacred objects. But ignoring religious context and meaning when exhibiting religious images or objects is hardly neutral. Neutrality in a museum should not result in silence about religion; neutrality should mean, in a word, fairness.

- *What does it mean to be "neutral and fair" within the civic framework of the First Amendment?* At a minimum, it means including how religious people themselves understand the sacred object or image. Fairness also requires that a variety of perspectives be represented – religious and non-religious. This principle is especially important when teaching about religions through educational programs at the museum – and legally required if public-school children are involved. Properly done, teaching about religions (as distinguished from religious indoctrination) requires considerable academic preparation, an ability to teach with empathy and sensitivity, and a clear understanding of the First Amendment.

- *How should a museum respond when religious people invoke the Free Exercise clause, claiming that a museum exhibit or action violates their religious freedom?* Is there a valid free exercise claim if, for example, a museum allows a sacred pipe from a Native American tradition to be photographed over the objections of the tribe? In strictly legal terms, the answer is "no." Such claims can't dictate how museums display religious objects or discuss religious beliefs or practices. In fact, censoring or altering a public museum display or program solely because of religious objections might well violate the Establishment clause.

- *Does this mean that museums don't need to worry about free exercise?* No. For example, re-creating sacred spaces or sacred practices may risk violating the conscience of visitors or the integrity of the faith involved (and also may raise Establishment clause issues in a public museum). A claim of conscience might also be made by parents of school children involved in learning about religions in a museum setting. For that reason, schools and museums should have "opt out" policies when museum visits involve substantial teaching about religions. In these and other ways, museums should think about how to uphold liberty of conscience for all visitors – even if they are not required by law to do so.

What is at stake in getting this right? Our nation begins the twenty-first century as the most religiously diverse place on earth, and, among developed nations, the most religious. The task of sustaining – and expanding – this extraordinary experiment in religious freedom requires a shared understanding of the role religion plays in public and private life and a shared commitment to the core civic principles that bind us together as a people. By using the civic framework provided by the guiding principles of the First Amendment, museums can play a vital role in helping us to understand one another across differences that are deep and abiding. Museums can (and should) be our common ground – places where people of all faiths and none are treated with fairness and respect.

Curating the Sacral

Hazarding Questions of Language, Translation, and Representation

Submitted by
Meera Viswanathan
Comparative Literature and East Asian Studies, Brown University

Forty years ago, it was customary at museums throughout the country to exhibit the majority of objects, sacred or otherwise, with only the most cursory identification: "Bodhisattva, Gandhara, c. 3rd century." These holdings remained for the most part esoteric, the purview of scholars in the field or of the curious few inclined towards the recondite. With the redefinition and reshaping of museums over the last few decades toward public accessibility, education, and global exploration, museum curators have become by necessity translators and mediators, not merely of artifacts but of what they purportedly represent: belief systems, practices, and cultures. Keeping in mind the caveat implicit in the old epigram "*Traduttore, traditore*" (Translators are traitors), I would like to consider a number of issues related to language use specifically raised by the exhibition of sacred objects from disparate traditions in the context of a contemporary museum including:

1. The question of invidious comparisons and its obverse, the bogeyman of cultural relativism.
2. The twin dangers of explanation: misunderstanding/reductionism on the one hand and the problem of desacralization on the other.
3. Assumptions about language and utterance, i.e., the use of sacred languages; the implications of naming the divine; the relation of language to Truth.
4. Positioning the audience, for example from without the culture (e.g. as

ethnographer) or from within (e.g. as believer), raising the question of the ethics of religious simulacra.

5 Implications of venue and audience (i.e., what kind of museum? Natural history? Art? And what kind of audience? Rural? Urban? Northeastern? Southern?

Museum as Metaphor in a Pluralistic Society

The Politics of Contact Zones

Submitted by
Charles Orzech
Department of Religious Studies, The University of North Carolina at Greensboro

What is a museum like? A hoard of treasure? A book of history? A repository of great art? A time capsule? A salvage yard? A school? A personal narrative? A journey? A local narrative? How we answer depends on where – in what community – we stand, and while any answer has always begged certain questions, the increasingly pluralistic and global context of even small cities in the South renders a simple answer suspect. In a sense, the question is whose museum is it? Though all may use it, the terms of its use may now be open to negotiation. Museums have been likened to "frontiers" (Chidester) or "contact zones" (Clifford), places in which each party, each community, seeks to negotiate an identity. How is a collection like that in the Ackland perceived by different religious communities? How can a "majority" museum work with an audience of increasing cultural and religious diversity?

Museums as we know them are a creation of Euro-American culture, and while their voices may be distinctive (the voice of Chicago's Field Museum is distinct from that of the Ackland) they all speak the same language, a language steeped in the dominance of European culture. If we are to explore the use of museums and their collections by religious communities, we must consider two things: First, our discussions are about how we give voice to the objects in a museum and how we want to change that voice or make it possible for an object to have many voices rather than one. Such an undertaking demands reflection on the history of museums, consideration of our notions about the collecting and display of objects in a museum, and attention to the voices we have traditionally given objects in a collection.

Second, though religious artifacts are given space in a museum, their inclusion comes with the tacit understanding that they stand isolated from active religious practice. As Robert Harbison puts it, "to enter, an object must die, and a non-museum object chosen for a museum is enviable like a maiden elected for sacrifice."[12] If we wish a collection to be used by a religious community, if we wish to revivify the objects in it, then religious communities and museums must negotiate a new understanding of the museum space and the objects in it. How are we to proceed with such negotiations, and how can we facilitate the use of the public and pluralistic space of the museum by religious communities? My aim in this essay is to open a discussion of the impact of our increasing pluralism on this public yet private institution.

Museum Values

What Are They? What Might They Be?

Submitted by
Ruth Slavin
Curator for Education, University of Michigan Museum of Art

In her recent book, *From Knowledge to Narrative: Educators and the Changing Museum*, Lisa Roberts argues that American museums are confronting a paradigm shift about the nature of knowledge and accepted "ways of knowing." Roberts argues that these shifts have been prompted by new intellectual understandings as well as by social change. In particular, the new understanding that museums, as institutions, as well as their visitors,

12 Robert Harbison, *Eccentric Spaces*, p. 147.

are actively involved in meaning making has changed and posed challenges to contemporary museum practices. The emphasis on interpretation and narrative, rather than the amassing and presentation of facts, has posed new questions and issues about what narratives shall be developed and presented, and by whom. And the choices made by museums – in the selection and display of objects, the development of labels and other texts, as well as a myriad of other areas – have come under new scrutiny and assumed a new importance. During the same time period, the role of education in museums has also been greatly expanded, in part due to an evolving mission but also due to marketing and funding imperatives.

In short, then, as the ancient curse terms it: these are "interesting times" for museums, their staff, and their audiences or collaborators. Museum educators, in particular, are confronted with a wide and changing variety of goals and options in their day-to-day work. Indeed, noted educator Danielle Rice writes in her important article, "Museum Education Embracing Uncertainty,"[13] that the public function of museums, often indiscernible from the educative function, may be in crisis as the cultural authority of museums and other institutions has been so dramatically redefined in the late twentieth century. How should museum educators often serving as key links to diverse communities direct their efforts, and to what ends? What are the needs of the varied audiences today's museums hope to serve, and can the diversity of needs and interests be successfully addressed?

One interesting direction, urged by Roberts, is that museums strive to better understand and more clearly identify and present their own values, as opposed to adhering to the fiction of presenting an "objective" point of view. This is consistent with a trend in museum interpretation and teaching to acknowledge and embrace personal experience as a rich vein that has been insufficiently mined in past eras which focused on scholarship and facts. If museums accept the responsibility to enable what Patterson Williams called "personally significant experiences" for their visitors, how do they address their traditionally didactic role? Is it important, for example, when exhibiting an unfamiliar object from a particular religious tradition, that visitors be presented with factual information? How can visitors be motivated to learn about information or perspectives be-

13 The Art Bulletin, A Quarterly Published by the College of Art Association 77, no I (March 1995)

yond their comfort zone or outside their interests? Is such motivational work in the museum's legitimate zone of interest? If museums take up Roberts' suggestion to put their own values on display (which they have arguably been doing all along without stating this), do they undermine their potential to exist as a space for dialogue, open to all?

Roberts' suggestion that museums more honestly put their "own values" on display continues to bother and intrigue me. For this reason, as the title of this talk suggests, I hope to focus our discussion on the questions of what museum values are today (as exemplified by practice and experiences with museums), and what they might become. I hope to provide a starting point via two methods: posing some questions for the group to consider, and also, briefly presenting some current ideas, practices, and problems. In particular, I will draw attention to both promising directions and potential value conflicts. Finally, I will advocate that one important role of the museum educator within museums be to actively engage other museum staff and constituents in the work of clarifying and further developing a set of values for guiding contemporary interpretive practices in museums.

CASE STUDY 1

Mass and Masterpiece

Celebrating the Eucharist in the Renaissance and Baroque

17 September 2000 – 20 May 2001

In 2000, the Ackland received a four-year grant from the Samuel H. Kress Foundation's *Old Masters in Context Program* to develop four small teaching installations designed to suggest the original settings and functions of selected paintings in the Museum's early modern European collection. The first Kress "art in context" exhibition was *Mass and Masterpiece: Celebrating the Eucharist in the Renaissance and Baroque*, which centered on the Ackland's *Madonna and Child with Saints* (c. 1490) attributed to Jacopo del Sellaio and explored the important role altarpieces played in the celebration of the Eucharist in Catholic Europe from the fifteenth through the seventeenth centuries.

We installed *Mass and Masterpiece* in a discrete space within the Museum's large gallery of early modern European art. The idea of a "room with a view" (into a larger room) offered visitors an opportunity to make connections between works installed in the conventional museum manner and those installed in a way that alluded to their original setting. In this way, the installation provided viewers with interpretive strategies for understanding other paintings and sculptures with sacred content. As a teaching tactic, the idea of an installation within an installation was very successful. Just among university visits, for example, *Mass and Masterpiece* brought 1,260 students and faculty from eleven different classes across campus to the Museum. We have since adapted the same approach to installing other works of art, secular as well as sacred, in other galleries.

Mass and Masterpiece provided the Ackland with its first opportunity to test the premise of the *Five Faiths Project* with an art installation dedicated exclusively to the beliefs and practices of a single faith tradition, Roman Catholicism. The small installation, set within the Museum's permanent collection gallery, sought to engage viewers in two ways: interpretive texts and photographs presented information about the original context of altarpieces in Catholic Europe, while liturgical objects, piped-in sacred music (Palestrina, Monteverdi, Gabrieli), and subdued lighting evoked an "atmosphere" of faith that suggested to viewers the experience of worship in Renaissance Italy. In addition, in conjunction with *Mass and Masterpiece*, we sponsored two public programs: *Sacred Masterpieces: A Celebration of Music and Art*, a performance of church music by The University of North Carolina Chamber singers and UNC Concert of Viols, and *Stories of Faith*, a storytelling program of narratives from the Catholic tradition performed by local Catholic practitioners.

Although we had not had the benefit of colloquy discussions about defining a boundary between endorsement and empathy when we installed *Mass and Masterpiece*, we were quite sure that it was best practice to *evoke* rather than *recreate* a sacred setting for the Sellaio altarpiece. The steps we took to do this were modest, but suggestive. We raised the altarpiece six inches and placed it on a new base so that it approximated the height it would have been in its original setting behind an altar. In addition, we placed two (unlit) candles on the protruding base, much as they would have appeared on an actual altar. We also considered placing a prayer stool in front of the altarpiece, but we were uncertain about the constitutionality of seeming to invite prayer in a public institution and refrained from doing so.[14]

Because the liturgical objects we borrowed from Monsignor Tim O'Connor – a monstrance, a chalice, a chasuble, and two Roman missals – were valuable, there was no question of arranging them so as to indicate their sacred functions. As responsible museum curators, we placed the objects in standard museum plexiglass cases, which of course meant that we privileged their aesthetic over their ritual value.

Mass and Masterpiece installation.

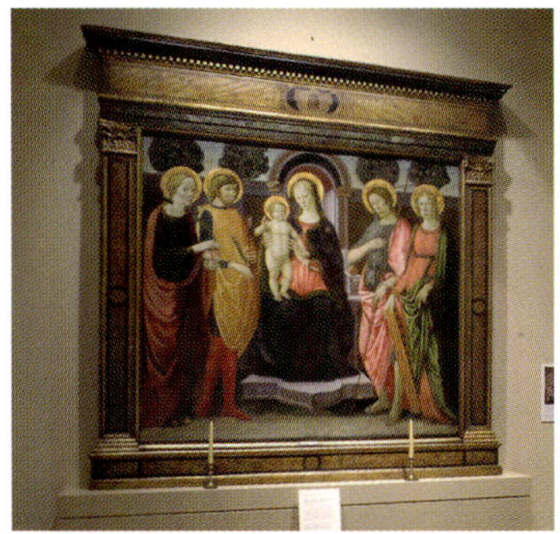

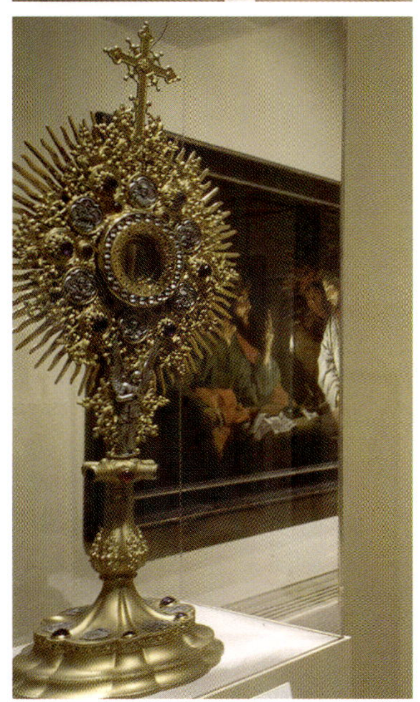

14 In a later Kress *Old Masters in Context* exhibition *(Spectans Specula: Reflecting on Princely and Priestly Perfections)* we did place a prayer stool under a sculpture of the Corpus. By then we had learned from discussions in two Colloquies and were confident that this did not cross the boundary from empathy to endorsement.

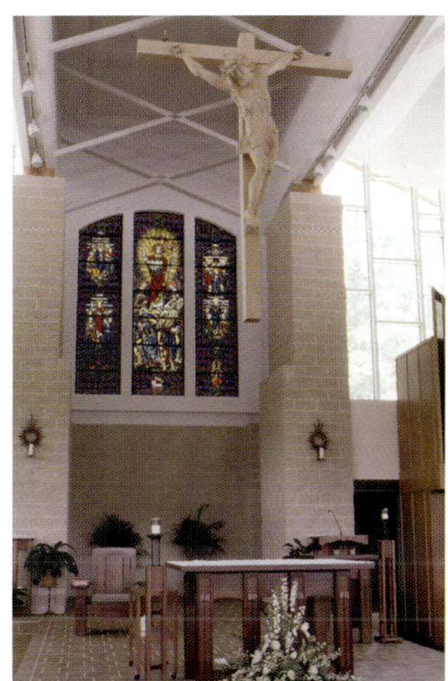

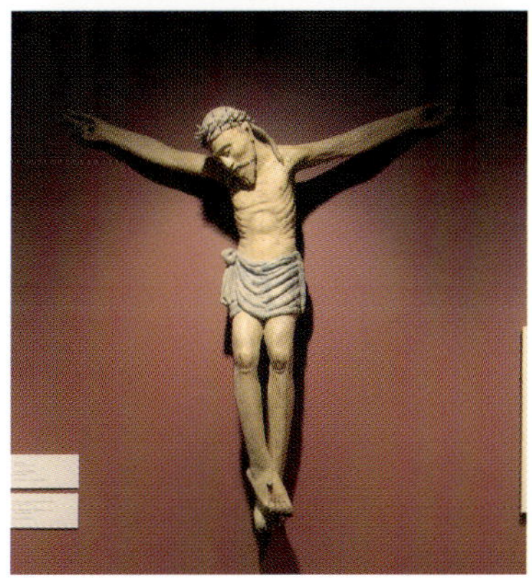

Church of Saint Thomas More in Chapel Hill.

CRUCIFIX CORPUS
Unknown
Tyrolean, 15th or 16th century; painted wood. Gift of Stephen B. Baxter. 2002.20

As part of our planning process for *Mass and Masterpiece*, we consulted with two Catholic priests, Tim O'Connor (Church of Our Lady of Lourdes, Raleigh) and John Durbin (St. Thomas More Catholic Church, Chapel Hill). We invited them to critique our ideas and identify any concerns about our use of language and our interpretation of the objects on display. We also asked them to identify any ideas they felt it critical for us to convey about Roman Catholicism. While both generously gave of their time, they were not in agreement about the exhibition's goal and how we set about achieving it.

O'Connor, a church historian, readily supported our goal to make the past "present" and accessible to museum visitors. Durbin, however, called this goal into question. In his view, we should be as attentive to the current context for understanding Catholic worship as we are to the past. He feared that our predominantly Protestant visitors to the exhibition would presume that past practices (in particular the reliance on images in worship) persisted into the present day. To preclude the possibility that our historical works of art might suggest a faith that was both stagnant and strange, we posted in the exhibition a large wall text written by Durbin about current worship practices in the Roman Catholic Church and an interior photograph of St. Thomas More, which had white-washed walls similar to most Protestant churches. It had never occurred to us, in our wish to educate and promote understanding, that we might unintentionally "exoticize" a tradition, by focusing on the "then" and "there" and excluding the "now" and "here."[15]

15 Father Durbin's fears were grounded in reality. As William Powers observed in the Raleigh *News and Observer* (November 17, 2003), "the deep South remains the least Catholic section of the country." In 2003, when 20% of the U.S. was Catholic, less than 5% of North Carolinians were Catholic. He noted an endemic opposition to Catholicism in North Carolina.

Mass and Masterpiece, the Ackland's first exhibition to consider a single faith tradition, introduced us to a number of issues later considered by the religious studies scholars, faith leaders, and museum professionals of the Five Faiths Colloquies. We learned how difficult it is to negotiate the sacred ground of a faith tradition and the common ground of the art museum. We also learned the benefit of consulting more than one faith leader or community in order to best represent the diversity of opinions and beliefs within each faith tradition. And certainly we discovered the wisdom of presenting both the "then and now" and the "there and here" when introducing audiences to the beliefs and practices of a minority faith. Perhaps our biggest lesson was that our good intentions might have unexpected consequences. We were alerted to the need for a more considered and reflective approach to the *Five Faiths Project* and its activities.

CASE STUDY 2

Word and Worship:

Approaching Islam through Art

15 August – 29 December 2002

> ... our truths are crafted privately by combining and recombining our experiences with the experiences of others.[i]

> For me, prayer is 24 hours a day, and the hours are full of praying. There is no time without praying. When I speak, I use *Insha'allah*, which means "God willing." In the morning when I wake up, I begin my day with God's name saying, *Bismi Llah ir-Rahman ir-Rahim*, or "in the Name of God the most merciful, the most compassionate." Feeling Allah's protection and love around me makes me happy.[ii]

In 2002, the Ackland collaborated with local Muslim faith communities on a small exhibition, *Word and Worship: Approaching Islam through Art*, which drew on the Museum's collection of traditional Islamic art to introduce visitors to three subjects central to understanding the beliefs and practices of Islam: the Qur'an, calligraphy, and prayer (*salat*). The exhibition coincided with Colloquy I and served to focus participants' discussion on a fundamental question: What are the implications of inviting communities of faith to participate in the interpretation and presentation of sacred objects?

The exhibition also coincided with a summer reading program at UNC-Chapel Hill for which the text was Michael Sells' *Approaching the Qur'an: the Early Revelations.*[16] The selection of Sells' book received national attention and provoked controversy around the issues of First Amendment rights. To our knowledge, neither the Ackland nor the

---

16 *Approaching the Qur'an: the Early Revelations/introduced and translated by Michael Sells.* First ed. Ashland, OR: White Cloud Press, 1999.

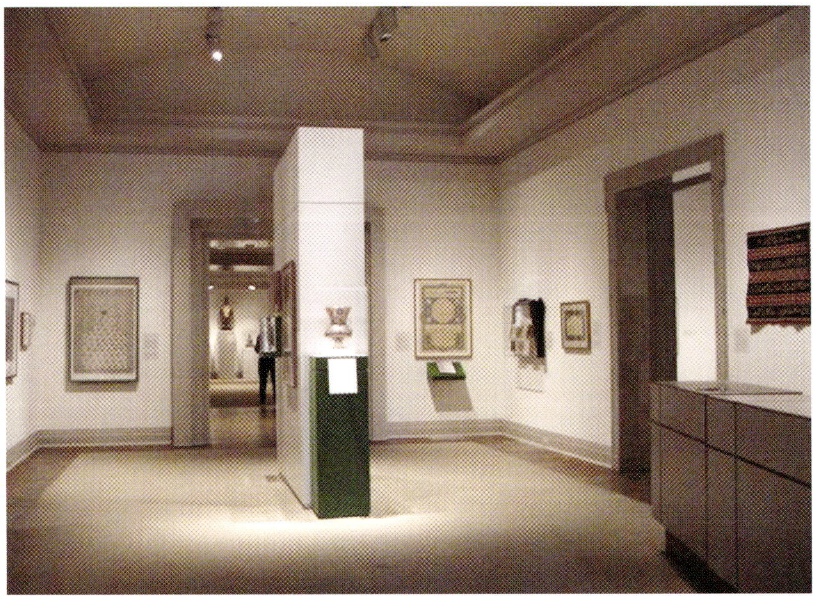

Word and Worship installation.

University anticipated the heated debate and national press coverage prompted by the reading assignment. Still, local Muslim groups on and off campus were pleased about the exhibition and readily agreed to assist the Museum by reviewing our interpretive texts, contributing personal perspectives on selected objects, and participating in public programs.

The Ackland conceived *Word and Worship: Approaching Islam through Art* in part to test the premise that museums were safe places for respectful conversations about faith and that works of art were effective vehicles for encouraging such conversations. While the controversy around the reading assignment continued well into the fall semester, the Ackland exhibition seemed to calm the conversation and engage new voices in the debate. Of course the Museum was concerned about being an institutional face for the argument, particularly because of the location of the Museum on the edge of campus, a bridge between "town and gown." We did what we could to prepare for any questions about our motives and our intentions.[17] In referencing Sells' title in the exhibition's subtitle, our hope was to make it clear that our intent was not to define Islam, rather to map several paths for attaining some understanding of it: by presenting ritual objects and objects with sacred content; by providing insider perspectives; and by making connections between the Museum's traditional objects and current practices among local Muslims.

For help in charting these paths, we arranged to meet with three Muslim communities in advance of the exhibition: the Islamic Center of Raleigh, a large *masjid* and school in the capitol-city suburbs comprised predominately of Muslims from the Middle East; Ar-Razzaq Islamic Center in downtown Durham, a store-front masjid whose members are African American; and the Muslim Student Association at UNC-Chapel Hill. From each community we gained enlighteningly different perspectives on the exhibition and the possibilities it presented for approaching an understanding of Islam.

Labels and Language

The members of the Islamic Center of Raleigh who gathered to talk with us were most concerned about appropriate language in the presentation of the objects in *Word and Worship*. We began our conversation by showing slides of the works proposed for the exhibition, describing standard museum label texts and methods of display, and asking the group for their opinions about both.

The critical lesson learned – and later confirmed by conversations with other faith communities – was that, above all else, one must be sensitive to the nuances of language. For example: one of our standard labels states "Qur'an, 19th century." For those of us accustomed to identifying any edition of the Bible as "the Bible," we assumed this was accurate. For this faith community, however, there is only one Qur'an, the one believed to have been directly imparted to the Prophet Muhammad by the Archangel Gabriel. All others are copies of the original and must be identified as such. Our object label now reads "Copy of the Qur'an, 19th century." Being sensitive to linguistic nuances extends to taking care to use terms in their original language, not only as a courtesy to the faith tradition, but also to avoid words laden with cultural baggage.

17 For example, all staff members, including our security staff, were given talking points in response to media requests for comments.

This was a point argued strongly both by the Islamic Center and colloquy participants. Among the Islamic terms that frequently appear in label texts for sacral objects, we were cautioned to use *masjid* rather than the French word mosque; *sura* rather than the English word chapter; *Qur'an* rather than the anglicized Koran.

The afternoon spent with the Islamic Center had a larger benefit in that it confirmed our premise that conversations centering on objects allows for free discussion and inquiry about faith practices and beliefs. Because we conversed about "third party" objects, we safely shared our preconceptions and misconceptions without offending and without the frustra-

This watch and compass combination indicates both the time and the direction for Muslim prayer. A Muslim prays at least five times a day: at dawn, midday, late afternoon, sunset, and evening, while facing in the direction of Mecca. Originally manufactured in Switzerland, the watch was adorned with invocations and prayers in Arabic calligraphy, by artisans in a workshop in India. The intricacy of the calligraphic arabesque design of the case is accentuated by four concentric bands of blue, green, red and white enamel which form a star in the center. The face of the watch is framed with an Arabic calligraphic band of invocations. (The star and a crescent is a trade mark, perhaps of the workshop where the decorating was done). The inscriptions in the center of the face include Al-shehada (the profession of faith), the first of the five pillars of Islam which translates as follows: "There is no god but God and Muhammad is his Prophet." The name of the original owner also appears. This man, Sheikh Hadji Rahim Bakhsh, was a Shi'ite gem merchant from Ludhiana, a market town in the Punjab.

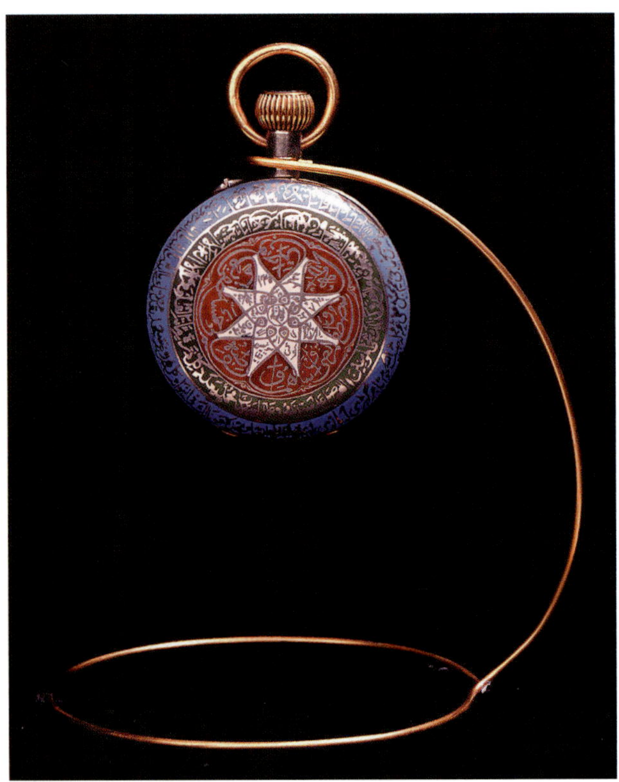

WATCH AND COMPASS
Unknown
North Indian and Swiss, late 19th century; brass, enamel, silver overlay and glass. Ackland Fund, selected by The Ackland Associates.

Islam is not something that just appeared suddenly from foreign shores. It has been part of American history for at least two centuries, and part of European history for over a thousand years ... there have been Muslims in America, including a very famous one in North Carolina, Omar Ibn Sayyed [Said] who, in the early 1800s, wrote his autobiography in Arabic while enslaved on a North Carolina plantation. An exhibit at the Ackland Art Museum at UNC includes a photograph of Sayyed and a document in his handwriting, in Arabic, that is actually an Arabic translation of The Lord's Prayer from the New Testament, that includes blessings on the Prophet Muhammad.

CARL ERNST
DEPARTMENT OF RELIGIOUS STUDIES, THE UNIVERSITY OF NORTH CAROLINA AT CHAPEL HILL

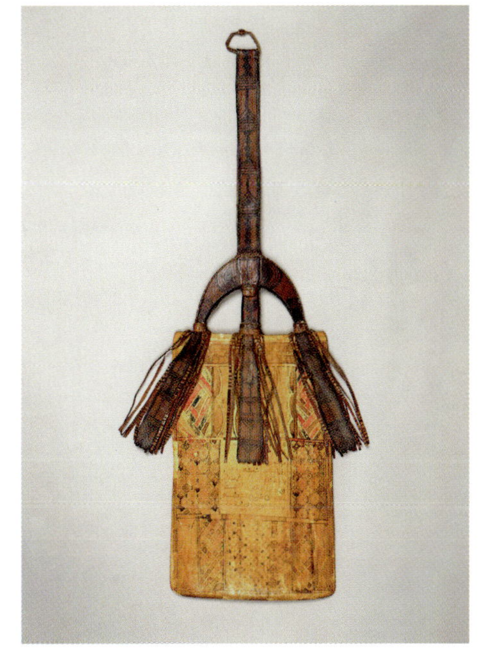

QUR'ANIC PRAYER BOARD
Unknown
African (Nigeria?), 20th century; ink on paper, leather, and wood. Ackland Fund purchased for study purposes.

tions and vehemence that often mark discussions of deeply held beliefs and practices.

Past and Present

In designing *Word and Worship*, we were committed to linking the works in the exhibition, mostly distant in time and geography, to present-day faith practices and practitioners in order to ensure that Islam would be "approached" as a living, local, and evolving tradition. Our meetings with Imam Abdul Waheed and others of the Ar-Razzaq Islamic Center provided the means for bringing Islam into the present day and familiar places. Among his many commitments to his community of faith, Waheed held a strong and personal mission to interfaith dialogue. From his impulse for sharing came a number of images and interpretive materials for use in the exhibition. The photographs we took of the storefront masjid in Durham and the people who worshipped there allowed us to show visitors how objects similar to our traditional works – a prayer mat and a copy of the Qur'an, for example – were used in familiar settings by North Carolinians. The images also served to suggest the diversity of Muslims in terms of their cultural, ethnic, and social backgrounds. These images, presented as "snapshots" without beautiful framing and careful gallery lighting, also provided an important visual dialogue with a photograph of the grand masjid in Pakistan. Even without the aid of contextual labels, the pairing of images suggested one of the many internal diversities of Islam.

Curatorial and Confessional

Our experience with the issues of continuity and change in *Mass and Masterpiece* encouraged us to include photographs of a worship service at Ar-Razzaq; images of ritual objects in use by local Muslims; and labels written by faith practitioners in *Word and Worship*. These very personal perspectives allowed visitors to connect with the faith tradition through illustrations of the "lived experiences" of people in our local community.

We also broadened our standard museum "information sharing" labels to include personal perspectives. By doing so, our labels provided museum visitors more than the traditional models of response to the works of art. They allowed for and validated the subjective *and* the objective access to understanding; the confessional *and* the curatorial.

Canzuel Zulfikar's personal response to the theme of prayer in *Word and Worship*, for example, which she communicated in a *Perspectives* label for the Ackland's prayer mat, offered visitors insight into its meaning through the deeply-felt experience of faith. Because this and other *Perspectives* labels in the exhibition identified the authors and their religious commitments, visitors were clued in to the personal, as opposed to institutional, basis for the label content.

In response to the *Perspectives* labels, Mimi Gates suggested that all texts, including traditional object labels, should follow the *Perspectives* format by identifying authors and their affiliations – curator, religious studies professor, faith practitioner, and so forth. David Power, OMI, agreed, observing that the great advantage of "signed" labels is that they signal to visitors that even object labels are not objective; they present a particular curatorial, or academic, or faith-based approach to the content provided.

Colloquy members readily embraced interpretive inclusiveness from their particular perspectives. Thomas Tweed was drawn to the idea that the Museum could be a forum for discussion: "What [museums] need is a kind of "poly-vocality," with all of the messiness – the conflicting points of view and the inconclusiveness – that comes with it." Rabbi Sharon Mars was intrigued by the idea that works of art could be like pages of the Talmud in which "an object is the central text, and all around it are the commentaries and perspectives of multiple generations going so far back, that you hear reverberations of people who have witnessed it before you ... You don't come to it alone ... You hear the echoes of the past."

Of the many benefits to engaging multiple perspectives in the interpretation of works of art, the most significant for the colloquy participants was the potential of this approach to surmount the most problematic aspect of a single work of art: its inherently reductive nature. As Yaakov Ariel asked, "How can one object, a Torah scroll from western Europe, for example, convey the different practices and beliefs within Judaism?" Multiple perspectives and images of diverse peoples and practices assist museums in suggesting, albeit obliquely, the richness and diversity, and the changes over time, within each faith tradition.

---

i David Carr, *The Promise of Cultural Institutions*, 2003, "Museums and Public Trust," p. 126.

ii Canzuel Zulfikar, Chapel Hill resident originally from Turkey, responding to a prayer mat in *Word and Worship: Approaching Islam through Art*, Ackland Art Museum, August 15 – December 29, 2002.

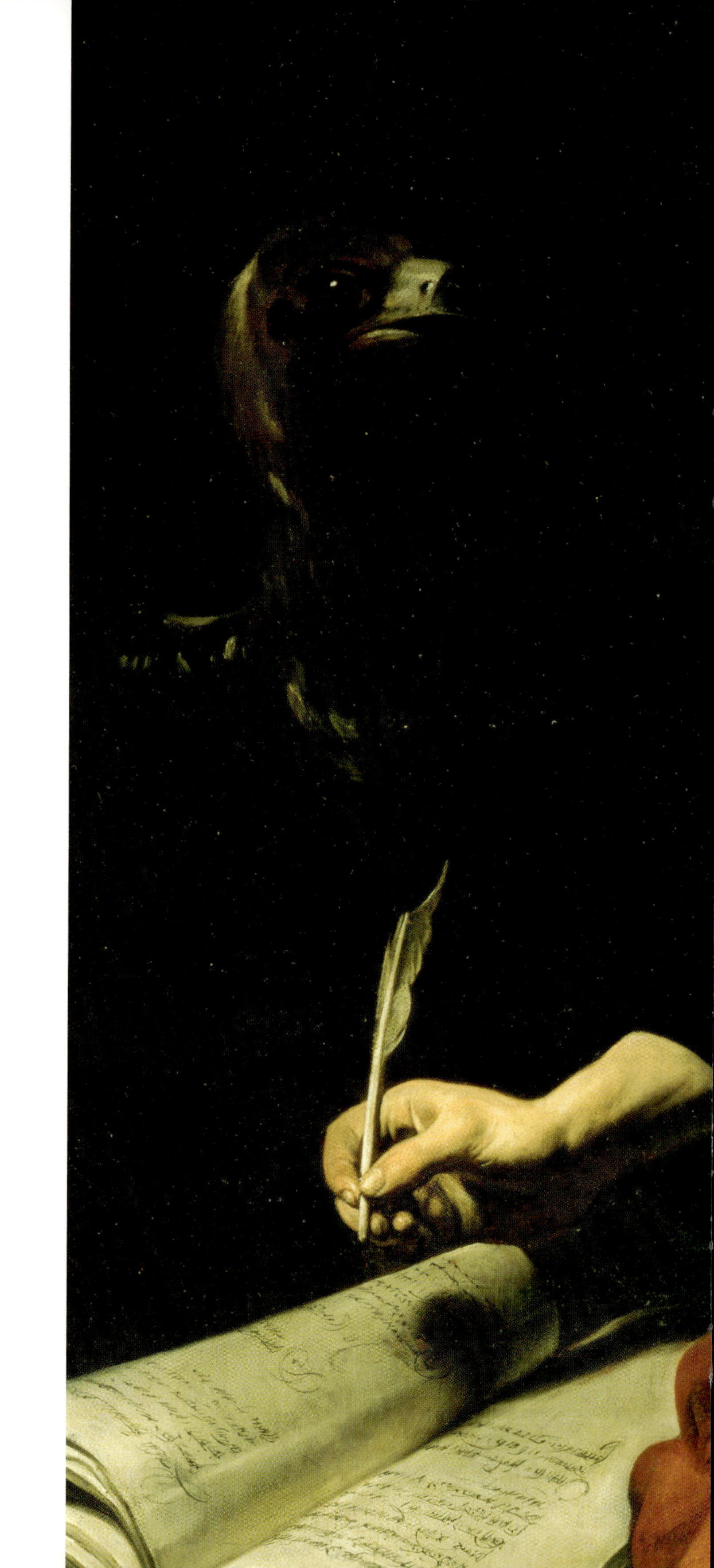

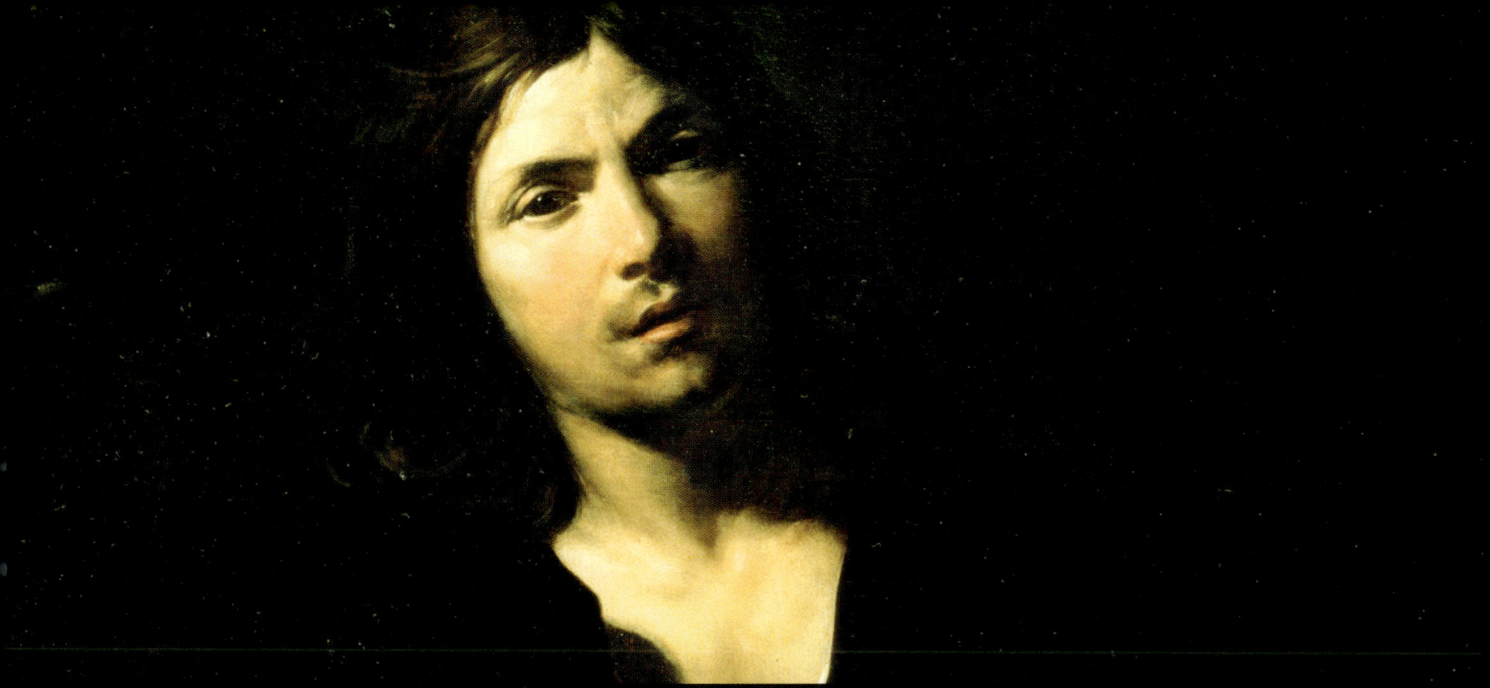

ATTEND TO THE ISSUES OF LANGUAGE:

aim for impeccable precision

allow for the inclusion of new and traditional vocabulary

creatively frame new questions in order to prompt new answers

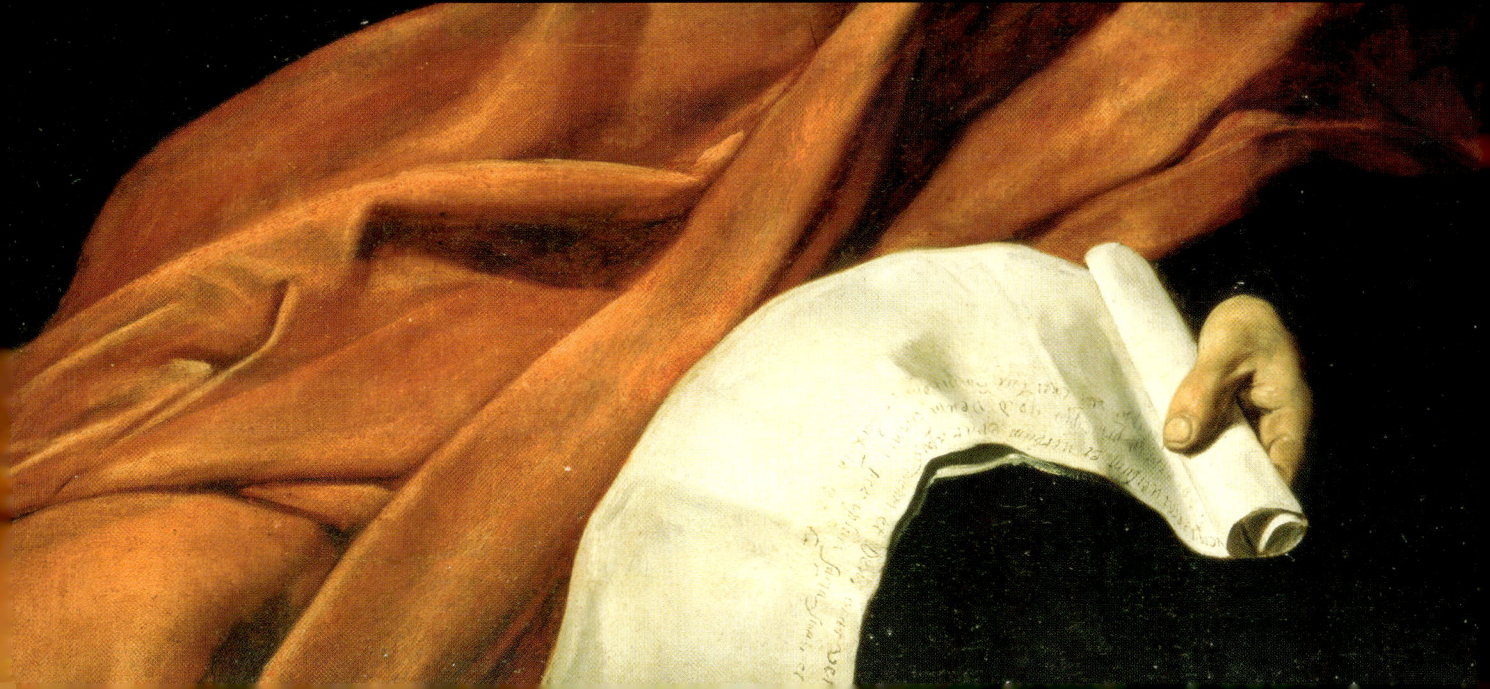

ST. JOHN THE EVANGELIST
Valentin de Boulogne
French (active in Rome), 1591-1632: c. 1622; oil on canvas.
The William A. Whitaker Foundation Art Fund, 63.4.1.

Accompanied by his emblem, the eagle, John sits with pen in hand between an apparently completed book, possibly symbolic of the Old Testament, and a scroll on which he has written the first sentences of his Gospel. As he looks upward, light from an invisible source picks out his face, his writing hand, and the scroll as the dominant elements in the picture.

Colloquy II

CONSIDERING THE LIVES OF SACRED IMAGES

> If we wish a collection to be *used* by a religious community, if we wish to revivify the objects in it, then religious communities and museums must negotiate a new understanding of the museum space and the objects in it.[i]
>
> We are, above all, custodians of works of art.[ii]
>
> The curator has the power to decide whose needs are met, how an object is defined in a given space and time, and which objects are more highly regarded.[iii]

At the end of the first Colloquy, Charles Orzech encouraged the Ackland to venture further than the limited ways in which the *Five Faiths Project* originally sought to engage faith communities through outreach.[1] His suggestion prompted us to consider some of the first assumptions of the *Project*, and led us to wonder whether the *Project* had been overly exclusive in selecting participants for its early activities. For example, the Museum did not invite Protestants (as a type) to participate in the *Visions of Faith* exhibition. We

---

1 The conversations of year one prompted many re-considerations of the origin and early history of the *Project* with the benefit of hindsight. We raise this only to remind the founders of new projects to assess their own assumptions and biases by adding voices and opinions in the early stages of planning that might otherwise have been excluded.

did invite Roman Catholics. Was this because Catholicism continues to be perceived as an "exotic" religion in North Carolina, with more in common with Hinduism and Buddhism? Or was it because the Museum assumed that its members and visitors were predominantly Protestant and therefore already engaged and in no need of special consideration? Interestingly, the two Protestant churches, Baptist and Methodist, that flank the Museum in downtown Chapel Hill did not participate. In fairness, the *Project* was designed to increase the involvement of immigrant communities, but (for example) not all Cambodian immigrants are Buddhist; also important to recall is that in North Carolina as in other parts of the country, many (in this case Cambodian) immigrants were hosted by Protestant faith communities at the time of immigration. Similarly, not all Latino immigrants are Catholic or Arab immigrants, Muslim.

Projects like the *Five Faiths Project* are not conceived *in toto*, but rather follow the directions created by the interests of those who readily engage in the process of a new initiative. Those who have engaged in community outreach know that one can hope to find interested collaborative partners in every encounter, but it happens only rarely and for a multitude of reasons. At the Ackland, the direction of the *Project* was shaped by its original goals as well as the responsiveness of its early partners. It was also limited by the objects in our collection and the objects available to the Museum.

The Ackland knew that practitioners could offer the *Project* a much deeper understanding of our objects and their use in ritual practices and personal devotions. But Orzech also asked for more. He wanted the *Five Faiths Project* to "set these objects free" from the constraints of curatorial practice and watch what might happen. By the end of the first Colloquy, we were talking about who owns the object, who uses the object, and who understands the object. Participants had come a long way from the question that launched the Colloquy: what are the limits and potentials of art in serving as teaching tools for understanding world religions? Now, it seemed, it was time to imagine strategies to integrate even more diverse and divergent perspectives whenever museums present works of art.

Another concern shaped our consideration as we prepared for the second Colloquy. The founder of the *Project* knew from his initial interactions with public school children that the Museum's sacral objects would give minority and immigrant communities a welcome touchstone in their new environment, and might establish the Museum as a resource for them. While it is true that members of these communities participated actively in early programs, after six years, even the most involved never embraced the idea that works of art within the Museum setting were of sustained value to their communities. Faith leaders did not send their youth groups to the Museum, nor did priests, rabbis, imams, and teachers from these traditions engage the collection in order to instruct the faithful in doctrine and tradition. It seemed the *Project* needed the religious communities more than they needed our objects, no matter how high the exhibition value of these objects might be and how much each community seemed to value the *Project*. The faith communities may have shared our goals for outreach, but while they were not restricted to object-based strategies for promoting understanding, the Museum was. Orzech was right when he asserted that faith communities do not need a museum quality Shiva Linga to experience *darshan*, the Hindu word for the sacred experience of seeing and being seen by the divine in encounters with sacred images. On the other hand, the Museum needed the faith communities in order to represent accurately and fairly the belief in that possibility.

Similarly, the *Five Faiths Project* started with a deep truth claim of its own: our historical objects, because they are rare, exemplary, or valuable, regardless of their original locations, will resonate with contemporary practitioners of each of the traditions. That is, North Carolina Catholics will recognize and appreciate the devotional properties of an Italian fifteenth-century altarpiece, and an eleventh-century Thai Buddha head will be meaningful for any one who practices Buddhist meditation. The Project seemed to have underestimated the particularities, and perhaps the limitations, of its own time and place.

Among other considerations, the Ackland began to question why the *Project* presented so many of these objects a-historically: why, for example, it often used as its starting point core tenets of belief, as though these were universal and enduring, or passages from sacred texts, as though the texts were uncontested and presented factual, historical records of events. Colloquy participants consistently reminded us that all five faiths changed over time, were self-reflexive, and adapted to new circumstances. They reminded us – and one another – that many of the assertions found in object labels were hotly contested truth claims, both historically and in contemporary communities.

Thus, for Colloquy II, with these questions in mind, participants brought their expertise and insights to bear in consideration of five objects as case studies for applying the recommendations of Colloquy I. We distributed images and current interpretive texts, and asked participants to examine the objects from their distinct perspectives. We asked them to think like stakeholders, and to be rigorous about asserting what each considered the essential information to be if a walk-in visitor was to understand their object accurately. What we learned was that much of the Museum's interpretation currently presented was neither essential nor accurate. Participants spent two and a half days imagining, articulating, and applying strategies for including both the sacral and the curatorial in presentation and interpretation.

What began as a community outreach project became a museum in-reach project. The possibilities for engaging objects and communities seemed limitless and the potential for museums becoming contact zones seemed undeniable. The question now was would museums welcome in-reach and how would they manage it? How much interpretive territory would curators and directors yield to new immigrants to museum culture?

For our part, as the "curators" of Colloquy I, we controlled the agenda, carefully orchestrating the conversations so that they followed one another in a logical sequence. In curating Colloquy II, however, it became necessary to cede territory to now deeply engaged colloquy participants with their own agendas. We responded to Patrice Brodeur's and Vivian Mann's requests to present ideas from their own research and included them in the program. With more than two dozen deeply engaged and highly motivated participants, "it was a messy business," to borrow a phrase from Colloquy I. Loose threads and unanswered questions made the *Project* more sensitive to the strains of this in-reach and to the demands on time and resources required to implement new directions suggested by new voices. Were the aspirations of Colloquy I attainable? Could a museum-based project develop a new, syncretistic language? Could the Museum apply to all traditions the interpre-

"Curators should honor faith voices pertaining to the objects on display. But they should not necessarily privilege them as the final or ultimate voices. If we brought someone from the Morrisville Hindu temple to the Museum to talk about the Shiva Nataraja, *I would be interested and respectful, but I would also reserve my own right to talk about the history of the* Nataraja.*"*

RICHARD DAVIS

"In the classroom and in academic research, as well as in the museum setting, we must work to make room for religious ways of seeing in the presentation of religious ideas and images."

CHRISTOPHER WILSON

tive principles used for one tradition? Could we present the biography of every object in every gallery?

The keynote speaker was Richard Davis whose *The Lives of Indian Images* had impressed us. Davis's presentation on the long history of the *Dancing Shiva* prompted a new set of concerns about what, traditionally, has been omitted from museum labels. The addition of the object's biography suddenly seemed essential. Patrice Brodeur's presentation on language and methodology suggested new approaches to objects from the perspective of certain universal principles, and prompted spirited debate about whether it was possible to define any sacred universals. The conversation raised more questions than it answered. Vivian Mann presented what she considered to be the essential content in objects from the Abrahamic traditions as a kind of road map for objects of all faiths. Her hope to apply norms that might make the presentation of sacral objects more manageable met a tactful and quick move away from what appeared to be a problematic premise: models derived from Jewish or Christian perspectives could have universal application. Every session ran long and every presentation prompted new questions and challenged old assumptions. The excitement was palpable and conversation fast paced. Over the course of two and a half days, the participants generated remarkable materials with which to approach objects in the Ackland's collection.[2]

Summary

Richard Davis's presentation focused exclusively on a single work, and by doing so, increased awareness of the power of the narratives through which we approach an object. By tracing the more than one thousand-year biography of the *Dancing Shiva* from community devotion, to protective burial, to an archaeological museum, to a private collection, and finally to its present location in an inaccessible storage vault, Davis challenged the timeframe used in typical museum interpretations and presentations. He also stressed the importance of particularities: "look at different types of relocations, and dis-

---

2 For us, the authors of this book, ceding territory was nerve wracking but transformative. Because of these chaotic conversations, inclusivity and intellectual hospitality became cherished ideals that have helped us to address our work, and assess our successes and our failures in meeting the challenges of this *Project*. These conversations also helped build empathy for the burdens of museum administration. Directors carry institutional responsibilities that must temper even the most visionary leadership.

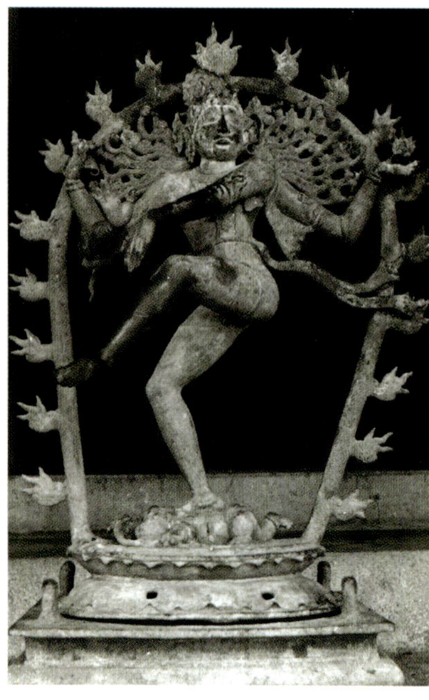

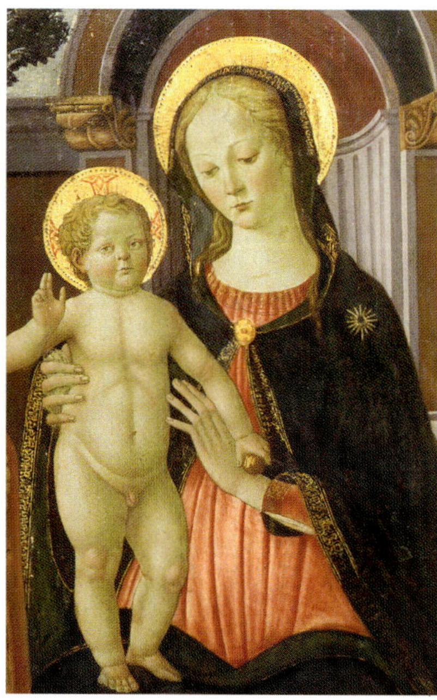

"I believe these objects, often the immigrant residents of the non-Western galleries of our museums, call out to us with important challenges. As privileged viewers of the collected, often expropriated, art objects of the world, we owe it to these relocated objects to understand the religious worlds from which they have come. And I argue we must also acknowledge the varied identities these objects have assumed, and the human activities and processes by which they have been brought before us."
RICHARD DAVIS

ruptions, and fabrications, and re-evaluations over time and relate those to different kinds of audiences." As Davis noted, every understanding of an object is unstable and conditional. When museums present objects, typically they present only one moment in a life subjected to shifts and changes, to vagaries of taste and value. Accustomed to heeding the careers of artists, it was a revelation that we should also attend to the careers of objects.

The career of the Ackland's altarpiece, *The Madonna and Child with Saints*, for example, has been varied. Most recently, after decades on view as a valued teaching object and a favorite among visitors, *The Madonna and Child* was moved to storage. More than the limitations of our gallery spaces informed the decision to move the object. Works of art are subject to curatorial preferences, exhibition opportunities, and the changing scope of a collection. Nam June Paik's *Eagle Eye* experienced a reversal of

SHIVAPURAM NATARAJA (DANCING SHIVA OF SHIVAPURAM)
Unknown
South Indian, central Tamilnad, late 10th century CE; bronze.
Icon Centre at Tiruvarus
Photo courtesy of the Institut Français de Pondichéry and Ecole Française d'Extrême-Orient.

THE MADONNA AND CHILD WITH SAINTS
Attributed to Jacopo del Sellaio
Italian, Florence, ca. 1441-1493; tempera and gold on wood panel.
The William A. Whitaker Foundation Art Fund, 63.18.1. (detail)

EAGLE EYE
Nam June Paik
American, 1932-2006: 1996; antique slide projector, aluminum, computer keyboards, eye chart, neon, nine 5-inch televisions, two 9-inch televisions and DVD player. © 1996 Nam June Paik. Ackland Fund, 99.8.

ENDLESS VICTORY
John F. Simon, Jr.
American, born 1963, 2005; software, Apple Powerbook G4, and acrylic plastic. © 2005 John F. Simon, Jr. Ackland Fund, 2005.19.

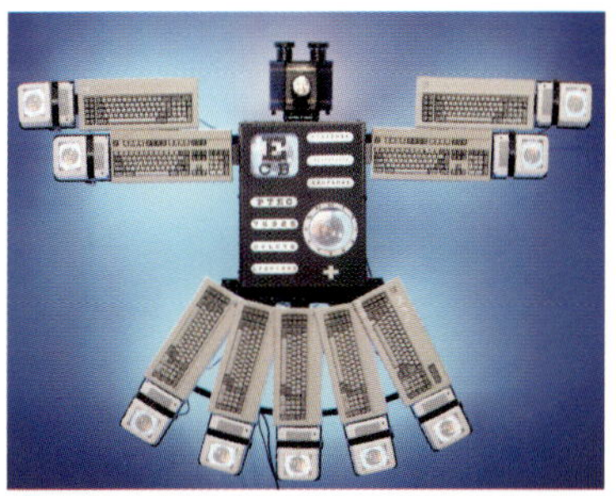

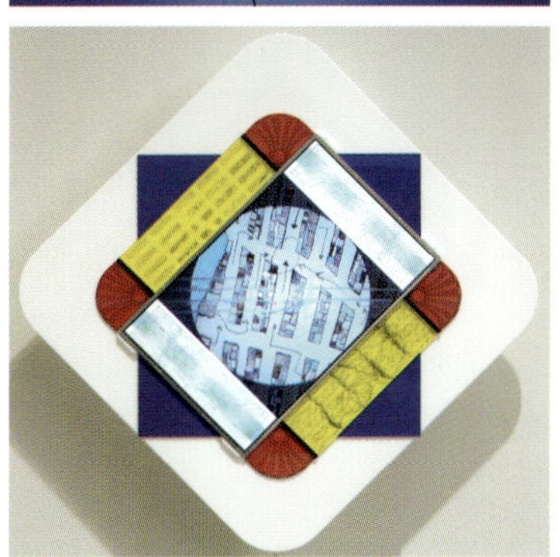

fortune when Ackland curators acquired John F. Simon's *Endless Victory*, a newer work with more advanced technology.[3] This is not to say that these works will not find favor in the future, only to point out that judgments about display or storage are regular occurrences in museum culture. Davis strongly advocated that we share with visitors this value transience by making the particular history of each object transparent. The potential meanings of each object are limited by a lack of information about the object.

Davis brought the postmodern world into focus, acknowledging that everything is contingent, nothing is static, not even the value and meaning of works of art. His presentation was a powerful reminder that approaches to objects, like relationships among human beings, are informed by histories, our own and others.

Vivian Mann's presentation countered postmodern contingency by insisting that it is both possible and beneficial to identify enduring commonalities across traditions and across time. Mann was not the first to encourage the *Five Faiths Project* to employ comparative strategies in presenting objects with sacred content.[4] However, she usefully shifted comparisons of beliefs to comparable questions about beliefs. By applying the same questions across the traditions, the questions themselves form a common ground on which to consider diversities and particularities.[5]

---

3 Paik's *Eagle Eye* employs various technologies that were once high tech (a DVD player with rapidly changing still images) juxtaposed with other objects that we now think of as antiques (a lantern slide projector, for example). Simon uses computer programming to create ever changing, non-repeating images in *Endless Victory*.

4 The content reviewer for the Islamic Council on Education insisted that comparison was an essential strategy for teaching about world religions. The Ackland heard from classroom teachers who wished that the stories included in the *Voices of Faith* project contained comparable content. How, one asked, can you compare a Jakata tale of the Buddha with a memory of a holiday meal?

5 See pages 191-217 for one example of the Ackland's attempt to apply this principle to volunteer gallery teacher training.

Patrice Brodeur revisited the problem of language first addressed in Colloquy I. He based his presentation on his experiences in attempting to find common ground and coming to an understanding about sacred objects and faith traditions through parallel questions. Despite skillful attempts, he found these parallel questions remained problematic because the language used in framing the questions remains restrictive and biased. For example, the words "sacred," "faith," and "religion" are, he reminded us, European constructs, derived from Jewish and Christian perspectives, and, therefore, are not uniformly applicable to Hinduism, Buddhism, and other non-Western traditions. As Brodeur proclaimed:

> Goodbye to the notion that we can ever achieve a neutral language, an objectivity that we will all agree upon, despite our deeply ingrained human desire for universals.

Since no single definition suffices, and objects are both bearers and transmitters of multiple meanings, we need a "dialogical methodology" that will bring together various stakeholders to uncover (and discover, in many cases) the coexisting meanings related to any "sacred" object.[6] He was describing, in fact, the methodology of the Colloquy series and anticipating the approach taken in the subsequent activities of Colloquy II.

All three presenters personified the objects, asking museums to set them "in relationship." Davis asked museums to establish the relationship of the object to its time line; to its history and its potential future. For example, visitors should know that the Ackland's statue of Parvati in her early life would

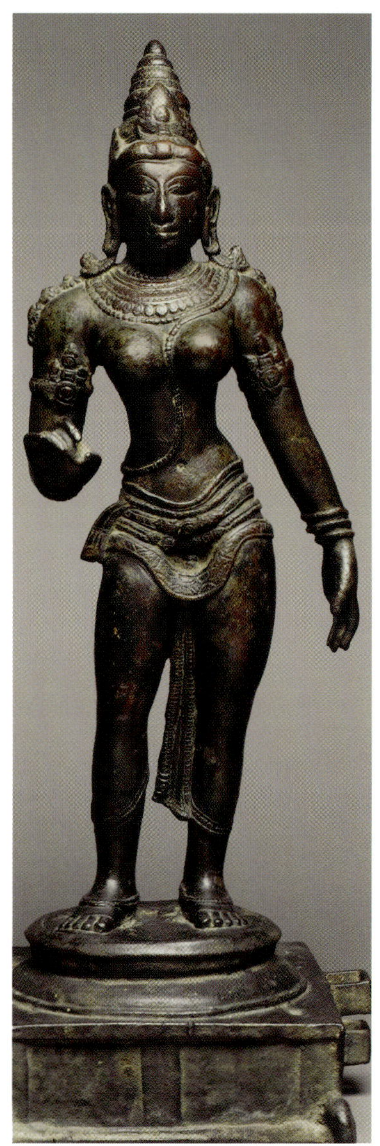

CONSORT GODDESS/PARVATI
Unknown
Tamil Nadu, Kavera delta region, mid-to-late 10th century; bronze. Gift of F.B. Vanderhoef in honor of Charles W. Millard, 91.23.

6 Brodeur's approach is comparable to Viswanathan's introduction of Assman's syncretistic translation: from sustained dialogue a new language will emerge.

KIDDUSH CUP
Hieronymus Mittnacht
German (active in Augsburg), died 1769: 1759-1761; silver-gilt, engraved, and chased. The William A. Whitaker Foundation Art Fund, 99.21. (detail)

JEWELED CHALICE
Barkentin & Krall
British (London): 1907-08; gilded silver, amethysts, and peridots. On loan from Rhoda I. and Roger M. Berkowitz. (detail)

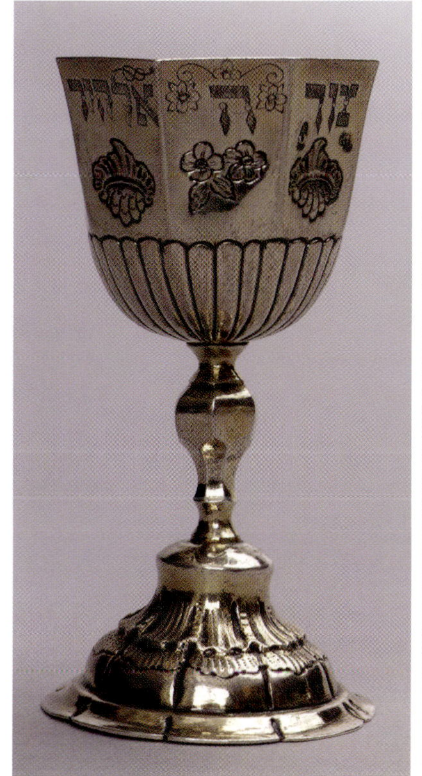

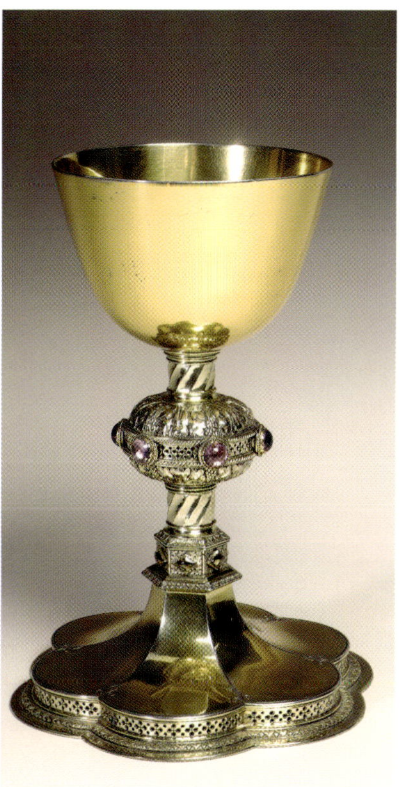

never have appeared as she is in the Museum, unclothed in public. They should also know that, while the Ackland long understood her to be Parvati and told Parvati's stories routinely in gallery lessons, new research calls that identity into question. She is likely not Parvati at all, but a consort goddess, with a completely different life story.

Mann asked museums to establish the object in relationship to other objects with comparable functions to build understanding across faith traditions. The Ackland's *Kiddush Cup* and the *Jeweled Chalice* could be presented as having comparable functionality – both hold wine for use in ritual – and therefore can be comparably regarded.

Brodeur asked museums to establish the object in relationship to the language we use to talk about it. For example, does the object title, "Burmese Buddha" convey anything about how the object might have been used, what stories it references, or why it might be considered sacred?

Everyone shared the conviction that the Museum must attend to the issues of language by aiming for impeccable precision, by allowing for the inclusion of new and traditional vocabulary, and by creatively framing new questions in order to prompt new answers. The stage was set for what Brodeur called the "battle for human meaning unfolding in museums today."

While the discussions gave rise to theoretically intriguing and often practically impossible models, they did compel the museum professionals to review their practices. The activities designed for Colloquy II gave everyone a chance to apply some of their new awareness. The idea behind the activities was not only to test the participants' theories, but also to test standard museum practice, and to bring everyone closer to workable models. The activities served to balance and adjust curatorial scholarship – on which museums typically rely in interpretive materials – with faith perspectives. In doing so, the activities successfully introduced nuances of meaning that prompted careful consideration of language in the Museum's interpretive materials.

Having reviewed the material sent in advance of the gathering, small-group members worked to reach consensus on the essential content for five objects. Then, they were invited to compose labels incorporating as much of that content as possible. They were encouraged to limit the length to 200 words (long for a standard museum label) and to attempt to keep the vocabulary appropriate for walk-in visitors (approximately tenth-grade level, as in *The New York Times*). Each small-group, composed of different stakeholders, worked on one object.

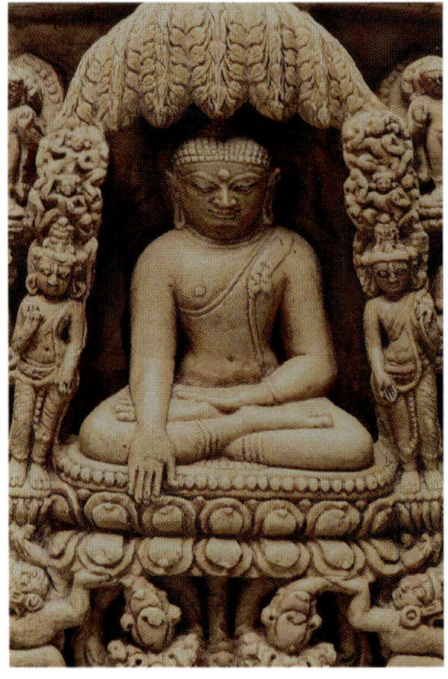

BUDDHA CALLING THE EARTH TO WITNESS
Unknown
Burmese, Myanmar, probably from the city of Paga around the 13th century; andagu stone (pyrophyllite). Ackland Fund, 97.14.1. (detail)

Of course, the label actually refers to this work as "Buddha Calling the Earth to Witness." But, the insider habit of referring to this as the "Burmese Buddha" as though that were a sufficient descriptive caught the attention of Colloquy participants. Even "Calling the Earth to Witness" does little to explain the object's significance or its use. And it does nothing to clarify the many other stories depicted in the carvings that surround the central figure.

Three examples are noteworthy:[7]

In the first, which centered on the *Shiva Linga*, faith practitioners and scholars took issue with the Ackland's presentation based on current scholarship. In their view, the Ackland curators had made serious errors in interpreting the linga. The original label focused on a post-Freudian understanding of the shape of the linga; noted the four visible faces, while disregarding the invisible fifth; and presented the object as representing one of Hinduism's "gods," thereby reinforcing a Western approach to Hinduism as polytheistic.

In the second, which considered the Islamic *Book of Blessings* and *Copy of the Qur'an* (displayed together), practitioners identified ways in which the labels and the installation misrepresented the objects' significance. The original label stated that the blessings expressed "devotion to Muhammad." As the faith practitioners pointed out, they are in fact prayers *to* Allah *on behalf* of Muhammad. The side-by-side installation of the two books also disturbed the practitioners. With that installation, the Museum had not given the copy of the Qur'an a privileged status above the *Book of Blessings*: the Qur'an was not elevated, it was on the left of the *Book of Blessings* rather than the primary right, and it was behind a curtain that visitors had to open in order to see it. Museum preparators designed the curtain to protect both books from light, but faith practitioners felt it implied a kind of secrecy inconsistent with the practices of Islam.

In the third, which addressed the altarpiece of *The Madonna and Child with Saints*, faith practitioners questioned the Museum's teaching strategies that center on Mary and devotion to her as a distinguishing feature of Catholicism. The faith practitioners emphasized the liturgical function of the altarpiece, in which Mary serves simply as an attribute of Christ, who is the medium and the message in the painting. As they noted, the title of the altarpiece both indicates the Museum's misunderstandings and assumes insider knowledge. Do our visitors know who the Madonna is? Who the child is? What, they asked, makes someone a saint, and how can one tell which saints, among the many

7 In order to make the rigors of this set of activities clear and to engage the strains of selecting what might be included or excluded, we have included extensive selections from the presentations and conclusions for all five objects selected for the activity. Each sample includes the original label and the new labels drafted in small-group sessions. Some additional materials are included in three of the five case studies as exemplary of the processes engaged by participants.

hundreds of possibilities, are depicted?

Following the small-group discussions about essential content, the five groups then grappled with the challenge of prioritizing and incorporating their diverse perspectives (scholarly, faith-based, and curatorial) into 200-word labels for their objects. Out of this activity, the groups proposed several strategies for developing inclusive labels – or not. One strategy, for example, was to limit the information provided in the label and to ask questions that directed viewing, thereby avoiding any conflicting perspectives. Sharon Mars suggested another approach based on the idea of the Talmud: surround the object with multiple labels, each from a different perspective:

> My mind keeps returning to the metaphor of a page of the Talmud because what you have [in the object] is the central text, and all around it are the commentaries and perspectives of multiple generations going so far back, that you just hear reverberations of people who have witnessed it before you. You don't really come to it alone ... You hear the echoes of the past.

However, as the same group also acknowledged, this strategy loses the splendid isolation that holds so much appeal for museum curators and visitors alike and may restrict deep appreciation of the aesthetic value of the object.

A third strategy selected essential content from each of the three stakeholder perspectives and clearly identified the perspective from which each type of content came: curatorial (or exhibition value), scholarly, and faith (or cult value, as one participant described it). This strategy appealed to participants because it clearly indicated to visitors that there is more than one way to understand a single object. Still, there was the issue of transparency. The tripartite label employed an omniscient curatorial voice, an omniscient scholarly voice, and an omniscient faith voice. The problem of transparency had not been solved; it had multiplied.

Museum culture already has a solution for this issue, although gallery texts rarely employed it at the Ackland. The standard practice for collection publications in which several authors contribute catalogue entries is to identify the writers of each entry, thereby holding them accountable for the information they chose to present. Again, the colloquy participants turned to their recommendation in Colloquy I, simply that label writers identify themselves by name and affiliation and thereby be held accountable for the interpretation(s) presented. As one put it, "This will help Museum visitors understand that they are reading one person's perspective on the object and one person's choice about which types of information to include."

By the end of Colloquy II, transparency was of paramount importance if the *Project* was to achieve its goals. Works of art may have the potential to build and sustain understanding about world religions, but only in as much as museums are willing to welcome new perspectives, bring outside voices and concerns into the curatorial process, and remain transparent about the authorship of all interpretive materials.

The Dancing Shiva of Shivapuram:

Cult and Exhibition in the Life of an Indian Icon

Submitted by:
Richard Davis
Religious Studies, Bard College

In his influential essay, "The Work of Art in the Age of Mechanical Reproduction," Walter Benjamin distinguishes two principal ways humans receive and value art objects. The first he terms the "cult value" of an object embedded within its tradition, whose value consists in the role it plays in a ritual setting. He contrasts this with the "exhibition value" of a work of art, where the value of an object derives from its availability to the gaze of an audience, and the degree to which it repays a viewer's visual attentiveness.

Benjamin's distinction provides a good starting point for examining a category of objects we find in every North American and European art museum: objects that have been removed from their original ritual settings, relocated in Western museum displays, and in the process transformed from religious objects into works of art. In Benjamin's terms, the earlier "cult value" of such an object for its original community has been replaced by the "exhibition value" it holds for a new audience with very different convictions and expectations. I believe these objects, often the immigrant residents of the non-Western galleries of our museums, call out to us with important challenges. As privileged viewers of the collected, often expropriated, art objects of the world, we owe it to these relocated objects to understand the religious worlds from which they have come. And I argue we must also acknowledge the varied identities these objects have assumed, and the human activities and processes by which they have been brought before us.

My own method for approaching these challenges has been a biographical one. Starting from the Indian premise that consecrated icons are alive with an animating divine presence, I have tried to retrace the lives of particular Indian religious objects over time, as if they are indeed alive. Benjamin would call this the "aura" of an original art object, which he defines as "the essence of all that is transmissible from its beginning, ranging from its substantive duration to its testimony to the history which it has experienced." Preferring less metaphysical language, I speak of life narratives. Objects have life stories, just as humans do. Many objects are born and live their entire lives without leaving their own villages, just as many humans do. But some objects experience lives of travel and change, disruption and transformation, influence and celebrity, and it is the lives of such mutable objects that make for the most interesting biographies. I believe a biographical approach can help us question both cult value (i.e., original intent) and exhibition value (i.e., aesthetic quality) as constituting the unique and essential identity of an object. Biographies highlight the ways that identities can be reframed in different settings and renegotiated in encounters with different audiences, without necessarily privileging any one identity.

Here I wish to tell the story of one Indian religious image that led a particularly eventful life. After an early life spent in a small South Indian village temple, and then buried underground for several centuries, the *Shivapuram Nataraja* enjoyed more than its fifteen minutes of fame in the early 1970s when it was sold to a wealthy art collector, Norton Simon, for nearly one million dollars. It then became a disputed object in a highly publicized repatriation case pitting Simon against the government of India. After an out-of-court settlement, it now lives in quiet retirement back in South India, though I for one hope that this is not the final chapter in the life of the Dancing Shiva from Shivapuram.

The Nataraja as Cultic Icon

Shivapuram is a small and ancient village in the fertile rice-growing delta region of central Tamilnad. The temple to Shiva there goes back at least to 800 CE, when two famous Shaiva poet-saints visited and celebrated the shrine. Sometime in the late tenth century, the bronze image of Nataraja was fabricated and ritually installed in the Shivapuram temple, along with another new icon representing Shiva in a different manifestation, Somaskanda.

For medieval South Indian worshippers of Shiva, this temple and many others like it were places of divine presence, where Shiva made himself physically present in material icons, so that his human worshippers might offer their tokens of devotion and honor. Neither Nataraja nor Somaskanda would have been the primary cult icon in the temple at Shivapuram. That role was occupied by a Shiva-linga, a plain, non-anthropomorphic cylindrical shaft that, according to Shaiva theology, represented Shiva in his most complete manifest form. In Shivapuram, as in nearly all South Indian Shaiva temples of the period, the Shiva-linga stood in the center of the temple sanctum, and received the primary daily offerings of worship. At the same time Shaivas believed that Shiva could manifest himself in a great multiplicity of material supports: consecrated icons, fire, water-pots, human priests, books, and many other physical objects. Ritual texts set out a hierarchy of divine supports ranked in terms of subtlety. According to the Shaiva guidebooks, the Shiva-linga as an abstract object was more subtle and therefore superior to the anthropomorphic bronzes that represented and supported Shiva in a more comprehensible form. Higher still was Shiva in a completely formless aspect, as Paramashiva, but then this aspect of Shiva was not visible to humans.

Visibility and accessibility were the purpose of a bronze image like Nataraja. As Chola-period temples on the one hand became more restrictive, with only certain persons able to enter the sanctum, there was reciprocally a growth in festival processions, when Shiva would venture forth from his sanctuary to see and be seen by his devotees. Since the fixed stone linga was immobile, Shiva would inhabit his mobile bronze icons such as Somaskanda and Nataraja during these regular parades. Festivals offered moments of sumptuous display. The processional image was beautifully dressed and ornamented, decked with flowers, and surrounded with all the pomp suitable to Shiva's lordly stature. Devotees responded to the spectacle as the visible manifestation of the god on earth. Exhibition value, it would appear, merges with cult value in the temple procession.

Concealment

Some people sail through life on a straight course. For others, disruptions like divorce, unemployment, disease, and war bring about major changes in their lives, and may lead to personal transformations. So, too, with religious images. Many Chola-period bronzes are still in their original temple locations. But not at Shivapuram. The disruptions that would alter the life of the *Shivapuram Nataraja* and several of its companions began with a layoff from ritual employment. At least five bronze icons were removed from the Shivapuram temple and buried.

The burial of religious icons must have been quite common in South India, for many hundreds have been accidentally discovered in the last century, often by farmers plowing rice fields or workmen digging foundations. These interments have nothing to do with death; "dead" metal images, those no longer suitable for religious purposes, are generally melted down in a fire, much as human corpses are cremated rather than buried in India. Instead, burial was a strategy of image concealment. "When there is danger on account of thieves or enemy armies, or when there is disorder in the community," advises one medieval ritual text, "one should conceal the metal images used for festivals, bathing rites, processions, and tribute offerings."

We do not know for certain when the community leaders of Shivapuram decided to bury their valuable festival icons, including the Nataraja and Somaskanda images. Many observers have suggested the fourteenth century, when the armies of the Delhi Sultanate invaded South India and plundered wealthy Hindu temples like Cidambaram and Sri Rangam. I am wary of the reflexive tendency to blame all disruptions to Indian religious sites on "the Muslims," however, and I would note that threats to valuable temple possessions may come from many directions, local as well as foreign. For example, one inscription on the Shivapuram temple wall, dated 1239, records that a temple priest and his accomplice stole the jewels worn by the temple goddess and gave them to their concubine, took the temple gong, hid a temple image, and when the king's agents came to serve a summons on them, the thieves beat them and threw them in the water. Over the centuries there have been ample opportunities for threats to temple property from many different sources.

Though we do not know precisely when the underground concealment took place, we do know something about how it most likely was done. According to one medieval Vaishanava text, the *Vimanarcanakalpa*, the defensive burial of threatened icons involves careful ritual procedures. After the priest has a pit dug and prepared with a bed of sacrificial grass, he approaches the Vishnu image in the temple and makes a solemn request: "As long as there is danger, O Vishnu, please lie down in a bed with the goddess Earth." The priest then transfers the animating energy from the icon to be buried into a *kurca*, a specially prepared bundle of fifty blades of sacrificial grass, which will serve as a temporary object of worship while the icon hides underground. The icon itself is lowered gently into the pit. Incense is burned, mantras are recited, and the hole is filled with grass and dirt. The divine icon goes into hibernation.

For medieval Hindus, a supreme god like Shiva or Vishnu was by definition eternal, but the material embodiments that god inhabits on earth are inescapably subject to decay and destruction. The Shaiva ritual texts recognized that images of Shiva could become unsuitable for his divine presence from a variety of causes. If broken or burned or defaced or worn out, if improperly made in the first place, if dislocated by flood or violent attack or theft, or if simply left unworshipped for too long, an icon will lose its animating presence. In some cases, as when an image loses its identifying features, the loss is irrevocable and there is nothing to do but melt down the bronze. Images that remain relatively intact are recoverable, however, and the texts spell out a ritual of re-consecration, known as *jirnoddhara*, to restore a disrupted icon to its proper ritual status.

The cult value of an icon, for the Shaivas, has to do with divine presence, which requires both physical completeness and regular human interaction. Ritual status may be temporarily lost, and then regained through renewed ritual attentions. This is the premise behind the ritual burial of an icon. As soon as danger is passed, it is assumed, humans will recover the icon, ritually reconsecrate it, and return it to normal worship. However, things may happen above ground that prevent the icon's timely disinterment.

Rediscovery

Evidently the residents of Shivapuram were unable to recover their buried bronzes, because the icons remained underground for centuries. In 1951, Kasturi Rangaraiya Annamuttu come upon the hoard by chance while carrying out renovations to the temple. Like Rip Van Winkle, the Nataraja and its companions had slept a long time, and the world around them had changed dramatically. Not so much may have changed in Shivapuram, perhaps, which remained a small rice-growing village with an active Shiva temple. In the world beyond the village, however, new institutions offered new possibilities for an ancient bronze image like the Nataraja.

Two developments were especially important for the subsequent life of the Shivapuram bronzes. By the mid-twentieth century, the international world of art – with its own networks of exchange, institutions of acquisition and display, and disciplinary forms of knowledge – had embraced ancient Indian religious sculpture as a legitimate and desirable category of art. Chola-period icons could now be treasured beyond India, not as consecrated supports for Shiva's divine presence, but for their sculptural beauty. At the same time, local agencies of preservation and display had been created in South India. In southern India, the Government Museum in Madras had been founded initially by the colonial British, and was celebrating its centennial in 1951 as an avowedly nationalistic institution in newly independent India, charged with educating the people of southern India about their glorious heritage. In the era of decolonization, independent India could value religious objects of the distant past in a new way, neither as cult objects or aesthetic ones exactly, but as part of its cultural patrimony.

With all these possible lives and identities to choose from, what would happen to the *Shivapuram Nataraja* and its companions? An old colonial-period statute, the Indian Treasure Trove Act of 1878, specified what *should* happen. Under its provisions, the finder of buried treasure should bring the recovered materials to the attention of the proper local authority, the District Collector. If the Collector determines that the object has been buried for over a hundred years, he can make a determination as to the subsequent ownership of the treasure. Of course, this procedure is not usually to the benefit of the one who happens to find a buried antiquity. What often happens is that the finder, observing the still older principle of "finders keepers," makes other unofficial arrangements, and the object enters the underground art market as a commodity. In the case of the Shivapuram bronzes, however, Annamuttu followed the legal route, and the Tanjore District Collector, T. K. Palaniappan, arrived on the scene to play his role in determining their fate.

Two parties made claims for the bronzes. P. R. Srinivasan, curator of archaeology at the Madras Government Museum, sought to acquire the bronzes for the museum's display of great works of South Indian metal sculpture. As a repository of antiquities the Museum had amassed a collection of over eight hundred bronzes, the large majority coming as treasure trove finds. In the 1950-51 administrative years alone, the Museum added forty-seven metal images to its collection, forty-three of them from treasure troves.

Muthuswami Mudaiyar, trustee of the Shivapuram temple, also put in a plea that the bronzes be returned to the temple. The temple officials wished to reconsecrate the bronzes and return them to their former liturgical roles.

Palaniappan had a political decision to make. Would he give greater weight to government officials from the state capital, or to local residents of a small village in his district? His decision would also determine the ensuing lives of the objects themselves. In effect, the District Collector would decide whether the Shivapuram bronzes would be honored in Madras for their exhibition value, as part of a display of traditional Indian sculpture, or in Shivapuram for their cult value, incorporated back into local temple liturgy. Palaniappan resolved in favor of Shivapuram.

Celebrity and Duplication

This could have been the end of the story. The bronzes might have returned permanently to uneventful lives as processional icons in a rural South Indian temple, holy only to the local devotees. But like a 1950s Hollywood starlet spotted at a drugstore soda fountain, the Shivapuram bronzes had been discovered. In 1959 P. R. Srinivasan published a report in *Lalit Kala*, an Indian arts journal, on the Shivapuram bronzes. He warmly praised the Nataraja and Somaskanda images as masterworks of the early tenth century, and singled out the Nataraja for its "boldness of conception and dexterity of execution."

Srinivasan's dating of the Nataraja was especially significant. By assigning it an early tenth-century date, he estimated that the Nataraja was one of the very earliest examples of this particular iconic form of Shiva. Since the early twentieth century, historians and connoisseurs of Indian art such as E. B. Havell, A. K. Coomaraswamy, and Auguste Rodin had proclaimed the Chola-period bronze rendering of Shiva Nataraja as the most elegant and profound of themes in Hindu sculpture. So to claim the *Shivapuram Nataraja* as possibly the earliest known realization of this theme was to place it among the most important and valuable of all works of Indian art. We should note here that Srinivasan's assessment, which set the terms of subsequent discourse concerning the Nataraja, involved placing the image in a chronological and aesthetic canon of other Indian art works, according to archeological and art historical disciplinary practices. Though the Nataraja was, in 1959, a cultic icon, Srinivasan characterized it entirely in terms of its exhibition value.

In 1961, Queen Elizabeth visited Madras. This required proper commemoration, and state officials hired Lance Dane, a retired British officer, photographer, and amateur art collector living in India, to prepare a souvenir volume for the visit. Dane photographed the *Shivapuram Nataraja* and placed it on the cover. Dane's visit to Shivapuram apparently set in motion the next great shift in the lives of the Shivapuram bronzes, their duplication, or in Benjamin's terms their "mechanical reproduction." He suggested to the temple officials in Shivapuram that their bronzes were in poor condition and needed cleaning. They sent the icons out to Ramasami Sthapathi, a reputable bronze maker in the nearby city of Kumbhakonam, a center of icon manufacture. However, instead of simply cleaning the bronzes, Ramasami fabricated exact duplicates of them. He returned the shiny counterfeits to the temple, for which "cleaning" he received Rs 500. Then he sold the originals to a low-level antiquities dealer named Tilaka for Rs 17,000.

Ramasami's duplication of the Shivapuram bronzes highlights issues of originality, authenticity, and what Benjamin calls the "aura" of the art work. In principle, any work of art is physically reproducible. Bronze sculpture can be manufactured in quantity, as the Greeks did, by casting multiple copies from a master mold. However, South Indian bronze makers have always used the lost-wax method, which ensures that each bronze icon is the outcome of a unique sculptural process. Ramasami's innovation in creating an exact duplicate of an ancient original, and passing off the duplicate as an original, required knowledge of new worlds within which Indian bronzes could be valued. He understood, or was told, that original authentic icons of the tenth century were coveted in a new way by a cosmopolitan audience. By doubling the Shivapuram icons, Ramasami could enable the icons to serve two ends simultaneously: the duplicates would serve the cultic needs of village devotees in Shivapuram, while the originals could meet the aesthetic desires of international art collectors and viewers. And he could realize a tidy profit in the process.

Will the real *Shivapuram Nataraja* please stand up? The 1960s game show, "To Tell the Truth," depended on the premise that only one individual could truthfully embody a particular life story. Other claimants therefore must be impostors, and it was the task of the interrogators to identify the honest contestant. So too with art works, as Benjamin argues, only an original work can claim "its unique existence at the place where it happens to be," its own distinctive history and aura. Reproductions lack that aura. For the international market in antiquities, this distinction between authentic original and inauthentic reproduction matters a great deal. The original *Shivapuram Nataraja* eventually reached the United States and realized a sales price of $900,000, but if Ramasami had tried instead to send his duplicate Nataraja it would not have gone far in location or value. For exhibition value, authenticity of the original is all-important.

Is the same true with Indian cult objects? After Ramaswami returned his duplicates to Shivapuram, they were incorporated into the ordinary ritual life of the temple. Neither the priest, officials, nor worshippers raised any objection, initially. It was a visiting British art historian, Douglas Barrett, who first observed in 1965 that the icons being worshipped in the Shivapuram temple were duplicates, not originals. Barrett noted that the original Nataraja from Shivapuram was currently in Bombay, displayed in a private collection. It is not certain whether this revelation made any difference to Shivapuram villagers. Theologically perhaps it did not, since Shiva graciously manifests himself equally in icons old and new, well and poorly made. However, one later indication that the expropriation of their ancient images did dismay them was a "local tradition," that several persons involved in the investigation reported to me. As it happened, Ramasami Sthapathi suffered paralysis not long after duplicating the bronzes and could no longer practice his trade. Lance Dane was jailed, and the Bombay art collector died. According to the locals, these afflictions were the result of Shiva taking his vengeance on those who had trifled with his icons. Perhaps authenticity is just as important to Shiva as it is to a wealthy art collector.

Pursuit, Dispute, and Return

I will skip briefly over an important chapter in the life of the *Shivapuram Nataraja* – its decade as a highly prized art commodity. There are various versions of how it made its journey from India to the United States, and I am not able to adjudicate among them. For this talk, suffice it to say that the icon traveled from South India to Bombay, passed through the hands of several art dealers at rapidly escalating prices, and finally emigrated to the United States in 1969. Norton Simon, a wealthy entrepreneur and energetic art collector, purchased it in 1972 from New York art dealer Ben Heller for $900,000, the highest price paid for any work of Indian art at that time. Simon also bought its old companion from Shivapuram, the Somaskanda, for considerably less in a subsequent deal.

Meanwhile, since Barrett's published observations, the Indian government had begun to pursue its errant icons. In 1969 the Commissioner of the Hindu Religious and Charitable Endowments office filed a complaint with the Tanjore district police superintendent, which set in motion a police investigation that would retrace the journey of the Nataraja and eventually catch up with it in the U.S. We should not take this decision to pursue for granted. The illicit trade in stolen Indian antiquities is huge, and Indian law enforcement agencies with limited resources cannot investigate every case. However, in the 1970s the Government of India chose to prosecute several high-profile thefts, in hopes that a few well-publicized recoveries might help discourage the market in stolen Indian art. The *Shivapuram Nataraja* was one of these cases.

By 1973 the Indian investigation had caught up with the celebrated Nataraja, and at this point the story becomes very complicated. In addition to Simon, Heller, and the Indian police, other parties became involved. Lawyers were engaged. Suits and countersuits were filed. Officials from the Indian embassy in Washington represented the interests of the Government of India. Daniel Moynahan, American ambassador to India, mediated in the negotiations. The Metropolitan Museum and its director, Thomas Hoving, had planned to put on a show of Simon's Asia collection, with the newly purchased Nataraja as its centerpiece. Conservationists at the British Museum were called upon to treat the Shivapuram icons for insidious metal disease. Even Shiva himself got involved as a legal plaintiff. Newspapers featured the story of a Hindu god suing for the return of his image. The *Shivapuram Nataraja* enjoyed brief celebrity as a legally contested object of great value. At the heart of the dispute, though, lay the conflicting desires of two suitors, who saw very different virtues in the object of their desire, and who ultimately sought to lead the Nataraja to two very different lives.

Norton Simon had become interested in the art of South Asia during a 1971 honeymoon in India with his second wife, the actress Jennifer Jones. Simon pursued this new interest with characteristic gusto, and with a connoisseur's eye for artistic quality. He particularly appreciated the sensuous, voluptuous qualities in Indian sculpture. Simon quickly acquired well over a hundred works of South and Southeast Asian art, and he saw the *Shivapuram Nataraja* as the crowning trophy of his remarkable collection. Heller had proclaimed the bronze as "the finest rendition of the most important subject in Hindu art," and Simon shared this view, along with a good number of scholars of Indian art. He publicly stated his opinion that the image had been smuggled into the United States. "Hell yes it was smuggled," he told a *New York Times* reporter. "I spent between $15 and $16 million over the last two years on Asian art, and most of it was smuggled." This did not prevent him from wishing to make the Nataraja his own.

While the connoisseur Simon sought the beautiful Nataraja for its exhibition value, the Indian government claimed it sought the religious icon for its cult value. The government claimed it would return the bronze image to its original community and to its ritual life in the Shivapuram temple. This is the basis upon which Shiva became involved. As part of the Indian government's strategy, the god Shiva as legally recognized proprietor of the Shivapuram temple would sue for the return of his own processional property, and India would act as Shiva's legal agent. Honorable as these intentions may have sounded, the stronger interest of the Indian government lay in the politics of cultural heritage and the antiquities market. The art historical reputation and purchase price of the Nataraja turned it into a prime trophy of cultural heritage, and their hope was that a successful repatriation of the celebrated bronze might have trickle-down effects on the large illegal trade in Indian antiquities.

To make a long legal story short, Simon and the Government of India finally agreed to an out-of-court settlement. The *Shivapuram Nataraja* would return to India, but only after Simon had enjoyed it on loan for ten years. In addition, India relinquished any claims against other objects in the Norton Simon collection – including the Shivapuram Somaskanda, every bit as much a smuggled antiquity as its old companion. The press largely portrayed this settlement as a humiliating defeat for Simon, but others have pointed out that the deal maker made out pretty well for himself. He got his $900,000 back by suing Heller, he retained the Nataraja as a showpiece for a decade, and he guaranteed the rest of this collection against all future claims. The power of Shiva's curse evidently did not extend over Simon, though it did over Heller.

Incarceration

In May 1986, M. S. Nagaraja Rao, director of the Archaeological Survey of India, traveled to Los Angeles to escort the Nataraja back to India. One might hope that this celebrated icon, successfully recovered as a masterwork of ancient Indian imagery, would return to a life of proper honor. But, as most 1950s starlets will remind you, celebrity can be fleeting indeed. The problem for the Nataraja was that the temple at Shivapuram, like many other small village temples in South India containing immensely valuable bronze sculptures, cannot be adequately protected. In the 1980s, the Tamilnadu state government constructed an Icon Centre at Tiruvarur, to house these valuable, vulnerable images. The Nataraja, too valuable for its own safety in Shivapuram, went there. Unfortunately the Icon Centre is neither temple nor museum. Priests and devotees cannot enter to worship the icons, and visitors cannot gain entry to admire them as works of art. When I visited in 1995 to pay my respects, two guards with guns chased me away and would not even permit me to photograph the outside of the facility. There resides the Nataraja, deprived of both cult value and exhibition value in the eyes of the world.

The Somskanda image from Shivapuram, on the other hand, currently enjoys a happier situation, as an expatriate masterpiece of Chola-period sculptural art at the Norton Simon Museum in Pasadena, California.

As we have seen, though, the lives of Indian images may take abrupt and unexpected turns, and I end this biography with the hope that its period of incarceration in the Icon Centre will not be the final chapter in the life of the *Shivapuram Nataraja.*

Defining Sacred Universals and Particulars:

Competing Relationalities in the Nature, Function, Ownership, and Meanings of "Sacred" Museum Objects

Submitted by:
Patrice Brodeur,
University of Montreal

Defining the Sacred is problematic. Defining is problematic. Why? Let me briefly explore five reasons. First, the act of "defining" is restrictive, often distorting, and always fluid.[8] There is no definition that is not linked to a power dynamic of one sort or another. The act of defining an object, in our case a "sacred" object, is always tied to a mul-

---

8 Thomas Beebee, *The Ideology of Genre: A Comparative Analysis of Generic Instability*, (Philadelphia: Pennsylvania State University Press, 1994).

titude of definers or stakeholders who view, own, use, manage, clean, etc. this object according to their respective interpretations of them.

Second, in the English language today, there is an automatic link made between the word "sacred" and those of "religion," "faith," "holiness,"[9] and "spirituality." That was not always the case. These close associations in meaning reflect a particular historical trajectory that has unfolded over centuries. These meanings only make sense in relation to one another. Changes in meaning generally happen slowly within any given language. These words form a unique set of interrelated meanings. It is very difficult to translate this set of words from the English language into other languages, especially non-cognate languages. Moreover, the translation process is bound by power dynamics affecting which meaning will eventually impose itself, as it was the case with the word "religion" linked to both colonial and post-colonial history. The process of translating into English a word or set of words from a very different linguistic world is equally difficult. For example, the Shiva Linga is a *murti* object that does not have a direct equivalent in English. The same is true of the Arabic word *din*, which is usually translated as "religion" even though its associations to the concept of "judgment," among other meanings, make for rather different conceptual associations and overtones than those of "connecting" associated to the Latin *religare*, which is one possible root for the word "religion."

Third, in the English language today, as in any human language, there is an unavoidable danger of unconsciously collapsing the *language about* the sacred with the *experience* of the sacred. This is particularly true in a museum space where the latter is usually not welcome, especially in publicly funded institutions in countries that practice separation between state and religious institutions.

Fourth, with language comes a universalizing tendency linked to the normal human attempt to represent linguistically experiences that transcend both the conceptual and experiential meanings of ultimate reality. The experience of God's totalizing presence in one's life often ends up generating a concept of God that is believed to be universal. Yet the concept of "God" can only point towards a universal reality; it cannot be equal to it by definition, since a word can never be the same as total reality. It is therefore useful to distinguish between three things: one's own definition of a concept of universality,

9 W.C. Smith, *The Meaning and End of Religion*, (Minneapolis, MN: Fortress Press, 1991, first ed. 1962).

the possibility of a concept of universality, and whether or not there actually is a universality beyond my limited human perception of it.

Finally, the fifth reason why defining is problematic, especially defining the "sacred," is linked to how languages, like definitions, function within power dynamics that remain limited when facing ultimate reality. In other words, the fifth reason is a combination of the third and fourth when it comes to defining the "sacred" in particular. For example, in the course of the later half of the twentieth century, the American language has become the normative and often hegemonic reference point with its own unique set of linguistic representations for "ultimate reality." This set reflects a variety of meanings to explain and make sense of humans' experience of life and reality in a way that is universalized and too often implicitly made equal to ultimate reality, when it is in fact limited to America's collective discourse on matters of ultimate reality.

I point this out not because any of this knowledge is new or because I want to engage in a Don Quixote battle hermeneutically. I simply want to ensure that we constantly remain aware of the invisible dangers of linguistic privileges that often translate into injustice towards various "minority" languages,[10] especially when those languages are central to the representation of the five faiths included in this project. Indeed because English speakers, not just Americans, live in an English-American language that is embedded in global power dynamics that lend it privileges of meaning, they implicitly universalize the meanings they implicitly ascribe to the concepts of "religion" and "the sacred," or that of "God" for that matter. This unconscious projection means that they too often misunderstand religious worldviews that are imbedded in other linguistic frameworks. From these five reasons, I therefore deduce that any so-called "universal" will remain a "particular," at least at the linguistic level. We can never achieve a neutral language, a definitional objectivity that we will all agree upon, despite our deeply ingrained human desire for universals.

But do not despair! A bit like the dancing Shiva of Shivapuram that now lies hidden in a human-built vault in India, this is not the end of the story. These five reasons that make defining so difficult are not, in my opinion, problems to be overcome. Rather, they

10 I put "minority" in quotation marks because some of these languages, for example Chinese and Sanskrit, are not at all minority in terms of demographic numbers!

are part of how we, that is certain postmodern academics, perceive reality today. These reasons point to issues we will have to address as we relate to objects referred to as "sacred" in any particular context, ours being that of a university museum of arts. Indeed, we amply emphasized earlier that objects are understood as sacred by some and not by others. This recognition implies, of course, that objects are invested with several meanings at once, some more "sacred" than others, leading to the concept of multiple voices. Objects are both bearers and transmitters of multiple meanings,[11] which depend not only on their location, but also on their "ownership." How museum curators in particular and those deemed to be "experts" manage those multiple meanings reflect how they manage the power that is invested in a particular object by multiple stakeholders at once. Each stakeholder relates differently to the object. Say, for example, from Christ to Christies in the case of the Sellaio *Madonna and Child.* "Christ," as a religious stakeholder and "Christies" as a curatorial or collecting stakeholder have two radically different referential points of view, which we may reductively call the insider/outsider tension. They represent a parallel to the struggle about how to integrate both the possibility of the presence of Shiva looking back at the seer of a consecrated Shiva Linga and the Ackland's Shiva Linga as a material object with a particular historical and aesthetic value.

In short, one may conclude that these different co-existing meanings, the multiple voices defining whether an object is "sacred" or not, simply mean that any definition of the "sacred" is relative. The danger with this conclusion is twofold: first, such a conclusion can easily marginalize the importance of the claims to universality which a definition may carry for insiders; second, and more serious in my opinion, a rapid dismissal of universal claims end up contributing to a difficult power dynamic between "believing" insiders and "expert" outsiders. These outsiders can easily hide behind a false neutrality, reproducing scientific, reductivist, intellectual tendencies rooted in a set of particulars linked historically to the European Enlightenment paradigm. The reverse danger is equally problematic: insiders dismissing any relevance to truth claims made by "expert" outsiders about objects to which they claim full ownership and sole hermeneutical authority.

---

11 David Carr, "Five Thoughtful Exercises Among Faith Objects," (Lecture presented for the Five Faiths Henry Luce Foundation Colloquium I, August 2002, at the Ackland Art Museum at The University of North Carolina at Chapel Hill), pp. 2-3.

In order to avoid these two dangers, I propose to talk about definitions of the "sacred" as not relative but relational. The "sacred" is always eminently relational to a particular power dynamic resulting from the conjuncture of a set of five particulars: the nature of the "sacred" object, its location within any space (i.e., which delimits its possible functions), the variety of its stakeholders (i.e., those who claim some form of ownership), the multitude of potential interpretations (i.e., its meanings) for each stakeholder, and his or her knowledge of the history of the object. Relationality is what determines the attribution one may ascribe to any object, which carries at once several meanings for different people and at times even within one person (i.e., as many of us here who are scholar-practitioners). This relationality is not only between the different form/content and function of an object. It is also between competing "owners" and competing "users" who vie for their own privileged mode and reasons for relating to the object to be the dominant interpretation presented in the museum. In other words, in addition to multiple relationalities in terms of meanings and usages of a particular object, there are competing relationalities between all those individuals and communities who relate in one way or another to an object. Of course, the most well-known example of the second kind of relationality is that of indigenous communities' efforts to recover control over thousands of "artifacts" stored in museums worldwide.[12] Another example is that of the Dancing Shiva of Shivapuram. We may thus ask ourselves what might happen if the five religious communities included in our project were to embark systematically on similar reclaiming campaigns.

These competing relationalities beg for recognizing and managing plurality not only in the nature of "sacred" objects, but in their function, ownership, and meanings, all linked to their histories as well. This is why I chose to emphasize in my title the "sacred" as an adjective rather than as a noun: a noun requires a conceptual definition more than an adjective does. This also explains my emphasis on the plural form not only of the word "particulars" but also that of "universals." Upon locating the sacred in the interplay between the language games of the mind, the performances of the body, and the experiences of the spirit, it is thus also possible to understand the "sacred" relationally

12 Tamara L. Bray, ed., *The Future of the Past: Archaeologists, Native Americans, and Repatriation*, (New York: Garland Publishing, 2001).

within a mind-body-soul paradigm, recognizing that even this tripartite model is only one possible interpretation.

In the face of such limitations and complexities, what exactly is left to think, feel, and do in the competing universals of daily life and in the particulars of managing "sacred" museum objects? As the personal is political, so is the individual social. And the experiences of the sacred, its interpretations, and its values are not located in any essential location embodied in an autonomous individual, be it physical, emotional, or conceptual, but rather in their relational dynamics within a person-in-community.[13] The "sacred" is like power because it is power. As Dyrberg explained in his book *The Circular Notion of Power*, "power is not located anywhere, yet it is everywhere." [14] From this notion I derive my assertion that the sacred is not located anywhere, yet it is potentially everywhere. It all depends on the uniquely contextual relationalities that exist, in rarely static form, between our five particulars: nature, function, ownership, meaning, and knowledge of the history of "sacred" objects.

The "sacred," i.e., what is ascribed the meaning of being "sacred" (or its greater or lesser equivalencies in other languages and symbolic systems), upon closer academic examination does not seem to exist in isolation from its human interpretations or, if it does, as human beings we cannot talk about it independently of our human limitations, including those intrinsic to any language of representation. Human beings discover the sacred through their own social and environmental interactions, whether, for example, they are passed down through generations or discovered in cyberspace, with all the complexities we can think about, feel, and intuit. Yet, despite this hermeneutical cacophony, the doing of museum imperatives built around particular objects already owned, as is the case for the Ackland Art Museum, requires an expansion in the number of participants invited to the decision-making circle that manages the use of these objects. This, despite all the subsequent challenges in labeling, for example!

I therefore put forth my first proposition, which will come as no surprise since we together embody it: it is through a dialogical methodology that brings together the var-

13 "We define religion as any person's reliance upon a pivotal value in which that person finds essential wholeness as a person-in-community" in Robert C. Monk, Walter C. Hofheinz, Kenneth T. Lawrence, and Joseph D. Stamey, eds., *Exploring Religious Meaning*, (Englewood-Cliffs, NJ: Prentice-Hall, 6th edition, 2002), p. 3.

14 Torben Bech Dyrberg, *The Circular Notion of Power: Identity, Politics, Community*, (London: Verso, 1997).

ious stakeholders of any so-called "sacred" object that everyone together can begin to discover the variety of co-existing meanings related to any "sacred" object, pointing towards all its potential and often contradictory universals and particulars. Such dialogical modes of communication and therefore representation are particularly appropriate in a university museum space in part because dialogue has become a more common pedagogical method as part of a small but growing trend that recognizes multiple learning and teaching styles. In order to achieve this end of bringing together as many stakeholders as possible (and here, it may not be as much the mere number that is important as the variety in the kinds of stakeholders), it is also necessary to argue the case that the achievements of interreligious dialogue need to be brought within the purview of the field of museum studies. One problem, however, is that interreligious dialogue itself has not been sufficiently theorized to move from the periphery towards the center in the academic study of religion itself.

Therefore, my second proposition, which I have elaborated elsewhere,[15] is that interreligious dialogue be understood as the cornerstone of a new branch in the academic study of religion: the *applied* academic study of religion. It is not enough for scholars of religion to do what they do best: talk (another word!) about religion, describe it, analyze it, interpret it, and even sometimes prescribe it. The academy has become a central locus for the teaching of and about religion, consciously or unconsciously. Thus, First Amendment issues come up: What is "legal?" What is "right?" What is "appropriate?" There are questions about ownership of objects that are defined as religious, with all the power dynamics which "ownership" implies within the American cultural and specifically legal context. By acknowledging an object as "sacred" or "holy," are the museum owners not empowering members of those communities of faith to some form of spiritual ownership over those very objects? If so, is museum space appropriate for those objects? What happens when the same religious objects can be "sacred" to more than one community of faith? Is there a responsibility to bring community members into dialogue with one another, in order to make joint decisions about the myriad questions which surround the use of any object in a museum? There are also questions about who defines objects as "re-

15 Patrice Brodeur, "L'étude critique appliquée de la religion dans un monde pluraliste," in *La religion dans la sphère publique*, ed. by Solange Lefebvre, (Montréal: Presses de l'Université de Montréal, 2005), pp. 198-219.

ligious," "sacred," "holy," etc. There are questions about who invites and who is invited to participate in decision-making around issues of definition, choice, display, and even labeling of objects. Are museums in the business of empowering particular communities of faith, particular individuals within those communities, particular scholars of religion, etc.? All these questions point to the need to clarify what all the relationalities are because they do compete with each other all the time, starting with the very central question of what constitutes the "sacred." As James Livingston suggested in his own version of an academic quest for a universal definition of "religion:"

> We begin our exploration of the anatomy of religion with the observation that religion is a universal and abiding dimension of human experience. This is followed, however, by a rather embarrassing admission, for when we attempt to define this phenomenon, we immediately run into difficulties. We look, then, at the problems connected with some of the influential definitions of religion. We will see that, while none of them is fully adequate, they do give us valuable insight into some essential aspects of religion.[16]

The fluidity, if not the outright competition, in the variety of definitions that exist for the words "religion" and "sacred" is only reflective of the need to understand the power dynamics underlying any of the relationalities pointed out in this paper. In the end, many may need to admit that there is a parallel and competition between the implicit universals toward which most definitions of the "sacred" or "religion" point and the implicit universals toward which academics' own theories about "religion," the "sacred," the "divine," or the "ultimate" also try to point. The museum space is only one of the latest spaces where this battle for human meaning is unfolding today.

16 James Livingston, *Anatomy of the Sacred,* (Upper Saddle Division, NJ: Prentice-Hall: 6th edition, 2008), p. 3.

Our Conversations among Faith Objects:

A Statement of the Museum Problem

Submitted by:
David Carr
School of Information and Library Science, The University of North Carolina at Chapel Hill

The ideas I want to bring to this conversation are primarily informed by the way I see museums and other cultural institutions: they are problem-solving structures, places where people go because they anticipate that they will discover objects, ideas, and other resources, including living human resources, that will assist the evolving, cognitive, emotional, ethical processes of living one's life. These processes, and the anticipation itself, help to address the unfinished issues that configure a cognitive life; these are the things that inspire our wonder, the unknowns that seem to be our own continuous mysteries, and the questions that seem merely to evolve in detail and complexity – no matter how much we pursue them – and appear never to be reduced. Problems of faith and its expression are central to this concept of the guiding question that never appears to be resolved – and yet we love it no less for all its fragmentation and elusive grace. And of course we must learn to love it, and even cultivate it, because it never goes away; it is ours. In this way we construct for ourselves the crafted truths that allow continuities and commitments into an evolving life.

When we regard the faith object as something given in order to assist us toward insight and renewal, we are regarding a product of the human mind and hand, one that reflects a divine image emergent in the hand's work. Better, I should say that the faith object is inspired by the image of the ideal that is both hope and the belief of the religious. As a reflection of the ideal, the faith object mediates a direct experience of truth and devotion, without illusion, misdirection, or irony. It is a kind of intimate purity we rarely find in other contemplations of even the grandest secular artifact. Perhaps this is because it is possible to see the faith object itself as an answer to a problem.

Though the faith object is a material artifact like other objects, we accept it also as a vessel or host for the sacred voice or divine value, something given to us as an evidence that, through its remarkable excellence and grace, confirms the value of believing. In the presence of the great faith object, we see and feel its power to summon a felt response, to evoke a divine name or theme, to allow us to pause in awe at the tranquil certainty before us. How unlike it is to the experiences of uncertainty that challenge us all day. I think we are likely, leading problematic lives as we do, to admire that certainty even though we may not share it. Whether we stand inside or outside the faith, we want to know what people of faith experience in the presence of the object. We hope to grasp its logics and central constructs. We want to know or feel its mystery or inspiration in ways that illuminate the faith itself, which is to say, how it brings reconciliation, solace, contemplation, and hope.

And, because this is the way we learn, we want to go beyond the object, to the critical point in our observations when we tie it to something we have seen or understood in our minds and hearts before – when we use our experience of the object as a pause, or a clearing we have arrived at for ourselves (because no one else can do this for us). In even a small increment of this process – this going beyond – we experience a change in our problem, a step toward a new form of anticipation and hope. Such experiences are full of promise, and they bring us back for more, because we cannot do without such problems, and such problem solving, in our lives. This is a process that the late John Gardner described as self-renewal, the fundamental characteristic of human being – that is, being human.

How do museums create such situations, where mindful attention allows a museum user to think beyond the information given and so to craft, in Kierkegaard's words, a truth that is true for me? This concept – going beyond the information given – comes from Jerome Bruner, as does the idea that we are always in the process of renegotiating our relationship with our culture – just as I assume a faithful person is always renegotiating a relationship with the divine. How do museums create circumstances where we are given opportunities to reduce our confusions, confirm our abilities as mindful human beings, and articulate our places as creatures in a challenging universe?

We must have encounters with the unknown.

In museums, among objects of faith, we will have new encounters with objects unknown, outside, and exterior to our previous experiences. Conse-

For museums, the challenge is to assist museum users to move toward and engage the unknown by helping them to rearticulate and reconstruct what they know, or what they anticipate about their own destinies. Museum learning implies that who we are destined to

quently, our past interior experiences – memories, metaphors, and evocations of relationship – become useful tools for our critical task as interpreters.

become depends almost entirely on who we have already become, and what we have come to understand, so far.

In museums, our deepest experiences of powerful faith objects – experiences that evoke feelings of passion, reconciliation, ecstasy, solace, inspiration, and doubt – are private, singular, and invisible.

Consequently, for learning to happen, a tension needs to be present between the private experience and its public expression. What can be said in words? We must think of ourselves as questioners, always working on this problem of articulation. Perhaps we must come to realize that it is not the transfer of knowledge that the museum undertakes, but the transfer of awareness and attention.

How do we mediate authentically – that is, without compromising the integrity and privacy of the user – between the hidden inspiration and its connections to renewal? How do we assist the silent museum user to express (if only in private) a single critical insight and thereby unlock the energies of change?

(Perhaps it is far more useful to assist the user to articulate excellent questions, rather than strive to supply answers to questions that have not yet been asked.)

Among objects of faith, a similar tension is present between our formative knowledge of and belief – those parts of our experience we have used to construct and define our ideas, our ethics and values – and the opposite of knowledge: our formative ignorance, the fear and confusion that close us down, and tend to defeat our evolution in a changing world.

How do we explore our ignorance? How do we express and construct the conditions for our thinking and learning? Unless it is a place of trust, a museum cannot easily anticipate the knowledge of its users, their unknowns, their hopes or their interests, or where the open mind shuts down. How can we know these things? We must have conversations with users, to see where they are in the life course.

Every learner needs a fearless acceptance of personal evolution as the only alternative to stagnation and despair.

The structure and function of the museum sometimes create problems: virtually every object the museum holds is reduced and contained, disempowered by separation from its contexts. We must remember that the origins and artifacts of a faith appear in social, institutional, and personal contexts (families, churches, mosques, synagogues, religious schools, places of fellowship and reflection). The faith object, in its functional contexts, may be touched or seen by the faithful. It is present to the senses as a physical object, and as more than a physical object. The practice of the faith and the use of its objects take their greatest meaning in a world where loss, ambiguity, and crisis often create the need for solace and reconciliation.

Or a cycle of observances calls for expressions of joy and renewal. It is in such intense contexts that the individual person of faith experiences the object of faith; it is part of an immersion in religious expression. But the museum object appears outside all of these contexts.

How can we understand the multiple contexts of religious artifacts in a secular setting? Where have they gone? How do we recover them? How is the object different? What is the difference between the object in use – the object being held and touched – and the object at rest under glass? What is lost? Power? Passion? Continuity?

The object has a contextual biography; it is a kind of evidence that practices and meanings have been enacted.

The faith object has a purpose, a physical place in sacred practice, and a physical role in the spiritual system or structure, where it is likely to be part of an ensemble of related objects, charged with the power to summon and embody aspects of the faith.

What is the purpose of an object of faith? Is it a physical embodiment of a divinity? An evocation of religious narrative? An illumination of a spiritual tenet? What structure does it document? Is it a tool, or a container? Does it bear an essential message?

Whatever its character or function, the masterpiece faith object captures and makes visible to us the energies of belief. The power of the object transfers or deepens these energies in the observer and transfers some of its power through the sensory experience of being in its presence. The nature of both experience and language makes any expression of this depth problematic.

What is the nature of this capturing? What is the invisible energy moving in the object? How does our language capture the energies of belief, or the logics of a religious system?

How does our language inevitably fail to do this fully?

Over time and continuous engagement, the mind is capable of weaving multiple strands, telling comparable stories, and grasping examples of thoughts that transcend category. The museum needs to redefine itself in accord with the mind's capabilities, grounded by an inviolable assumption of service devoted to the mindful user, the user for whom change is continuously possible. Much of this recommitment depends on the flexibility and imaginative capability of museum minds – and the other minds the museum consults. As the capacity of a user increases, the museum and other cultural institutions ought to develop a place to turn, an expansive structure for collaborative support of independent inquiry.

And every museum needs to ask of itself, What is the capacity of this institution for dialogue? How permeable are we to other voices? The enemies of mindful engagement of a museum user are probably few, but first among them is what I will call reduction or condescension. The second, however, is the distortion of excessive scholarship. Perhaps the third is silence and discontinuity. (No one is comfortable in mid-air, the mind entirely concentrated on grasping the next thing, waiting for the trapeze that does not arrive.) All of these things are forms of arrogance, and so I suggest to all museums on the verge of arrogance just one word of advice: humility. Try humility.

Let us imagine that, across all faiths, for example, we may consider examples of the vessel, the lamp, the adornment, the decoration, the robe, the candelabrum, the text, the altar, the icon, the bell, even the holy place of worship itself, and how each follows a design and purpose that serves the values and variations of a particular faith. We can ask:

How might we understand and compare one among others?

How might we make the object permeable to the dimensions of both instrumentality and passion?

Let us imagine that, of the object, we can ask:

What is its conventional place and use in ritual pattern and practice?

What is its meaning in observances of birth, death, initiation, transformation, or other continuities of human life?

What is its relationship to sacred text or narrative, symbol or deity?

What is its comparative complexity among other objects of its kind?

Let us imagine that, of every faith – including all tribal faiths – we can ask:

What is the path of the faithful human toward the divine?

What is the human being, as an artifact of faithful practice?

How do such objects as these assist the human along this path?

WORKSHEET[17]

An exploration of the "Limits and Potential" of one object and one label:
"What can we learn about a faith tradition through the study of one object related to that faith?"

Introduction

All of the objects in the Five Faiths Collection have some relationship to a religious tradition. Although now distanced from that tradition, what can these objects teach us about the faith tradition from which they come? What does the average museum attendee need to know in order to understand and appreciate the object?

As you investigate these questions in preparation for writing a sample label, please record your answers.

Part One: What can we see?

1. With members of your group, look carefully at the object.
   List your observations.

2. Based on what you see, what do you think this object might have been used for in its original context?

3. What do you still want to know that will help you better understand the object's original use? List your questions.

Part Two: What resources are readily available?

Look at the contextual materials provided by the small-groups this morning.

4. What question(s) do you still have?

5. Where else might you look for answers to these questions?

17 David Carr developed these materials as interactive templates which may be used in other contexts once modified.

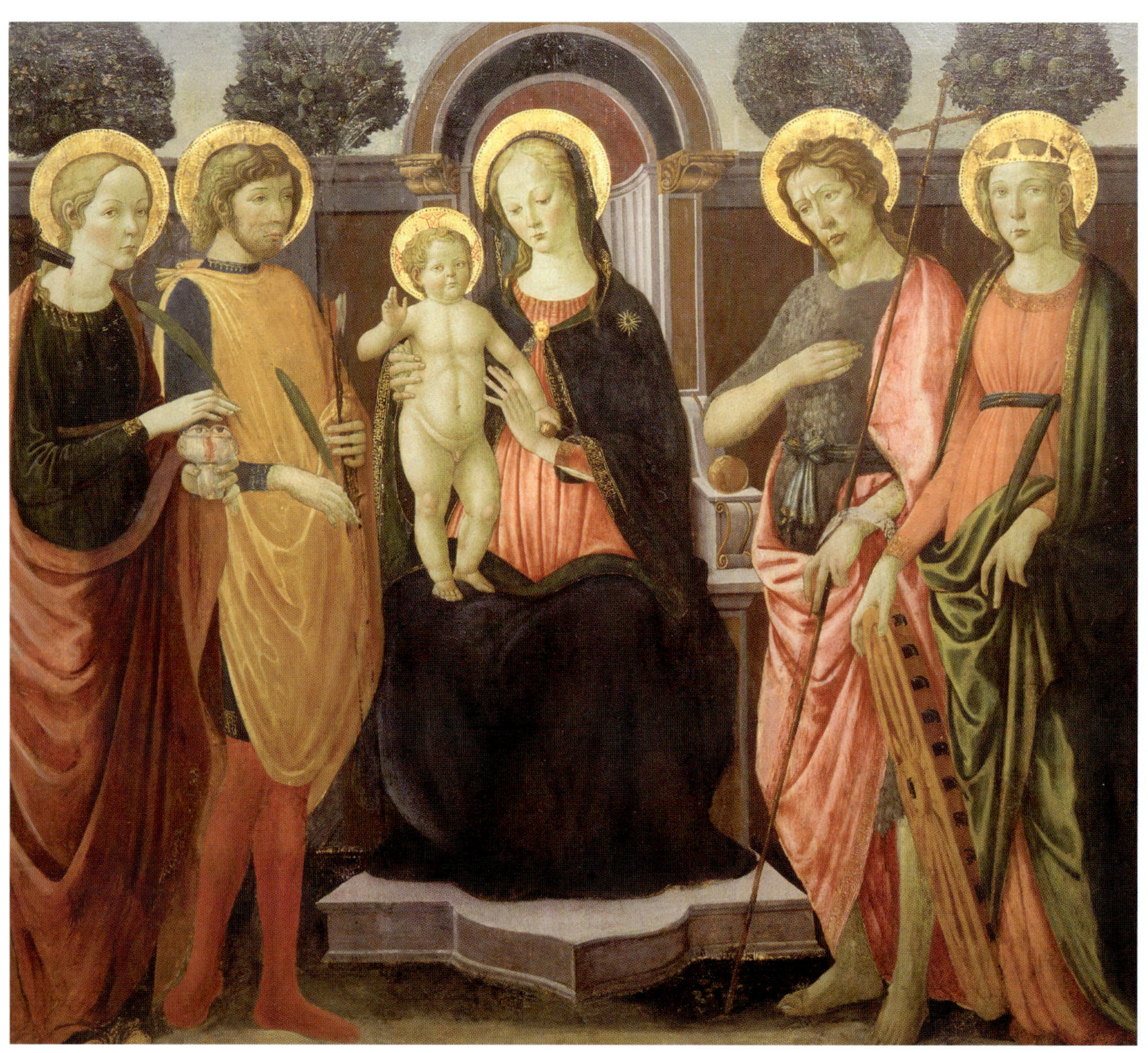

THE MADONNA AND CHILD WITH SAINTS
Attributed to Jacopo del Sellaio
Italian, Florence, ca. 1441-1493; tempera and gold on wood panel. The William A. Whitaker Foundation Art Fund, 63.18.1. (detail)

CASE STUDY 1[18]
MADONNA AND CHILD WITH SAINTS: LABEL WRITING EXERCISE

original label

This is an altarpiece, a large painting intended to be placed behind and above the altar in a church. It is mounted at the approximate height it would have had in its original setting behind an altar.

To worshippers in the Renaissance, the emphasis on sacrifice and salvation in the painting would have helped to convey the meaning of the Eucharist (Holy Communion) celebrated at the altar in front of it. Depicting saints with the instruments of their torture or martyrdom, it reminded worshippers of the pain they had endured for their faith. It also includes subtle reminders of Jesus' coming suffering: the child is naked and vulnerable, as he later would be at his death on the cross. Jesus' sacrifice is symbolized by the blood-red cross on the halo behind his head.

The artist balanced the theme of sacrifice with that of salvation. Jesus stands facing the viewer with his right hand raised in a formal gesture of blessing. When the priest at the altar elevated the Host (consecrated bread) during the Eucharist, Jesus would have appeared to be blessing it himself.

revised label 1

What strikes you about this painting?

Many museum visitors ask who are the people arranged around the central pairing of mother and child and what are the objects they hold. Visitors also struggle with the contrast between the stoic, calm expressions and, for example, the knife in the neck of the woman on the left.

For worshippers in the Renaissance, the saints arranged around Mary and Jesus would have provided a visual expression of the meaning of the Eucharist (Mass) celebrated on the altar. For this is an altarpiece, a large painting originally placed behind and above an altar in a church. The saints directing our attention to Mary and Jesus invited Catholic worshippers to participate in the sacrifice of Jesus for the salvation of humanity (text source) commemorated at the altar.

The saints reinforce the theme of sacrifice and salvation, by holding the instruments of their own torture (as Lucy on left with knife and eyes …), yet now transcending human suffering.

---

18 The process for these case studies is outlined in the text of the proceeding section, pages 78-79. To summarize: in advance of the Colloquy, each participant was asked to review objects, interpretive materials, and other resources from their perspective as scholar, faith practitioner, museum curator, museum educator, etc. They were then assigned to small-groups to share their perspectives and arrive at what they considered to be "essential content" as well as strategies to include this content in labels no longer than 200 words in length.

revised label 2

This painting was originally placed behind an altar in a Catholic church. Jesus and Mary, his mother, are flanked by saints, each of whom is distinguished by the instrument of their martyrdom and a palm leaf, signifying their status as martyrs.

In its original setting a priest would elevate the sacrament, visually uniting it with the infant Jesus. This association reinforces the symbolism of the sacraments as the body and blood of Jesus. His adult-like appearance and the cross on his chest prefigure his death on the cross. The blue, red, and green of Mary's garments are associated with hope, charity, and rebirth.

Considerations

1 Historical Time Period: Renaissance
   - human potential for perfection
   - ordered and stable universe
   - social and political hierarchy
2 Religion
   - devotion to Mary
   - devotion to saints
   - saintly virtues
3 Ritual
   - original context
   - role in celebration of the Eucharist
   - role of the patron

---

19 The authors chose to include this transcript for a number of reasons. First, it represents a deeply informed faith perspective – that of scholar and priest. As such, it is laden with insider references – from the use of Eucharist and Mass as words that do not require definition, to the clear use of honorifics, as in Christ, rather than Jesus throughout the text. But, equally compelling was the opportunity to demonstrate the depth of interpretation possible because of the perspective Power brought to his assignment. Not an art historian by training, nevertheless, his experience and his knowledge of Catholic practice and Catholic history afforded him approaches to the object that would have remained opaque to the Museum without his generosity. Finally, the authors included this piece because it deeply challenged some of the assumptions with which we had previously approached and interpreted the object. For many years, we had focused interpretive attention on the role of the saints. David helped us to return our attention to the central figure of the child Jesus and the functional role of Mary.

It is also noteworthy that this is an excellent representation of the kind of translation that multiple perspectives may require if they are to be incorporated into standard object labels. And, the amount of editing required. This text contains more than 1,100 words (four times longer than a typical extended label).

Other Considerations Submitted by David Power, OMI

I have been asked to react to this altarpiece from a faith perspective.[19] The faith context is established by the fact that it is an altarpiece, to be viewed therefore in a church with its furnishings and other visual representations, and chiefly by those gathered for Eucharistic celebration, the memorial of the mystery of Christ the Savior, of his death and resurrection. This means that I am unable to view the image in faith without recognizing that issues of exhibition and location are immediately involved. How can the meaning established by its original church setting be conveyed in a museum or art gallery?

It is some knowledge of art history that tells me that this image belongs within a church behind the altar where the Mass is celebrated and that it is seen within the context of a Eucharistic celebration. I also know that it is an altarpiece, rather than an apse mosaic, and so belongs to a period and place when priests stood with their backs to the people.

In the course of the Mass, it would be seen by the faithful, especially at the moment of elevation of the species which occurs once at the words of consecration and again at the doxology at the end of the prayers or Canon of the Mass. In looking at the species elevated, the viewer would encounter at the same time the elevated species and the painting: the visuality of the species and the visual painting complemented one another to bespeak the meaning of what was taking place.

Something else that I know about is that placing Mary and saints in images in the apse, in side paintings, and in altarpieces, was tied up with the increase of patronage. It has an initial meaning in the doctrine of the communion of saints and the principal commemoration of the communion of saints is the Mass; where they are mentioned in the Canon and where there is also reference to the relics of martyrs in or beneath the altar. Legislation often requires, moreover. that church buildings have their titles and patrons and this too had an influence on saintly depictions for the place of celebration.

If I look at it as one visiting a museum, viewing it outside its place in worship, it seems that the viewer's search for a religious and spiritual meaning may be invited by the central figure of the mother Mary looking at the child, Jesus. The other figures in the painting invite the beholder to look to Christ. Lucy and Catherine, the two figures closest to the viewer, look out from the picture but Lucy's right hand points in the direction of Christ. These two women saints point toward Christ. One is renowned for wisdom, the other for light, and both have their feast day within the season of Advent, the time of preparation for Christmas, when Christ is celebrated as the light of the world.

Following the movement embodied in the painting, one next encounters John and Sebastian whose eyes are turned to Christ, with Sebastian's hand, like Lucy's, pointing in the direction of Christ. John the Baptist is the precursor, the image who binds the Hebrew and Christian covenant, and Sebastian is wearing a robe rather like that of a deacon at the liturgy.

Mary's eyes are also turned to her child, as she holds on to him as he makes a forward movement, inviting the viewer to gaze upon him. If he were not sturdy enough, the child would fall in the somewhat precarious hold Mary has on him (compare the firm gesture of the right hand and the almost tentative movement of the left). The eyes of Christ himself are then turned towards the viewer, complementing the invitation given by Lucy and Catherine. This gives the impression that the viewer, in responding to the invitation to look, finds herself looked upon by Christ.

Though Jesus is presented in the body of a child, he is an adult figure and the mark of the Cross on *his* chest indicates that this child was born for crucifixion and sacrifice. But, he *is* strong and firm enough in his stance and in *his* gaze to show that the cross does not overcome him and in this way the resurrection is also presaged. The image of enthronement highlights this, for it evokes the biblical image of the Lamb of sacrifice enthroned in heaven. The uplifted right hand of the infant, a symbolic gesture of address, of one who speaks, together with the enthronement, indicates the nature of the child: the Word of God who has taken on flesh; Word and sacrifice even from infancy. Presenting him in the form of a child, born of Mary, is a way – as in Saint Luke's Gospel – to speak of the mystery of his *birth* for our salvation, of what the viewer *will* have learned to speak of as the mystery of the Incarnation. In its own way, the painting therefore bespeaks the mystery of the Trinity, since one inevitably asks, whence came this child, already sacrificed and triumphant in his infancy. One may well go back in face of this image to read the introductory chapters of the gospel of Luke.

The other figures, Mary and the four saints, speak to the painting's viewer of the mystery of the communion of saints, something likewise accentuated in the celebration of the Eucharist for which the painting was ornament and symbol. Mary gives him flesh and then recedes into the background, a clear presence whose whole purpose is to give the child to the world.

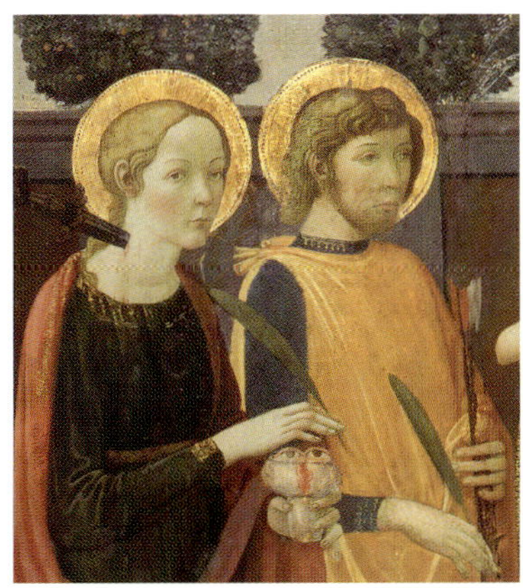

THE MADONNA AND CHILD WITH SAINTS
Attributed to Jacopo del Sellaio
Italian, Florence, ca. 1441-1493; tempera and gold on wood panel. The William A. Whitaker Foundation Art Fund, 63.18.1. (detail)

It is significant that the other four saints are martyrs, of both genders. It reminds us that the doctrine of the communion of the saints began with the veneration of the martyrs. It is by virtue of their martyrdom, or witness to Jesus Christ through their own suffering and death, that they are commemorated in the Eucharist and that they are held in honor.

Historically, I also know that this depiction of Mother and Child belongs to the artistic tradition of the *maiesta*, where mother and child are enthroned as symbols of divine majesty and of Mary's role as mother of the divine son. This particular painting lacks the tenderness of the relation between mother and child such as one often finds in devotional images, where the child is playfully tugging at his mother's veil or sucking from her breast. The difference may be due to the liturgical rather than devotional purpose of the image.

There were other ways of integrating the devotional and the liturgical, as seen in the example of an altarpiece by Piero del Francesca. The devotion to the Mantle of Mercy is central: the faithful find refuge under Mary's mantle. However, this is surmounted by an image of Christ crucified with Mary and Magdalen at the foot of the cross, and the narrative panels at the base recall for the Eucharistic participants, the events of Christ's passion, burial, and resurrection.

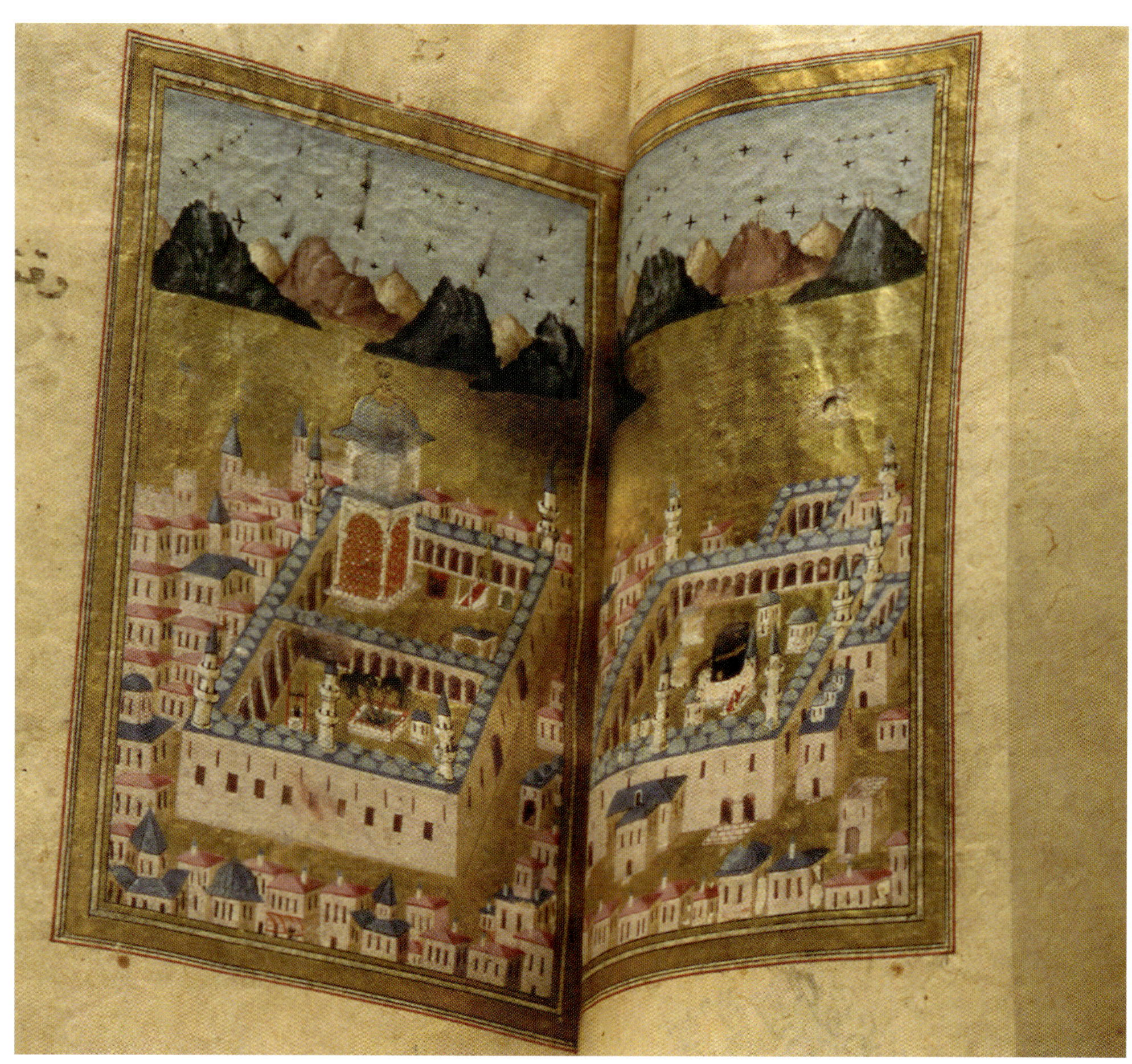

BOOK OF BLESSINGS
Unknown
North African, Algiers (Ottoman Empire), 1769; paper, gold leaf, ink, watercolor, leather binding. Ackland Fund, 96.4.2.

CASE STUDY 2
BOOK OF BLESSINGS: LABEL WRITING EXERCISE

original label

The "Guide to Blessings" (Dala'il al khayrat) is a collection of prayers for the Prophet Muhammad, a description of his tomb in Medina, and a list of his names. The work is attributed to the sixteenth century Moroccan sufi, Abu Abd Allah Mohammad Ibn Sulayman Al Djazuli. It is composed of invocations, litanies in devotion to Muhammad which were sometimes recited by visitors to the Prophet's tomb in Medina. The book has maintained a worldwide popularity among Muslims, particularly some members of the sufi orders who recite it as part of their daily rituals.

This manuscript was copied in naskh script by the calligrapher Ibrahim Jakeri Al Masri and contains two illuminated pages of drawings. The page on the right depicts the mosque surrounding the Kaaba in Mecca, which plays a central role in the ritual life of Muslims. According to Muslim sacred texts, the Kaaba was built by the Prophet Ibrahim (Abraham) as the first shrine for the worship of God. The Kaaba orients Muslims in their daily prayers and is the focus of their pilgrimage. The page on the left depicts Muhammad's tomb and mosque in Medina. In both drawings the artist used gold to mark sacred grounds.

revised label

Miniature Paintings of Makkah and Madinah[20] in a Book of Prayers

These two images, bound into a collection of prayers, depict two holy sites in Islam. According to Muslim belief, the Kaaba, located in Makkah and seen on the right, is the ancient house of worship established by Abraham to commemorate the worship of one God. A Muslim is expected to make the pilgrimage to Makkah once in his or her lifetime. On the left is an image of Madinah (literally, the city) where the prophet Muhammad built the first masjid (mosque) and established the ummah (Islamic community). When depicted together, these two images suggest that First Pillar of Islam in which Muslims profess: "There is no God but God and Muhammad is the Messenger of God."

These two images are set at the beginning of a book of prayers. In this book (Dala'il al-Khayrat/Guide to Blessings/Good Deeds) is a collection of prayers requesting God's blessings upon the Prophet Muhammad. It also includes a description of his tomb in Medina and a list of his names. It has been popular among many Muslims who recite it as a part of their daily rituals.

The compiler of this celebrated manual is the sixteenth-century Moroccan Sufi (a Muslim mystic), Imam Al-Djazuli.

---

20 Participants asked that we change place names to international spelling. Note the ways in which these participants offer definitions within the text.

Considerations

Oh Allah I have believed in our master Muhammad and I have not seen him so do not deprive my heart of a vision of him and provide me with his companionship and have me die on his way and lead me to drink after from his pool plentifully, blissfully, heartily, a drink after which we will never feel thirst. You are the power of all things.

Excerpt from the text provided by Amy Nelson

Description of Book

- Including title, author, contents
- Prayer directed to Allah, asking for blessings
- Upon the Prophet Muhammad and finally upon oneself

About the Illustrations

- Mecca – Kaaba
- Medina – Prophets, Mosque[21]
- two principle pilgrimage centers
- (Importance of Hajj within Islam)

About the Author

- (Left blank)[22]

21 It is interesting that this group reported their considerations using many of the language choices they recommended against: for example, "mosque" instead of "masjid," "Mecca" instead of "Makkah," etc. It is a vivid reminder that habits of language are difficult to break, and certainly what may seem like an easy change of use may be harder to implement than anticipated. Whether by intention or by default, this group returned to familiar usage when presenting to all the colloquy participants.

22 Presenters left this space blank although comparable information appears in the revised label. The revised text references the "compiler" rather than author of the text.

Other Considerations Submitted by Amy Nelson

1 *Definition.* What sort of "devotional book" is this? The Qur'an? A book of Diwan (devotional poetry/songs)? A book of Duas/prayers? What is the purpose of the picture(s) in relation to those prayers, words, or songs?

2 *La ilaha if Allah, Muhammadan Rasulullah/There is no god but Allah and Muhammad is the Messenger of Allah.* The two pictures convey "spiritual spaces" that are interconnected and essential in Islam. The Kaaba is the highest. It is "The House of Allah," the ancient house of worship established by prophet Ibrahim/Abraham. A Muslim must make the pilgrimage to the Kaaba once in his lifetime. If his intention is pure and he makes hajj, Allah will purify his heart in this life and reward him in the next. After visiting the house of Allah, the devotee must travel to the city of Medina to visit the prophet's mosque – the place where Muhammad (pbuh) established the Islamic message. The purpose of this life, according to the Qur'an, is to know Allah. Muhammad is the last in a long chain of prophets to show us the way to this knowledge.

I was a hidden treasure and I longed to be known (Hadith Al-Qudsi)

3 *Relationship to supplicant.* How do the pictures of the Kaaba and the prophet's masjid relate to the supplicant? I believe it is a device for conjuring up those spiritual spaces inwardly. To be reminded of that nearness to Allah we are all trying to achieve. There is a strong message here that these two spaces are interlocked based on the artists' decision to draw them next to one another. In reality, these two places are in two different cities: Mecca and Medina. These images, side by side, help to intensify and focus one's devotion to Allah, and commitment to the path as taught by the prophet Muhammad (pbuh).

4 *The picture.* In the background there are mountains and birds. In the foreground, walls encircle the holy sites. It is an aerial view. The message I get is one of protection. The natural world will protect these places as well as

the man-made walls which surround them. On an *outward*, or physical plane, the Kaaba represents closeness to Allah. How does this relate to the *inward* plane? In the Qur'an, Allah says: "We are nearer to him than his jugular vein" (50:15). If we are to say that the *heart of* the believer is an inward manifestation of the Kaaba, then the devotion of the supplicant is a protective barrier for his heart – as the mountains and walls are for the holy places.

Submitted by Shabbir Mansuri

The existence of such a Pilgrimage Manual indicates the high value placed on Hajj by Muslims in various lands. It may have helped Muslims visualize the possibility of fulfilling this obligation, despite the potential difficulty of traveling great distances.

The manual's inclusion of information about the Prophet Muhammad's alternative names (probably Mustafa, Ahmad, etc.) and prayers for the Prophet reflects the centrality of Muhammad as a guide and exemplar for Muslims. This is a consistent feature of Muslim religious practice.

The use of gold ink in the illustrations likens this work to a piece of calligraphy designed to glorify Qur'anic verses.

5 *Historical Perspective.* It seems likely that this manual is one of many that were produced historically. If that is a case, then the pilgrimage manual can be considered a specific genre of Muslim literature. The attribution of this work to Moroccan sufi AI-Djazuli suggests that Sufism or sufi perspectives were part of "mainstream" Muslim practice at the time the manuscript was produced (perhaps unlike today).

6 *Exhibition Perspective.* The Record sheet for this object lists it as "Turkish?." Though it was prepared in Ottoman territory (a political condition), the work itself is from the North African regional or cultural zone and should be designated accordingly. What makes the work Turkish?

Additional Considerations Presented by group members

The spellings of terms and names seem inconsistent in the exhibition materials, captions, and/or descriptions. (eg.. Makkah/Mecca, Muhammad/Mohammed, Ka'ba/Kaaba).

The description presents the Muslim belief that Abraham built the Kaaba as fact. This is a confessional view that may be borne out historically, but should be attributed as Muslim belief.

The description of the object could be edited for greater accuracy, meaning and relevance to a viewing audience. For example, the name Allah should be introduced in conjunction with the word "God" and "God" should be used thereafter.

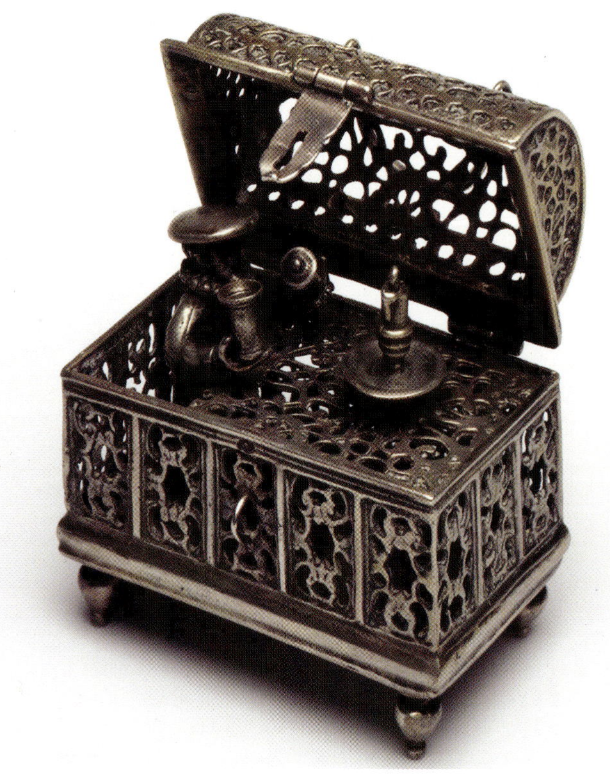

SPICE BOX
Unknown
European, Eastern, mid-19th century; nickel-plated brass. Gift of Elizabeth F. Gervais-Gruen in honor of the marriage of her son S. Daniel Gruen and Sharon Timian, 2001.5.2.

original label

Like the Kiddush cup, the spice box is part of Sabbath observance in the home. On Saturday after nightfall the Havdalah [separation] ceremony ends the Sabbath, and smelling the sweet spices in the box helps provide a gentle transition from the festive Sabbath to the ordinary routine of the weekday. A spice box is usually made of perforated metal so that the odor of the spices inside can come out, but the boxes vary widely in size and shape.

revised label

The spice box is used in a ceremony called *havdalah* (separation) that marks the end of the Sabbath and the beginning of the work week. Just as the Sabbath began with blessings recited over wine, it is concluded with blessings over wine, spices, and light. The light represents the return to physical creativity, and the smelling of spices fortifies the spirit after the Sabbath has ended.

Although *havdalah* is an ancient custom, the use of spice containers is known only from the twelfth century. A spice container is usually made of perforated metal so that the odor of the spices inside can come out, but the boxes vary widely in size and shape. The figure here is unusual because it shows a man performing the *havdalah* ceremony.

CASE STUDY 3
SPICE BOX: LABEL WRITING EXERCISE

This group did not present notes in the same formats as the previous presenters. Instead it spent considerable time discussing the authenticity of the object, as well as its actual intended use suggesting that perhaps it was meant only to be decorative, and not for use in the *havdalah.* Their revisions constitute a major shift nonetheless. By locating the object not only within the ritual use but within the historical practices of Judaism, the writers in this group expanded understanding of the changing preferences of religious communities.

Other Considerations Submitted by Vivian Mann

1 *Faith Perspective.* Jews refrain from creative physical work on the Sabbath in imitation of God who rested on the seventh day of Creation. The rabbis defined the work to be avoided as any of the thirty-nine categories of work performed in the Jerusalem Temple. Onc of thcsc was lighting a fire. The kindling of a light during the *havdalah* ceremony therefore signifies the resumption of creative physical work.

2 *Historical Perspective.* Use of a spice box is an Ashkenzi custom that began in the twelfth century. Rabbi Ephraim of Regensburg was reported to have kept his spices for *havdalah* in a glass container. Other Jews at that time used aromatic twigs or leaves, but no container.

3 *Curatorial Perspective.* This may not be a spice box. This is a problematic area. Although functional as a spice box, the Ackland example does not fit within any known historical group of such containers. It appears to be modern!

An activity in the gallery could contrast photographs of well-dated spice boxes with the Ackland example to reveal similarities and differences.

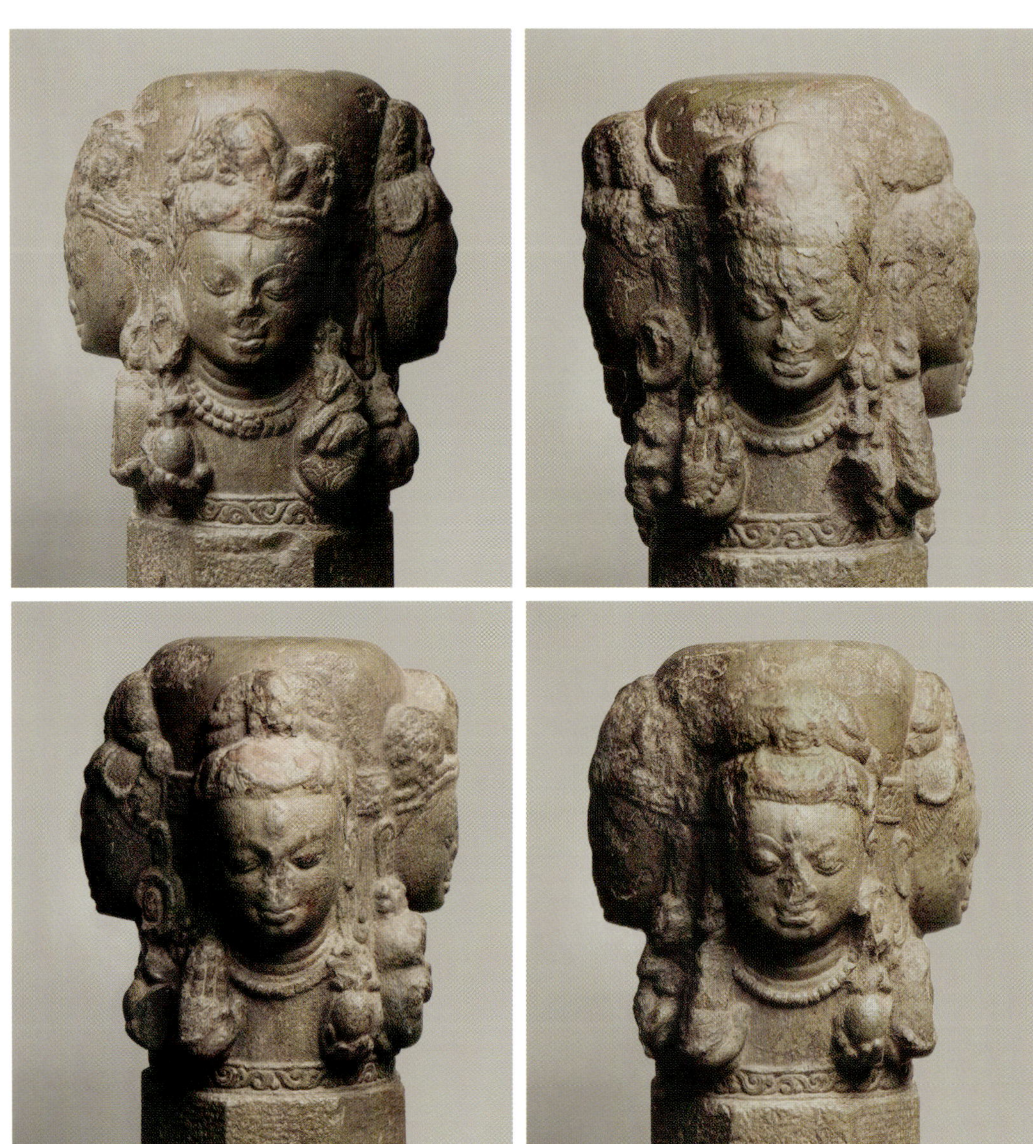

SHIVA LINGA
Unknown
Nepali, Transitional Period (879/80-1200), 12th century; green schist. Gift of Gilbert J. and Clara T. Yager in honor of our advisor Dr. Sherman Lee, 95.4.2. (details)

CASE STUDY 4
SHIVA LINGA: LABEL WRITING EXERCISE

original label

In Hinduism, Shiva is God of Creation and Destruction and is often worshipped in the form of the linga, a symbolic representation of male energy. Sometimes, as in this sculpture, the linga is embellished with four faces, oriented towards the points of the compass and representing different aspects of Shiva. Missing from this sculpture is the yoni, a cylindrical or octagonal base on which the linga is traditionally mounted. The yoni represents female energy. Together the linga and yoni portray the unity of male and female creative energies.

The square base and octagonal mid-section of the linga are taken to represent the other two principal Gods of Hinduism: Brahma and Vishnu. For followers of Shiva, he is the supreme God, crowning the other two, but at the same time all three Gods can be seen as different aspects of the one Supreme Source, known as Brahman.

revised label 1

Imagine this Shiva Linga in the center of a sacred temple in Nepal. It served as the principal focus of the worship of Shiva. Devotees visited the shrine to have *darshan* (to see the deity and be seen by the deity). Many brought offerings to Shiva such as flowers, milk, and vermillion powder.[23] Traces of this red powder are still visible on the object.

For Shaivites, Shiva is the supreme God who animates and sustains the cosmos. The four visible faces of the linga facing in the four directions – and a fifth invisible upraised face – represent Shiva's five fundamental activities: creation, preservation, destruction, veiling, and grace. Together they point to his transcendent essence/nature.

Although here we see the vertical shaft of the linga, it would have originally been embedded within an ovoid pedestal called a *yoni*. The combination of linga and yoni signifies the perfect integration of Shiva and Shakti, male and female principles and energies.

---

23 Note that the writers do not refer to *kumkum* in the label. Conversations with the authors revealed that they were concerned that learning about kumkum distracted from the object itself and that, perhaps, would contribute to a misunderstanding of Hindu practice as exotic or esoteric.

Considerations Submitted by Anantanand Rambachan

A faith perspective on the Ackland Art Museum display of the Shiva Linga ought to begin by taking note of the fact that the act of seeing a sacred object constitutes one of the primary Hindu modes of worship. This is of special significance since the museum experience is primarily one of seeing. The encounter with icons in a museum setting is still strange and unsettling for Hindus, accustomed as they are to knowing these objects in the altar/ritual settings of homes and temples. There is a spontaneous urge to adore and to revere, along with the restraint of a location that does not appear to invite such a response. The experience is intensified by the fact that Hindu icons displayed in museums are still a vital part of Hindu ritual life. They are not archeological remnants of a vanished tradition, and the implications of this cannot be overlooked. I think that it is still quite difficult for a Hindu to view an icon in a museum without the evocation of worshipful sentiments more typically aroused in the home and temple. For one who is accustomed to the visual apprehension of the sacred as a religious experience, it is difficult to see it otherwise.

Hindus typically speak of visiting a temple, a sacred location or a saintly person for the purpose of *darshan*. The word, darshan, comes from the verb root, *drs*, meaning "to see," and is used to describe the seeing of that which is endowed with religious meaning and significance. It is therefore better translated as "sacred seeing." The experience of seeing becomes darshan when the object awakens in us the consciousness of the divine. Many of us approach the icon (*murti*) with our eyes open, but as the awareness of the divine grows on us, we close our eyes in order to more fully savor the experience. Murtis are important to Hindus because they are capable of awakening us to the divine presence, yet Hindus do not claim that murtis are alone capable of engendering this experience.

Darshan is a dual mode of experience. While it involves a profound sense of seeing or being awake "to God's reality," it is, at the same time, a consciousness of being "seen" by God or standing in God's presence. In darshan, I see and know that I am seen. To enhance this experience, the eyes of the murti are usually prominent and opened by the artist as the final act during the ritual of consecration or establishing the life force (*prana pratishta*).

The Shiva Linga is Hinduism's most famous aniconic representation of the divine, and is the most popular form in which God as Shiva is worshipped. It is generally the only object of worship on the altar of a Shiva temple. While the origins of the Shiva Linga are lost in antiquity, there are very important differences between the faith-perspective and "seeing" of the Hindu and representations and descriptions of the Shiva Linga outside of the faith setting. For the Hindu, the linga is an ancient sign and symbol of the transcendent and invisible Shiva. A properly consecrated linga is also one of the ways in which God as Shiva becomes accessible for ritual worship (*puja*) in the temple or home. Such accessibility is an act of compassion and grace.

Outside of the faith-perspective, the linga is interpreted to be a phallic symbol through which Shiva is worshipped and it is the phallic character that is emphasized and treated as factual. The Ackland characterizes the Shiva Linga as a "symbolic representation of the male genitals," in the opening sentence of its description. The first paragraph of the Museum's article on the Shiva Linga speaks of it as a symbol of "sexual potency," a "phallic emblem," through which Shiva "directs his semen toward the highest life-force center (*chakra*), the head, converting sexual energy into spiritual bliss." The linga is also described as a "cult object" worshipped in temples. While Hindus are not prudish about the use of sexual symbolism in a religious context, it would appear that the museum visitor is directed to a form of seeing very different from the seeing of the Hindu. We must acknowledge with Diana Eck that European travelers and missionaries, who looked at the Shiva Linga and saw a phallic symbol, expressed moral outrage and condemnation of the Hindu tradition for its indecency.[24] It does not surprise us that Hindus are similarly outraged when told that the Shiva Linga is a phallic emblem. Whose seeing does the Museum represent in its depiction of an icon?

From a faith perspective, additional issues arise in the presentation of Hindu icons in the museum setting. One of these has to do with the plurality of icons and names for the divine. This issue arises directly in relation to the Shiva Linga under discussion since, as a *caturmukhalinga*, it depicts four faces of Shiva. In a monotheistic culture, this leads to the representation of the Hindu tradition as polytheistic and the use of the lower case "g" when speaking of the "gods" Shiva, Brahma, and Vishnu. While the narrative that accompanies the Shiva Linga concedes that "all three gods can be seen as different aspects of the same being," one must admit that the there is considerable ambiguity. Polythe-

---

24 Diana L. Eck, *Darsan: Seeing the Divine Image in India* (New York: Columbia University Press, 1996), pp.35-36.

ism, understood as the worship of a multiplicity of gods, each with limited powers and fields of authority, does not faithfully describe the Hindu self-understanding. The Absolute, as Hindus will tirelessly explain, is one and yet can be sought and celebrated under a variety of names and forms, each of which is understood as supreme. While the Ackland describes Shiva as a "Hindu god" and Brahma and Vishnu as "gods of Hinduism," Hindus understand God, whether called and imagined as Shiva, Vishnu, or Brahma, to be the God of all. It is appropriate to speak of a Hindu understanding of God, but not of a Hindu God. One rarely finds such a description employed in relation to the traditions of Judaism, Christianity, and Islam. While admittedly more difficult to capture in a brief narrative, museums must be aware of the broader cultural and religious context in which these sacred objects are exhibited, and strive to accurately portray a faith's self understanding.

Closely related to the matter of oneness of the divine and its multiple names and forms are problems arising from the descriptions of the ritual uses of the Shiva Linga. The Ackland describes it as the "primary cult object worshipped in temples." Along with a questionable connotation of "cult," one gets the idea that the Shiva Linga is the focus of worship and the stereotypical impression, prevalent in the minds of many, is that Hindu worship is therefore idolatrous. While accurate, the statement that the Shiva Linga was "cleansed during worship with liquids like consecrated milk, water, curds, and butter," is not really helpful. Again, one must keep in mind the wider religious and cultural disapproval of imaging the divine and the denunciation of ritual centered on icons.

Idolatry, strictly speaking, is the identification of the Absolute with the limited and finite. While the Hindu tradition affirms the immanence of the divine, it emphasizes that the divine is not identical with or limited to any object in the world. It is God, immanent and transcendent, who is the focus of Hindu worship and not any particular icon through which such worship is offered. Hindus do not simplistically equate the Shiva Linga with God and descriptions of the ritual use of the latter should not make this suggestion.

Museum displays of Hindu icons require an accompanying hermeneutic that takes into consideration the ways of seeing that users are likely to bring as well as Hindu ways of seeing. The aim must be to help us see, not merely through our own eyes, but also, as far as possible, through Hindu eyes.

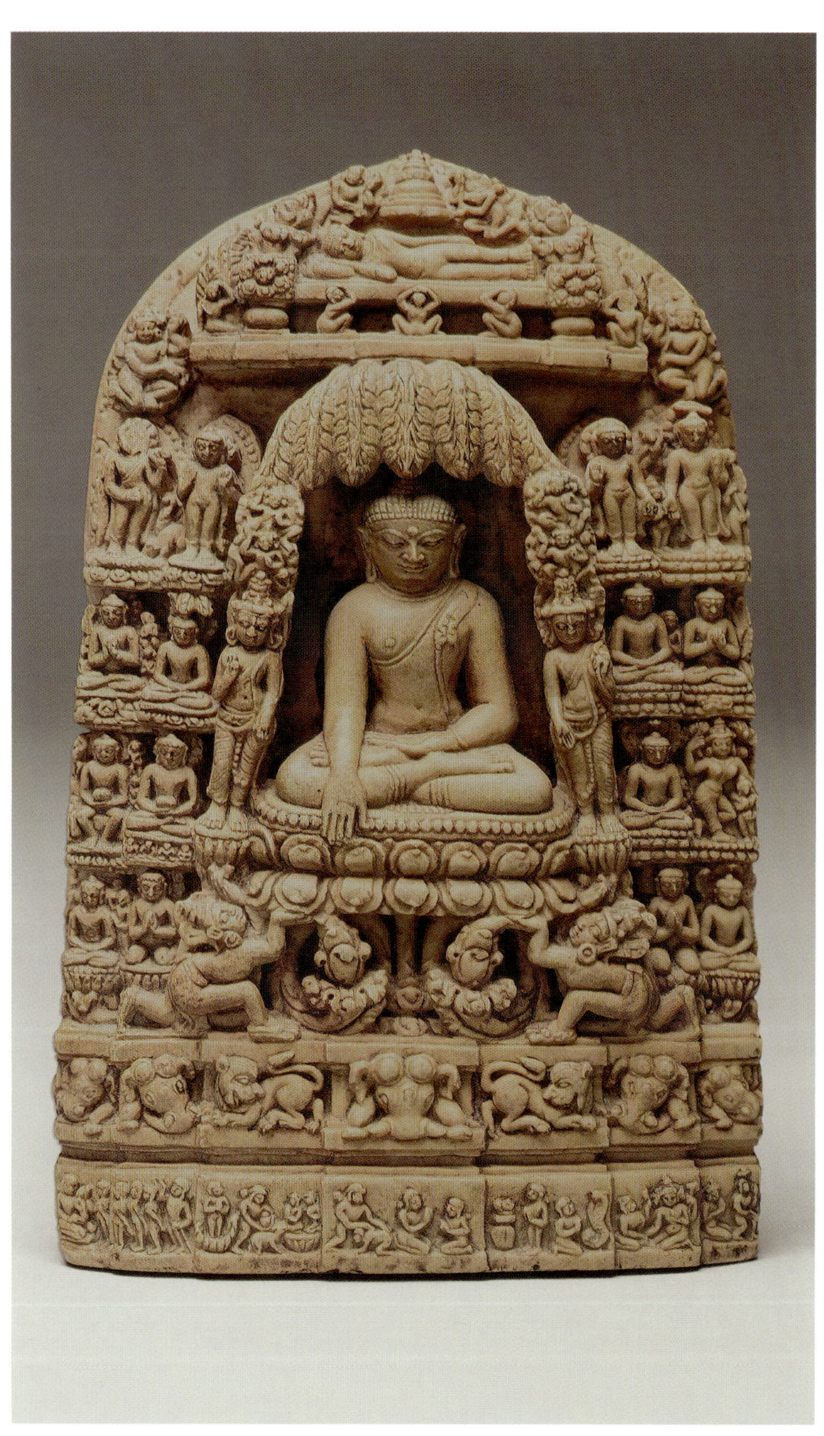

BUDDHA CALLING THE EARTH TO WITNESS
Unknown
Burmese, Myanmar, probably from the city of Paga around the 13th century; andagu stone (pyrophyllite). Ackland Fund, 97.14.1.

CASE STUDY 5
BURMESE BUDDHA: LABEL WRITING EXERCISE

original label

Prince Guatama Sakyamuni, born in 555 BCE in what is now Nepal, abandoned wealth and family to seek the meanings of life and death. According to Buddhist tradition, after years of meditation, he discovered the truth (*Dharma*) and became the Buddha (literally "awakened one"). This sculpture portrays him meditating under a sacred peepal tree (sometimes called *Bodhi*, which means enlightenment) and calling the earth to witness his moment of supreme insight. Also portrayed are scenes from the Buddha's life, including his first sermon and later, his death at the age of 80.

In his first sermon, "The Great Discourse on the Wheel of the Dharma," the Buddha noted that the world's pain and suffering were caused by negative passions and emotions. He also spoke of the remedies that were needed to establish harmony within this state of darkness and outlined an eight-fold path based on morality, meditation, and wisdom. Recognizing the emotional and economic realities of daily life, the Buddha advocated a lifestyle based on moderation that he called "The Middle Way."

This sculpture may have been associated with pilgrimages to holy sites, either transported or symbolically referring to sacred sites in India.

revised label

This beautifully carved portable shrine depicts scenes from the life of Buddha. At the center beneath the bodhi tree is the Buddha, his arm extended in the earth-touching gesture. This gesture recalls the earth quaking to affirm his worthiness of enlightenment due to virtue in this and previous lives. Depictions of some of these lives appear at the base. The reclining Buddha above represents his final entry into nirvana at death.

Some Buddhists interpret this image as Buddha's rejection of the extremes of self-deprivation or/and self-indulgence, and finding the Middle Way which acknowledges the interdependence of body and mind. This enabled him to practice with and awaken to the totality of his being. By referring to key events, all associated with sites in India and Nepal, this portable shrine is a visual model for the life of Buddha and the path of his teachings. Texts carried within represent the Buddha's teaching. This shrine may have been used for personal devotion and contemplation.

Questions and Considerations

What are the implications of size given the range of representations of the Buddha?

- The smallness of the work implies private use
- Required on a pilgrimage

What does the intricate carving on the stone connote?

- Great expense of work

What can we learn from the composition?

- Hierarchy of scenes from bottom to top
- Artist ordered the composition as a focus to the devotee
- Selections of eight scenes may indicate which type of Buddhism

Historical Considerations concerning Bhūmisparśa-mudrā [25]

Submitted by Charles Orzech

Four things dominate my initial perception of the object:

1. The obvious focus of the object is Siddhārtha reaching out to gently touch the earth.
2. Less immediate in written/printed form but immediate in person: this is a hand-sized object for personal, almost intimate piety and reflection.
3. Not obvious to the non-Buddhist: it is in the shape of a *stūpa.*[26]
4. Finally, I want to know the history of the piece, not simply in terms addressed in the excerpt given us (probably thirteenth century, perhaps Burmese, perhaps carved in Bihar near Bodh Gayā) but in the more ex-

---

25 As in the case of David Power's work on the Sellaio Altarpiece, the authors include this text because it demonstrates the contribution of scholars of religion. By paying close attention to the structure of Orzech's contribution, museum professionals may find things to admire and things to correct. Can visitors be expected to value the threat of Mara if they do not know who Mara is? Is "lord of death" sufficient? Perhaps. By way of contrast, this contribution engages the sacred texts that support this object in interesting ways, and challenges participants to remember what walk-in visitors do not, and perhaps cannot know. For example, note how Orzech walks the participants through an introduction to Buddhism with this one object. Also note his inclusion of diacritical marks.

26 Stupas are reliquary mounds and locations of practice in some streams of Buddhism. See page 132 for a more complete exploration of the origin and history of stupas.

tended sense of how this object, possibly bought on pilgrimage, has made a pilgrimage of its own to arrive before us in North Carolina at the beginning of the twenty-first century.

To touch the Earth

Although the image of Siddhārtha touching the earth (*Bhūmisparśa-mudrā*)[27] has long been used as shorthand for the entire enlightenment narrative, a Buddhist sees so much more. For this is not, technically, the moment of enlightenment (if indeed it can be conceived of as momentary) but rather the moment of Siddhārtha's victory over the forces of desire and death. According to the legendary accounts, Māra, lord of death and therefore of the world of *samsara*, tried in every way possible to derail Siddhārtha's meditative progress. At last, in frustration Māra asked by what merit could Siddhārtha claim the seat of enlightenment and thus triumph over the world? The sage's response was to touch the earth and in doing so to call the earth to testify to his innumerable past lives of virtuous action – his store of meritorious deeds. The earth obliged in the form of an earthquake, and Māra retreated, leaving Siddhārtha to complete his meditation. So what is not immediately obvious is that this is a lesson both about unshakable stability and an unshakable progress in the practice of good deeds. Thus for the pious Buddhist this is not solely, or even primarily, a call to mediation. Rather, in its allusion to Siddhārtha's past lives (the *Jātakas*) we are called to attend to the history of the practice of meritorious action and that history is illustrated at the base of the image with scenes from the widely know Jātakas. This is, in fact, a call for the Buddhist to tread a similar historical path.

Palm of the hand devotion

This is an object sized for personal piety and it is meant to be portable. Such objects abound in connection with pilgrimage sites and we all recognize that small images are one of the mainstays of the pilgrimage trade in many religious traditions. Whether carved at or near Bodh Gayā or in Burma near some local Burmese temple complex, it alerts us to a great cosmopolitan tradition whose forms and practices crossed political

27 *Mudras* are hand postures that signal certain stories and activities to those who know them. In this case, the activity of touching the earth is understood to reference a complete narrative, not a moment within the narrative.

and ethnic boundaries to encompass and create a community across much of Asia (in this respect it is much like Islam). Further, by representing eight key events in the life of Siddhārtha, it replicates in miniature the geography of the holy land and its chief Buddhist pilgrimage sites. Contemplation of this object is perforce an imaginary pilgrimage and a recreation of the historical geography of the religion.

Stūpa, Structure, and Typology

The object before us takes the form of a stūpa or reliquary mound. Also sometimes designated as *caitya* (having no relic) or *dāgoba*, these mounds were traditionally erected as shrines to inter the remains of rulers and saints, and they are the architectural inspiration of pagodas in East Asia. Stūpas are among the earliest iconographic signs of the founder and his doctrine and their symbolism is many layered. Early in the history of Buddhism in India stūpas became the locus of lay/monastic interaction and of royal patronage. Although early stūpas may have been unadorned, they quickly came to embody the equation between the physical presence of the founder and the didactic content of his *Dharma* or Teaching. Not only did large stūpas enshrine relics, many stūpas, even small ones like that before us, enshrined the Dharma – literally including a text as ours does. As the Buddha says in one early text, "he who sees my Dharma, sees me." At festival times monks would lecture the laity on Buddhist themes and on the life of the Buddha; and the Jātaka tales and key events of the Buddha's final life were illustrated by carvings on gates surrounding the stūpa and on the stūpa itself. Among the Jātakas or past life stories of Siddhārtha, ten stories became most frequently depicted and the eight key events in his biography became conventionalized. Whether in a large stūpa as the one at Sāñcī or Borobodur, or in a small one as the object before us is a kind of typological history and representation familiar to us from the stained glass windows in Christianity. While in Christianity events from the "Old Testament" (Hebrew Bible) are selectively read in light of exemplary events in the life of Jesus, in Buddhism past incarnations of Siddhārtha have been modeled on the exemplary deeds of the Bodhisattva.

Thus, the object before us, like many full sized stūpas, can be read synoptically, historically, and symbolically all at once. Read from bottom (Jātakas) to top (the *parinirvāna*) we have a "historical" biography that simultaneously maps soteriology. Read synoptically we have a geography that maps the conduct of a moral life.

Furthermore, the inclusion of motifs connected with kingship (including the use of the stūpa itself) and the symbolism of world sovereignty, imply Buddha's status not only as transcending the world of samsara but also as the "Lord of the Triple World" (he who, at birth is said to have announced that he was "best and highest in the world," and who has defeated Māra, former master of the world). Thus, throughout South and Southeast Asia the *stūpa* form is replicated in temples, royal palaces, and ceremonial cites (such as Angkor). The anthropologist S. J. Tambiah has used the term "galactic" polity to encapsulate this many-leveled symbolism. The owner of this object carried the Lord of the World and the world itself in his or her hand.

Pilgrim in History

Finally, I want to suggest we take a broader view of what history means in regard to an object in a museum. Traditionally, collectors of Chinese paintings set their seal on a work of art when it came into their collection. Thus a work would have a colophon or seal from the artist, and might be adorned with other seals indicating a history of ownership. In contrast, it has long been a practice in our museums that one might summarize the "native" history of an object or painting but keep the story of the object's pilgrimage through private western (or Japanese) collections safely in the archive. There are many reasons for this, but there are also some good reasons for providing museum goers with a fuller sense of how our pilgrim got here. This is particularly so if we want to see the museum become a space for faith-based activity.

---

i Charles Orzech, Colloquy I discussion.

ii Vivian Mann, Colloquy I discussion.

iii Heather Kane, Colloquy I evaluation.

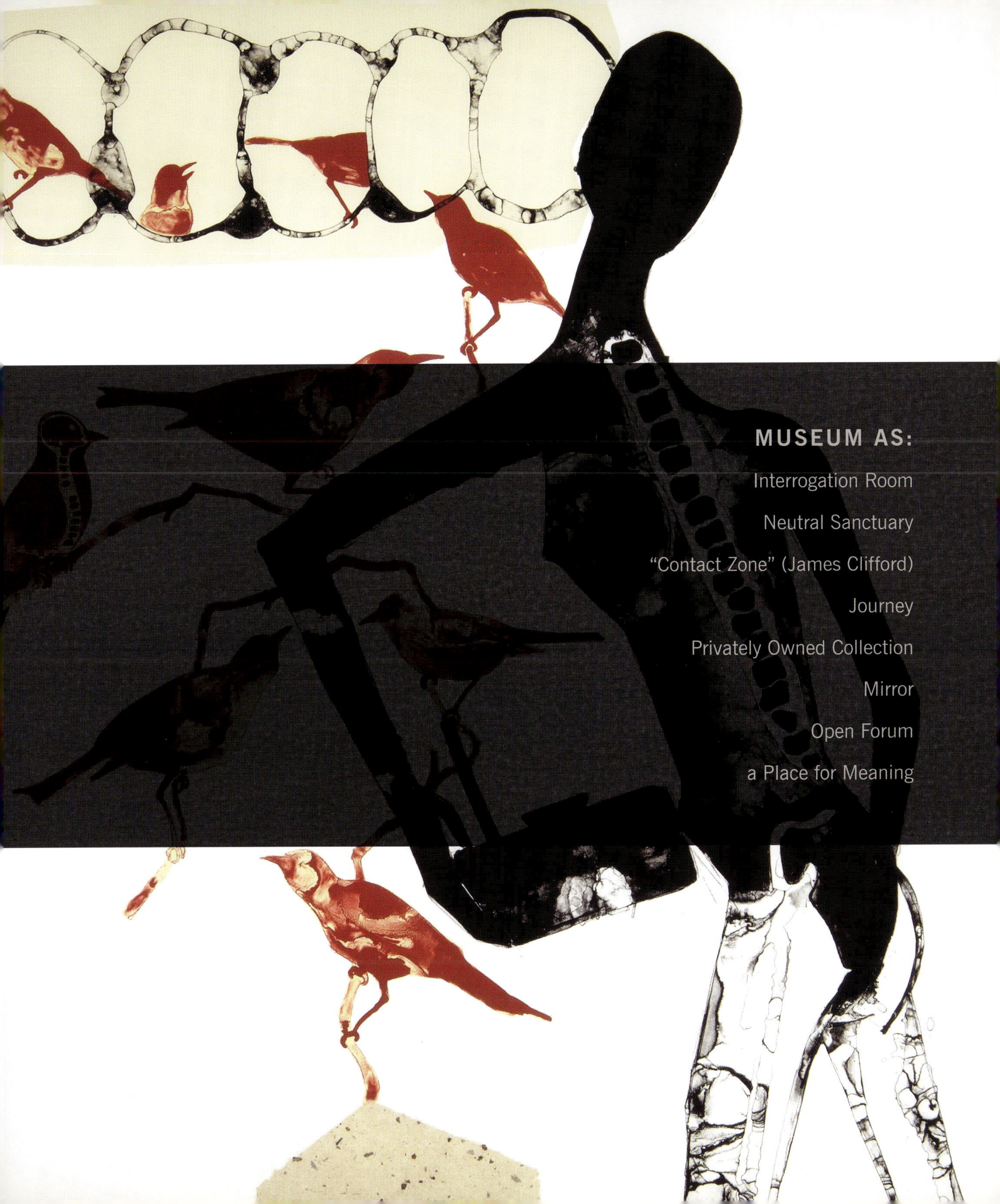
MUSEUM AS:
Interrogation Room
Neutral Sanctuary
"Contact Zone" (James Clifford)
Journey
Privately Owned Collection
Mirror
Open Forum
a Place for Meaning

SABARI WITH HER BIRDS

Atul Dodiya

Indian, born 1959: 2005; 4-color lithograph and Chiri Bark paper collage on handmade STPI cotton and linen. Ackland Fund, 2007.4. (detail)

Atul Dodiya, born in Bombay, has become one of India's most acclaimed artists. Experimenting in all media, he recently turned his attention to collage and printmaking in collaboration with the Singapore Tyler Print Institute. The result is a striking series titled *The Wet Sleeves of My Paper Robe (Sabari in her Youth after Nandalal Bose)*. Dodiya interprets a story from the Indian epic, *The Ramayana*: A tribal woman living in the forest as a hermit waits her whole life to be blessed by the crown-prince Rama, an incarnation of the deity Vishnu. In contrast to traditional depictions of Sabari as an old woman, Dodiya emphasizes her youthful sensuality. He fills the composition with graceful, yoga-like postures that reveal partial x-ray views of her skeleton. The artist's contemporary vision of an ancient figure personifying patience and devotion blends aspects of South Asian culture with modern abstraction.

Colloquy III

A PLACE FOR MEANING

> Museums have unexplored potential as places to experience "the Other" ... When sacred images are removed from their ritual settings and transported to museums, they require innovative approaches to communicate to the uninitiated visitor the profound emotional power they possess in their original context.[i]

> Museums are sometimes the only places where voices that challenge tradition, voices that are often silenced, may have space to be considered.[ii]

> The evocative nature of art opens the possibility of the museum becoming a truly transformative space, a space that can lead one to awe, to wisdom, to creative doubt, to affirmation, or to prophetic agency in the world.[iii]

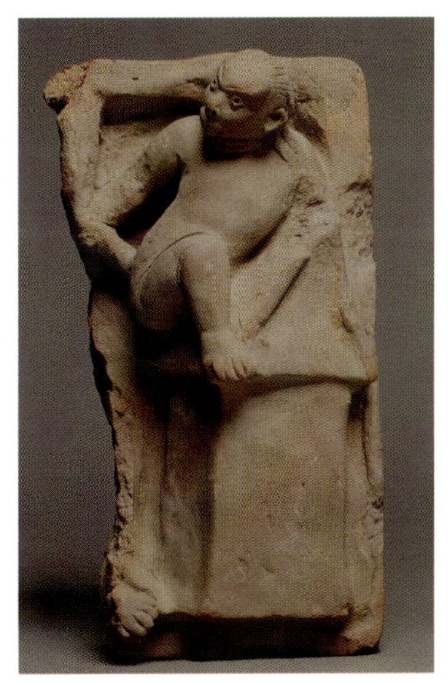

MONKEY ON A ROOFTOP
Unknown
North India, Haryana or Uttar Pradesh, 5th-7th century CE: terracotta. Gift of Clara T. and Gilbert J. Yager, 9036.

By Colloquy III, all the participants were invested believers in the value of the *Five Faiths Project.* Acknowledging that museums had great potential to be "contact zones" for traditions, values, and belief systems, participants began to extrapolate ways in which art museums in particular are uniquely suited to realize this potential. For example, they suggested that the core mission of art museums to present and interpret works of art (whether in focused collections and exhibitions or within broader installations of survey collections) resonates with the experience of visitors who encounter difference daily and try to understand these encounters. From the "do not touch" signs to displays that give objects "personal space," from protective cases that suggest extraordinary value to thoughtful groupings of objects that encourage visitors to approach works of art from multiple perspectives, the museum has a number of strategies in place that support respectful engagement. Even the overarching signage that informs visitors what continent or time period produced an object, without presuming that everyone can recognize an ancient Mediterranean object or a medieval manuscript page, suggests that many of the visible conventions of gallery installation hold strategies for fostering safe and civil encounters. The museum is in fact a metaphor for valuing difference and constructing a safe environment for the free exchange of ideas and beliefs.

Beginning with a panel discussion designed to restart our discussion of the promise of our museums, the panelists were asked to consider how to make museums places for meaning. David Carr, author of *The Promise of Cultural Institutions*, was the logical choice for moderator. The panelists were Mimi Gates, former director of the Seattle Art Museum; David Power, OMI, Catholic priest and scholar emeritus of The Catholic University of America; Meera Viswanathan, professor of comparative literature, Brown University; and newcomer Mark Bozzuti-Jones, Episcopal priest at Trinity Church Wall Street and poet. Unfortunately, Charles Orzech, professor of religious studies at The University of North Carolina at Greensboro, was unable to attend, but sent some materials to be read at the panel discussion. Each panelist presented an opening statement, with time allowed for conversation among them and questions from the audience.

Bozzuti-Jones began with very powerful truth claims about the museum experience:

> Conversion in religious terms is a change of heart, a shift in perspective, and while conversion is oftentimes considered a divine gift, I believe it is our responsibility to dispose ourselves to conversion. Viewers or observers in a museum might consider their interaction with exhibitions as disposing themselves to the unique conversion experience that turns on engagement with the other and with the different.

THE TRIUMPHANT CHRIST FORGIVING REPENTANT SINNERS
Johann Boeckhorst
Flemish (born in Germany), 1603-1688: about 1660; oil on canvas. Ackland Fund, 72.1.1.

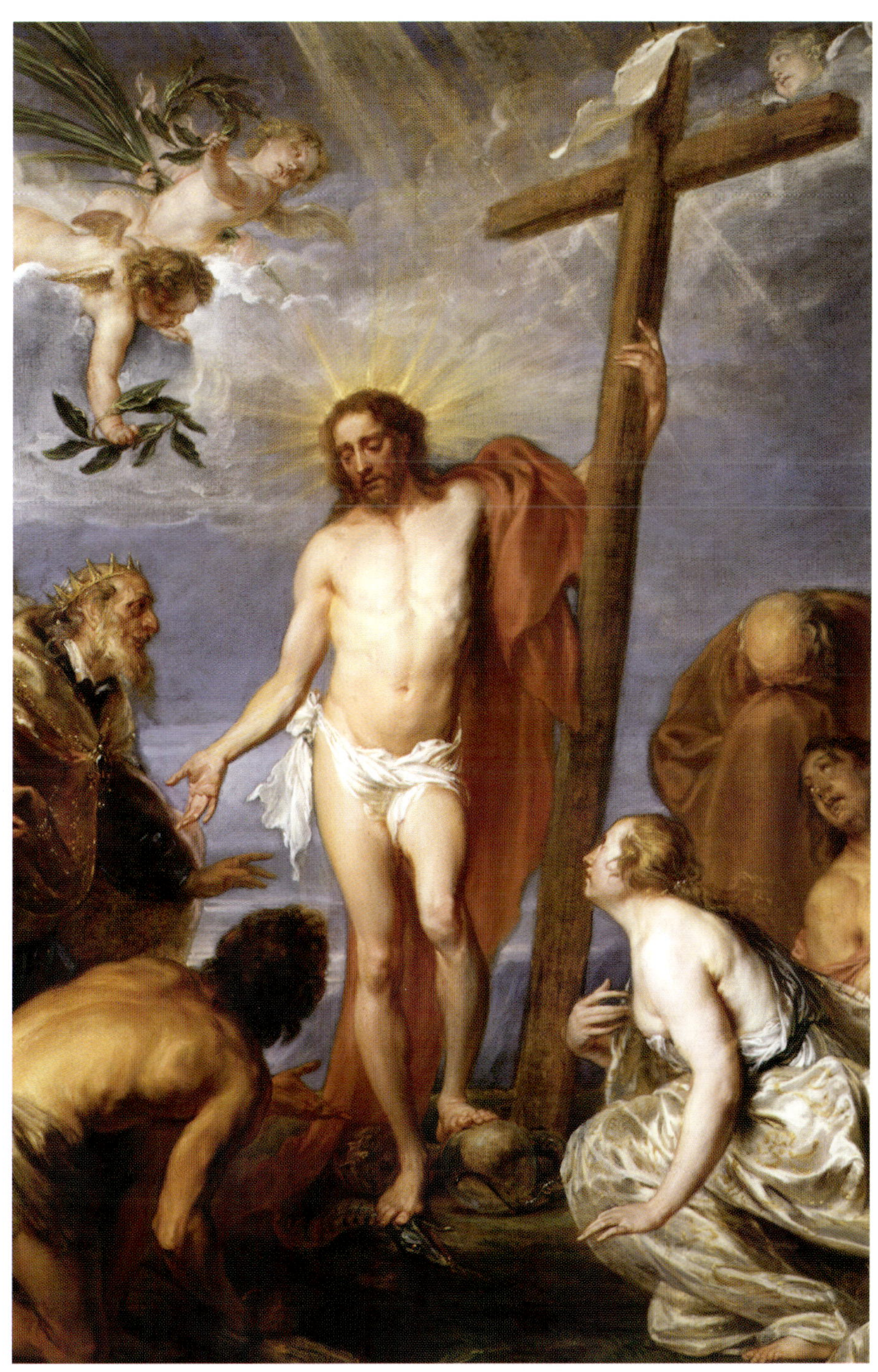

Mimi Gates extended the metaphor:

> I firmly believe that meaningful dialogue and rich, multisensory experience – maybe smells and bells – is central to museums. If we are to be vibrant centers of learning and centers of community, there is a need for change, for experimentation, and for greater risk-taking by museum professionals. We must transcend traditional museum practice and reject the response, "This is the way it is done." Museums need to go beyond "This is the way we have always done it" – and when appropriate, provide visitors with an engaging multisensory experience.

David Power, who professed to be a museum outsider with no background in art, examined the ritual aspects of museum visits and, in fact, asked a profound curatorial question: how, precisely, do museums encourage visitors to encounter, to turn to, to entertain these sacred objects?

Power reminded the audience and the participants that religious objects present a special set of issues for presentation. If you remove the objects completely from their world of origin, then they may become objects of curiosity rather than objects of veneration or religious significance.

> The museum must communicate something of the power of the religious world to which these objects belonged originally, while simultaneously engaging visitors in contemporary appreciation of their enduring beauty, value, or meaning.

Meera Viswanathan, whose academic training suited her well to discussions about making comparisons across perspectives and seeing tangential connections, suggested that the greatest challenge faced by the museum lay in the use of hermeneutic language.

> ... hermeneutic. It is such a ponderous and, in some ways, clumsy word, but I use it because I wanted to get at the idea of the Greek God Hermes. Hermes, who is known as Mercury or Quicksilver in Rome, is the messenger between humans and the Gods, he is the God of Travel and he is the God of Traffic. ... that is precisely what we do in museums. We negotiate traffic, and we need to think about the ways in which this intercourse happens.
>
> A hermeneutic notion of language is one in which language is not about declaring something to be so, but about asking questions, raising possibilities, allowing for a kind of modification, inundation, and change. The role of language in all of this must be

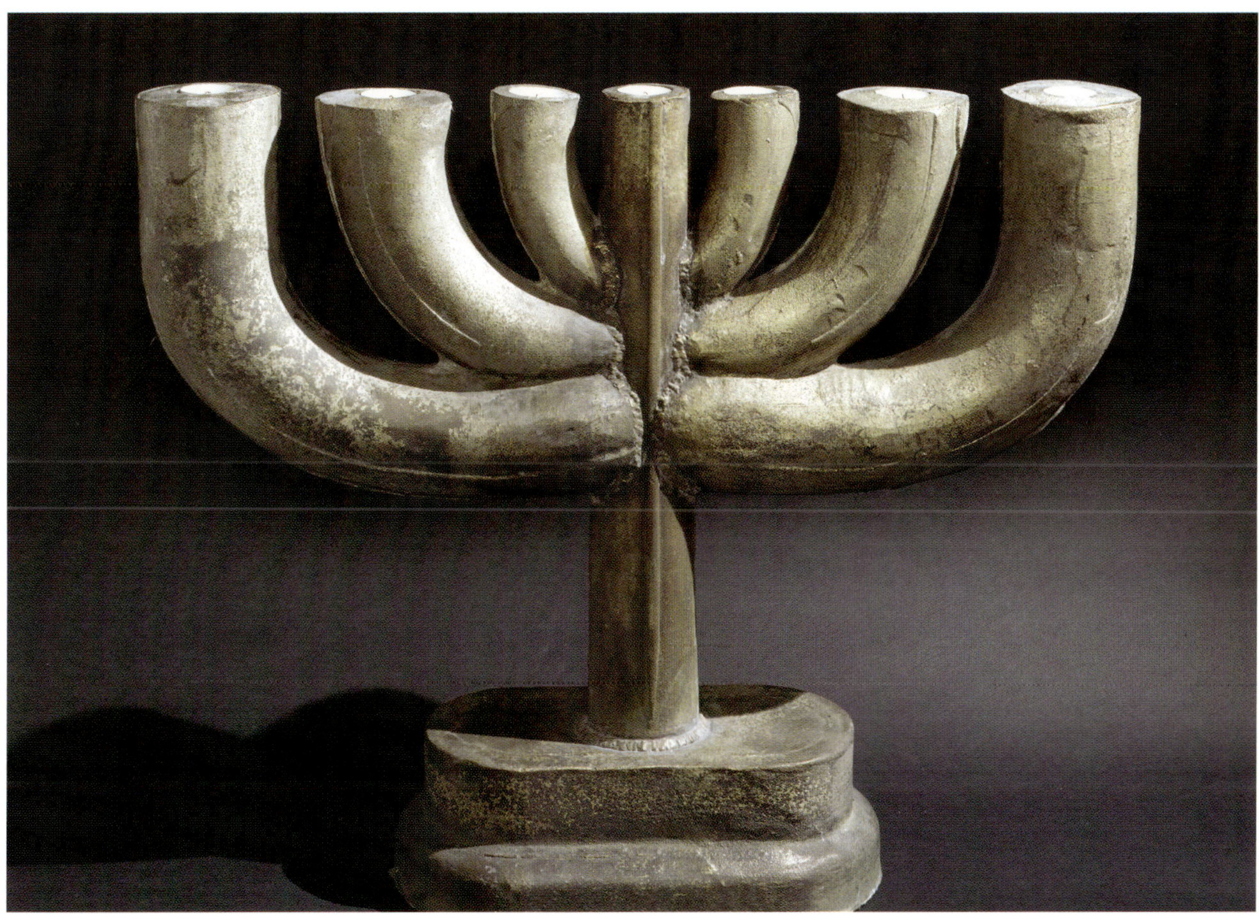

MENORAH
Anthony Caro
British, born 1924: 2000; brass, cast and welded. Gift of Charles Millard and Leena and Sheldon Peck. 2001.23.

hermeneutic: to juxtapose meaningfully, to mediate, and to uncover possibilities between and among. The goal is not identity but delineation. Rather than relying on its assertive function, in the museum, language calls attention to the provisional, contingent, and experimental nature of understanding itself.

The presenters were well past considering limitations. They wanted museums to do more than merely include multiple perspectives. In fact, over the course of the intervening year, it seemed that every participant had decided that museums should – and perhaps must – make a difference in the world.

Everyone referenced exhibitions they had visited in the last two years and the ways in which these exhibitions met or failed to meet the expectations generated by the Colloquies. Museums must be more than responsive and responsible to their audiences and their collections – they must take a more a proactive approach, be brave, daring, engage social issues of racism, injustice, immigration, a litany of social concerns. As one audience member announced at the end of the question and answer period, "I don't accept any of the disclaimers from the people on this panel who said that they don't have art or museum backgrounds. Everyone said wonderful, pertinent, valuable, and moving things ... art and religion tune our minds to higher planes and higher purposes ... the prescience of the project in relation to our current world situation is just astounding."

From the beginning, the Ackland had a conviction that works of art could serve as the focus for sustained inquiry. We believed that religions and the practices of these traditions could be critically (and compassionately) examined through works of art. Working from the premise that the quest for meaning may be a common concern that draws visitors into the museum setting, we watched as the enthusiasm of the participants affirmed that museums *do* matter, conversations centered on works of art *can* be transformative.

Bozutti-Jones suggested that Moses may have been the first museum visitor – taking off his shoes to allow a transformation that was only possible in the presence of a tangible object, the burning bush. In the final Colloquy, to pursue his metaphor, the participants had not only taken off their shoes, but they had rolled up their sleeves to create a list of suggested strategies for continuing the work of the *Five Faiths Project*, expanding its im-

"This is one of my favorite experiences, to think about what it would look like if museums got serious about the question: What is the most important role that we can play in the world?"
RAY WILLIAMS

"A museum is an environment in which serious thought is valued and exists in order to assist people toward perhaps the most reflective place outside the place of worship in their culture."
DAN PALS

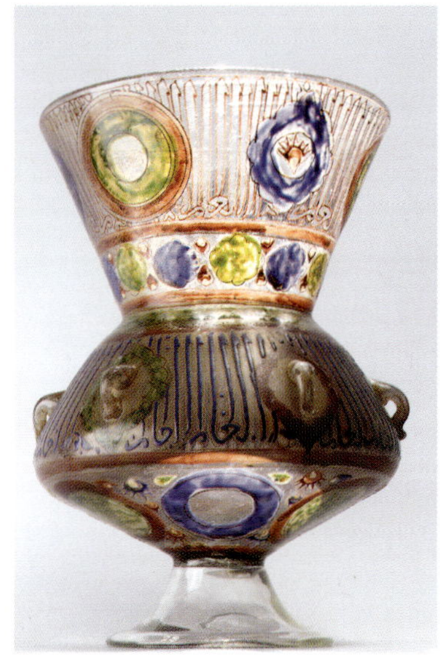

MOSQUE LAMP
Unknown
Syrian, 15th century; glass, polychrome enamel, and gold. The William A. Whitaker Foundation Art Fund, 97.13.

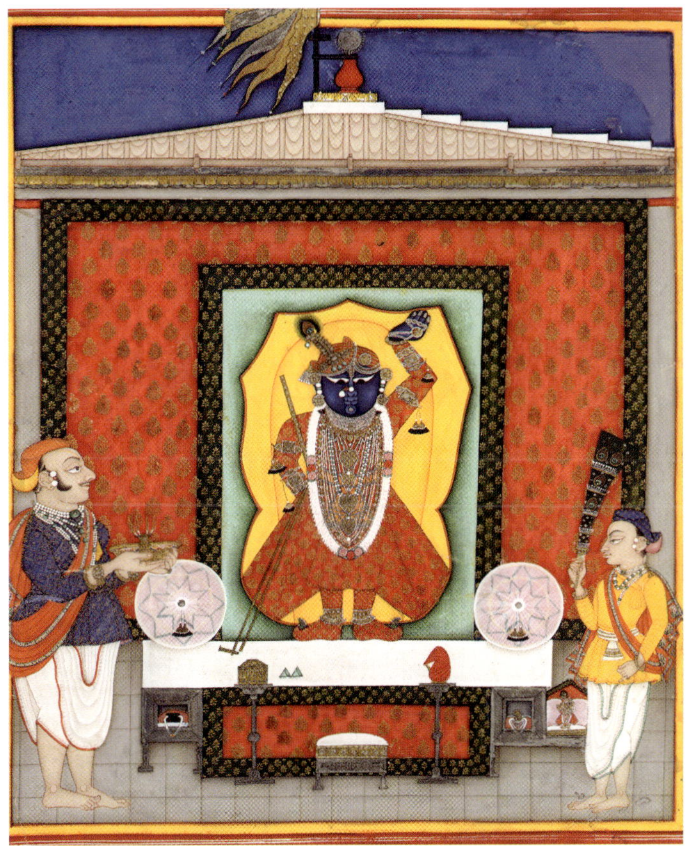

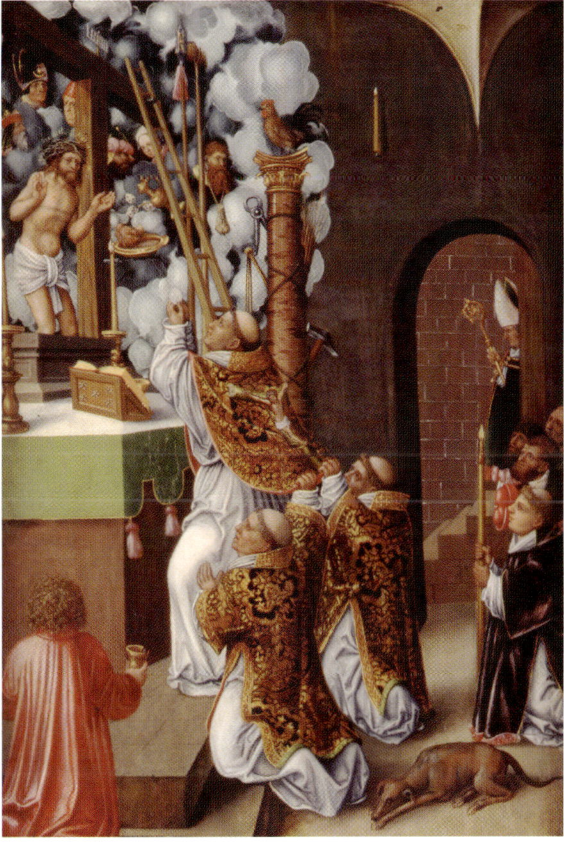

A HINDU PRIEST WORSHIPPING AT THE SHRINE OF SHRI NATH JI (KRISHNA)
Unknown
Indian, Rajasthan, Kota, about 1840; opaque watercolor, gold and silver. Gift of Clara T. and Gilbert J. Yager, 91.73.

THE MASS OF ST. GREGORY
circle of Lucas Cranach the Elder
German, 1472-1553, about 1550; oil on wood panel. Ackland Fund, 59.8.2.

plications for the Ackland, and promoting its influence in museums across the country.

These joyful and hopeful presentations – the language used, the suggestion made – framed the next day and a half of conversations. The first activity was a self-guided tour of *Five Artists Five Faiths: Spirituality in Contemporary Art.* All the colloquy participants were given an hour in the exhibition, alone or in self-selected groups, and asked to return with their responses. Having all become insiders to museum culture, they asked provocative and important questions of the exhibition curator Barbara Matilsky. For example, how and why were these works selected? Do they actually represent the five faiths in any meaningful way or are they individualized responses to the artists' individual faith experiences? Are these works emerging from the mainstream of Hinduism, Judaism, Buddhism, Christianity, and Islam or are they outliers and tangential? Participants wanted to know how these contemporary works related to the historical collection, and whether local communities were consulted in their selection? They asked about the editorial process at the Ackland: Who wrote and who edited the labels? What length limits were placed on the writers? Why were there so few text panels? Could you have included more information about the artists? What were the outcome goals for the exhibition? How are you measuring success in achieving these goals? After more than an hour of interrogation, Vivian Mann ended the session by congratulating the curator: "I think we should applaud the Ackland for this – for mounting this exhibition and then inviting us all to come and critique it! That takes a lot of courage."

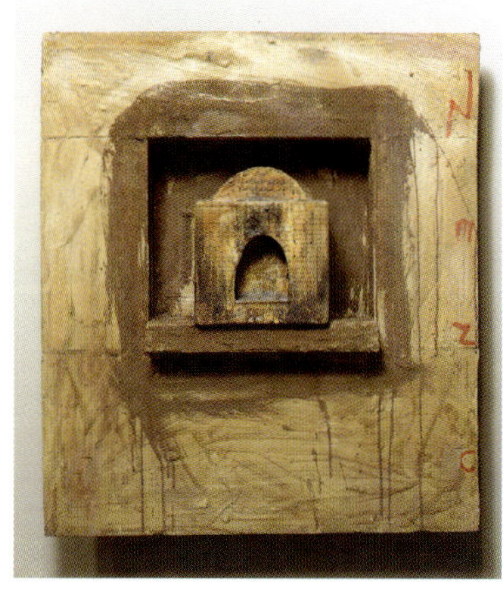

DO NOT BELIEVE IN YOURSELF
Jack Jano
Israeli, born 1950 in Morocco: 1995; painted wood, paper, wax, and other materials. Ackland Fund, 97.3.

The final exercise of the Colloquy series focused on the creation of an imaginary exhibition with the working title: *Avatars and Exemplars*. Participants were divided into groups assigned to create a curatorial approach to an exhibition of objects from the Ackland's permanent collection. They were told that they had a healthy – even substantial – budget, so for the purposes of the exercise they could be expansive in their thinking. Once they arrived at a basic approach, they were asked to consider what parameters they might place on the curatorial process. How might they, as the curators of this exhibition, realize the principles employed in its design and implementation? How would they teach from it? How might they replicate the process in other exhibitions?

The *Avatars and Exemplars* exercise proved to be extremely useful. While the groups considered the appropriateness of the

"There are so many kinds of dialogue: the dialogue of the object with the tradition which gave birth to it; the dialogue of the object with its own personal history; the dialogue of the object with the viewer; the Implicit dialogue between the object and the meaning it created; the dialogue of the viewers though they may view it individually; and the dialogue of the viewers with the curators and on and on and on ... we have a web of relations."
MEERA VISWANATHAN

"Be faithful to the object and say these are what we have and we are offering you what we have, and this is what we are showing. We are not pretending to be the whole tradition, but this is an aspect of the tradition which the object allows us to present, and that is hermeneutic humility."
DAVID N. POWERS, OMI

"Rather than using Western, Christian terminology that is framed on concepts that we've grown up with ... keep with the original language, but define it in English."
JOSHO PAT PHELAN

"How long do Muslim prayers take?"
AMY NELSON

title and the inclusion or exclusion of particular works of art, they also put forward principles and recommendations that might be applied to any exhibition or community outreach program. When the groups gathered in a plenary session, their presentations suggested specific and replicable principles that fulfilled one of the original goals of the colloquy series. After hours of deliberation, debate, and consideration, the participants drafted sets of guidelines that might be applied within the museum setting in order to enhance the Ackland's (and other museums') capacity to fulfill its institutional mission.

Faith Perspectives

1. Be faithful to the object on display.
2. Exercise hermeneutic humility.
3. Use language that is specific to the culture. If visitors don't understand the words, offer definitions.
4. Allow the art to speak for itself. Some works disturb and jostle, others promote contemplation. Don't apologize for either, and when possible allow visitors to experience both.
5. Notice what is missing and suggest some of it to visitors. Examples are: the *Shiva Linga* and its absent *Yoni*; the altarpiece without candles; the spice box empty of spices.
6. In describing ritual practices, museums typically note the how and the why, but not the how long.
7. Make the investment in local faith communities. Building trust takes time.
8. Exhibitions must acknowledge diversity within faith communities: whatever object is on display is not necessarily the authoritative representation of the community.

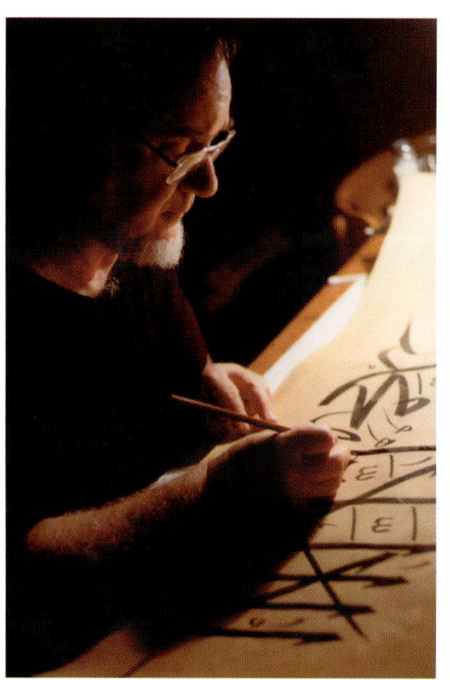

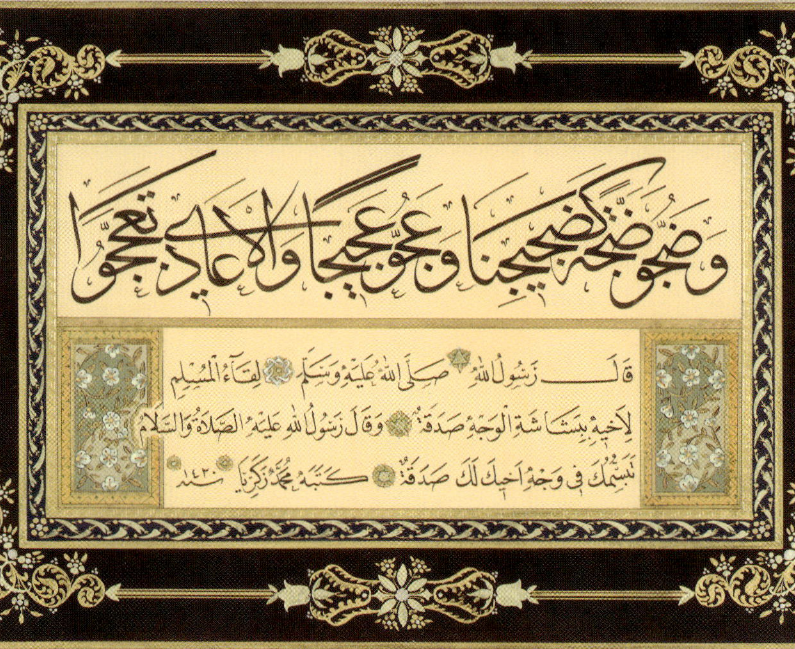

Zakariya described his work as follows. "This work is in the form of a kit'a, or small piece. The top line, which is written in a largish sulus script, is a favorite of calligraphers – a visual as well as linguistic tongue-twister that says, 'and they raised a loud noise like our noise, and they roared a great roar and the enemy also roared.' It is followed by two hadiths (sayings of the Prophet Muhammad): 'When a Muslim meets his brother with a cheerful face, it is a kind of charity' and 'Smiling to your brother is charity.'" The contrast between armies facing each other on the verge of battle and individuals greeting each other with a smile is mirrored in the contrast between the inscriptions: the first one bold, agitated and tangled; the other two neat, orderly and punctuated by floral ornament.

Teaching and Learning Perspectives

1 Acknowledge intra-religious variance: include the fact that within traditions there are different perspectives and views.

2 Consider object orientation (the prayer mat on the east wall; the altarpiece elevated to altar height; the *Copy of the Qur'an* on the right instead of the left; placing Ganesha and his parents, Parvati and Shiva, close enough to one another to establish the family relationship).

3 Layered interpretation ... poly-vocality: the material should be accessible to people on multiple levels.

4 Stay transparent: explain how objects were selected, what goes into decisions, what is the in-

> "... if by the word 'fairness' ... we mean, we will make sure there are different voices in the conversation, that opinions are presented accurately, and that each presentation acknowledges the presence of many other ways of understanding each tradition, then I think we could agree on the goal of 'fairness.'"
>
> CHARLES HAYNES

> "[In our small-group discussion] we compromised. We chose the less complex, more direct representations of the faith over the different, the more challenging, the more provocative, and richer – and more truly beautiful. We chose the mediocre, but accessible."
>
> DAVID CARR

> "Institutions get great examples of Jewish art from the past or Muslim art from the past, and totally ignore the current lived situation. I think that that's a terrible trap to fall into."
>
> CHARLES ORZECH

TONGUE-TWISTER KIT'A

Mohamad Zakariya

American, born 1942; ink, color, and gold leaf. © 2002 Mohamed Zakariya. The William A. Whitaker Foundation Art Fund, 2002.36.

tention behind the exhibition. It is important to let visitors in on these things.

5 Design, evaluate, and revise every exhibition.

6 Attend to parity of esteem and the problem of fairness in presenting multiple faiths.

Curatorial Perspectives

1 Art comes first: exhibit objects with respect, seeking to reanimate them with lighting, placement, and contextual material, so that visitors may respond affectively, spiritually, intellectually, alone or socially.

2 And not just any art, the best a museum can afford.

3 Offer a succinct explanation of the object's significance, allowing visitors to stop there or choose to go deeper.

4 Encourage audiences to encounter and respond to the objects in multiple ways, by including the voices, perspectives, and presences of insiders to the tradition, of scholars, of museum professionals, and others.

5 Provide interpretive materials that make the object accessible to visitors outside the tradition, that show the work "in motion" as it might be used by members of a living tradition, perhaps including – these are examples – passages of sacred text, information about the artist's relationship to the faith, multimedia, and/or multisensory materials.

6 Strive for fairness, clarity, consistency, and balance among the traditions, making the curatorial process transparent.

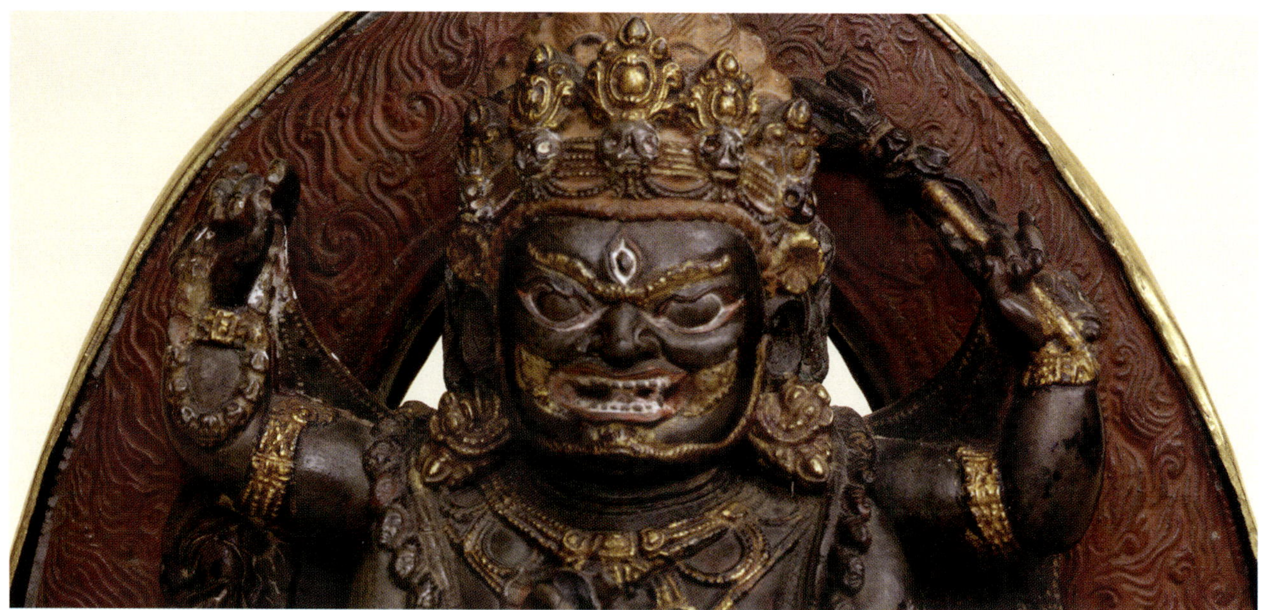

MAHAKALA
Unknown
Tibetan, South Central Tibet, 13th century; stone, pigments, gold, and gilded copper. The William A. Whitaker Foundation Art Fund, purchased in honor of Ray Williams, curator of education at the Ackland Art Museum 1985-2000, 2003.13. (detail)

In addition to these sets of principles, Viswanathan reflected on conversations about museums and their roles in society over the three Colloquies and summarized them as a series of metaphors:

1 *Museum as Interrogation Room*: a legalistic notion of discovering truth through witness and judgment; with an emphasis on "interrogating the artifact" and consideration of it as a document to be read and interpreted.
2 *Museum as Neutral Sanctuary*: "a safe place," a friendly and respectful setting for private exploration of beliefs and practices.
3 *Museum as "Contact Zone" (James Clifford)*: microcosm of society, a place where traditions, values, belief systems come into contact – sometimes collision – with one another.

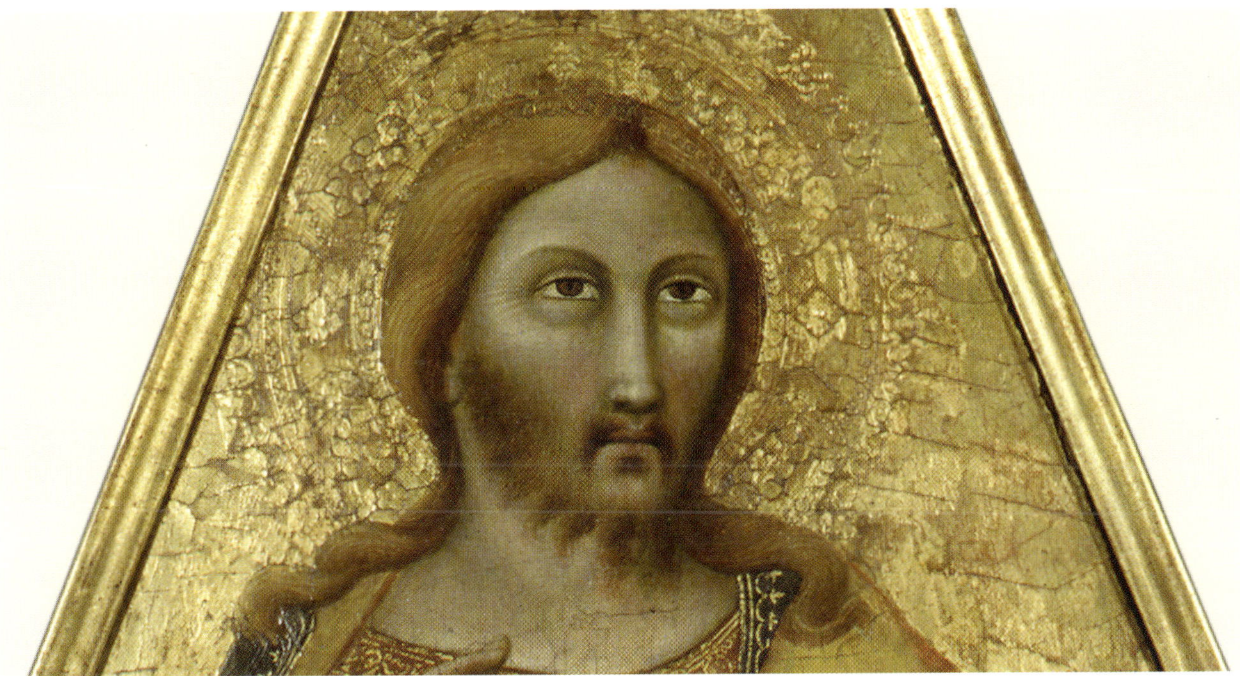

CHRIST BLESSING
Francesco Traini
Italian, Pisa, active 1321-1363, ca. 1335; tempera and gold on wood panel. The William A. Whitaker Foundation Art Fund. (detail)

4 *Museum as Journey*: traveling, a vicarious voyage of exploration, a journey in which we encounter "aliens" and "others" who may or may not be familiar or friendly.

5 *Museum as Privately-Owned Collection*: an historical Marxist materialist perspective in which museums attest to relations between competing owners and users of material artifacts.

6 *Museum as Mirror*: the objects reflect our consideration of ourselves; like the objects under consideration, we are incomplete artifacts in search of perfection and meaningful context.

7 *Museum as Open Forum*: a place in which dialogue between and among stakeholders of all kinds is fostered, encouraged, but never required.

Throughout the life of the *Five Faiths Project*, the Ackland has tried to balance the grand conversation with the practical conversation. The final session reflected this tension between the daily applications and the grandest aspirations for the *Project.* We proposed a number of directions for the *Project* in the future and asked for advice from the colloquy participants. One proposal was to publish a book on the colloquy proceedings. Another was to offer workshops for mid-career museum professionals, bringing more than one member from each institution: a director and a curator, a curator and an educator, etc. We also considered a second series of conferences: one, to explore the Americanization of the five faiths and, another, to consider the ethics of the five faiths with regard to medical practices.

Except for the book proposal, all of the ideas were hotly contested. Haynes, however, did plea that we continue to apply our energy to resources for public schools. "The art-centered nature of the *Five Faiths Project* has a number of pedagogical and educational values that other projects developed for public education do not have." The remarkable lesson for us was how very difficult it is to get consensus on any new proposal. We realized that the best idea often comes from one person with the conviction to pursue it.

In the intervening years, we have attempted to apply the principles we found the most compelling from the *Project.* Some have been employed successfully in a sustained way. For example, collaborative exhibition and interpretive projects are the norm at the Ackland. The *Project* taught us that if we are to realize our potential as a university museum serving the academic agenda for creating global citizens, we must create more opportunities and deepen the involvement of faculty, students, and the surrounding community in every aspect of the Museum's enterprise. When the *Project* began, fewer than three hundred university students were assigned a visit to the Ackland as part of their course work each year. In 2009, seven thousand students from more than twenty UNC-Chapel Hill departments will engage the collection. By creating a standard for meeting the needs of our audiences and involving them in decision-making processes, the *Project* enriched not only our university service, but every aspect of our interpretive plan. Over the years, the Ackland has been asked many times how we did this and what did it cost. Former director, Jerry Bolas, is quick to remind us, "One relationship at a time."

OFFICIAL TRANSCRIPT[1]

Making a Place for Meaning

Art, Faith, and the Museum Culture

Panel Discussion

with Mark Bozutti-Jones, Mimi Gates, Charles Orzech, David Powers, and Meera Viswanathan, moderated by David Carr

Ackland Art Museum – Hanes Art Center Auditorium

Carolyn Wood:

Good afternoon. On behalf of the Ackland Art Museum, it is my pleasure to welcome you to the third of our three Five Faiths Colloquies, funded by the Luce Foundation. Over the past three years, the Colloquies have brought faith leaders and practitioners, scholars of various disciplines, and museum professionals to the Ackland to consider the limits and the potentials of visual and verbal communication in relation to the display and interpretation of works of art with sacred content. The goal of these Colloquies has been to explore – and to make recommendations about – the ways museums might use their collections to promote tolerance and understanding of diverse faith traditions and cultural practices.

Thanks to those colloquy participants who have enlivened our conversations about faith traditions and the visual arts, who have raised and addressed issues that, when recorded, will surely inform colleagues across the nation who are becoming increasingly aware of their religiously pluralistic constituencies and of their constituents' confessional sensitivities. Making museums matter in diverse communities is a delicate matter and we've been honored at the Ackland to have colloquy collaborators devote their time and thought to the challenge.

1 This material has been edited for clarity only.

Thanks also and emphatically to the Luce Foundation for enabling us to convene, resolve, then reconsider, and now conclude the Five Faiths Colloquies, by making a place for meaning, by reevaluating the place of art and faith in museum culture. Indeed our panel presentation this afternoon is titled just that: "Making a Place for Meaning: Art, Faith and Museum Culture." Michael Gilligan, our friend, conspirator, and *inspirator*, thank you. Your good will and your clear thinking inspire us. And thanks also now to our new partner at Luce, Lynn Szwaja: thanks for making our museum and these conversations matter.

I am delighted now to introduce David Carr, who has embraced this project from the start and whose erudition, wit, and exceptionally good sense about museums, museum professionals, and, above all, museum visitor experiences have helped us reflect on our objectives and strategies from day one. He came to the University of North Carolina School of Information and Library Science in 1998 from Rutgers University, where he taught – as he does here – about cultural institutions as life-long educational environments and about information, its access and use in its cultural contexts. *The Promise of Cultural Institutions* is his new book, published in 2003 to critical acclaim for its generous thinking and its profound insight into the necessity of great cultural institutions in civil society. No one among us, I believe, is better positioned to restart our next discussion of the promise of our nation's museums than David. David, the prospect that we will all continue to use our collection to promote tolerance and to propel our visitors beyond the usual dimensions of experience, that prospect is in your hands, and I for one am gratified – as well as relieved. Thank you.

David Carr:

My observation is that the public conversations that we have held during intense two-day periods for the last three years – this is our third year – have founded innumerable moments of private reflection, private conversation, and those times when suddenly the world forms a coherent moment – perhaps you've had one or two of these in your lives? Almost always those coherent moments for me come through the remembered words of other people. This is an opportunity for those words to be spoken and for us to remember them, because much memorable conversation has occurred under the aegis of this program.

If you cast your minds back not just two years ago, but three, to August of 2001, who among us would remember or believe or come to understand the full dimensions of faith, the understandings of faith, the values of faith, the motivations of faith would have in the construction of the world we live in now? I read today in the *Times* a brief comment: someone said we will look back at the era from 1950 through the year 2000 as a kind of halcyon days, paradise as it were. Now, I grew up then and I don't remember it that way – but it is an era that changed. It changed not long ago, and we are in the midst of it, just in its beginning.

And in these conversations we have been talking about the very center of the future of our understanding, that is: the ways in which we can integrate faith into our conversations, the ways in which we can use objects and museums and cultural institutions to cross the boundaries of faith, authentic or artificial though they may be. And it gives us an opportunity to remind ourselves how everyday through faith, through intellect, through conversation and understanding, we have the opportunity to reconstruct new dimensions in the world, particularly those that will help us to understand the very large picture that seems so often so elusive.

What we are going to do today is to show you what these colloquy conversations have really included. We have done this by inviting four panelists. A fifth, Charles Orzech, could not be here because of illness, but I did want to acknowledge the invitation to him. We have asked each of the panelists to speak about their reflections on the *Five Faiths Colloquies*. Then there will be an opportunity for discussion among the panelists and the audience.

I will introduce the panelists now, and in each case, I will read statements that they have written in regard to lessons learned from the Colloquies.

Mark Bozutti-Jones is the associate rector of Christ's Church in Cambridge, Massachusetts. In his statement, he wrote:

> Mutual understanding and openness to other religious traditions happen when we recognize the limitations of all our representations/interpretations of the divine. The present day challenge for followers of all religious traditions is to guard against believing what is created or interpreted represents conclusive and ultimate meaning.

Mimi Gates is the director of the Seattle Art Museum. She wrote:

> Museums have unexplored potential as places to experience "the Other" in a non-proselytizing way that respects Americans' right to freedom of religion. When sacred images are removed from their ritual settings and transported to museums, they require inno-

> vative approaches to communicate to the uninitiated visitor the profound emotional power they possess in their original context."

Charles Orzech, who is not here, is a professor of religious studies at The University of North Carolina at Greensboro. He wrote:

> Museums are worlds in miniature, and like the world, they are the product of cultural and religious interaction. If museums are places of cultural and religious contact, and if we wish to promote a pluralistic encounter of religious voices in them, then we must strive to foreground this *social* interaction.

David Power, OMI of Catholic University of America, wrote:

> We have not talked much about how people may grasp the artistic value of objects displayed or of how the aesthetic may address viewers. While each object has its proper setting in its own faith tradition and information tells the viewer of this, may the object in its form speak to viewers and raise "meaning" issues? It seems that for all their particularity, religious objects (like texts) may say something beyond the limits of a people of a particular faith.

Meera Viswanathan, a professor of comparative literature at Brown University wrote:

> What does it mean not only to place objects from different faith traditions side by side, but also sacral objects amidst secular ones, as well as those that may be perceived to bridge or oppose the two domains? The role of language in all of this must be hermeneutic: to juxtapose meaningfully, to mediate, and to uncover possibilities between and among. The goal is not identity but delineation. Rather than relying on its assertive function, language in this context serves to call attention to the provisional, contingent, and experimental nature of understanding itself.

Mark, please begin.

Mark Bozutti-Jones:

A few thoughts: First of all, I want to commend the bold and important decision made by the Ackland Art Museum to design an exhibition (*Five Artists, Five Faiths: Spiri-*

tuality in Contemporary Art) premised upon inclusivity rather than exclusivity. The word "museum," as you know, means "the seat of the muses," and our musings that happen when we come to a museum can help us recognize, appreciate, and even integrate that which is different from and beyond our own religious identities.

This experience I believe can make us holier, stronger, and more respectful of other faith traditions. It might even model the necessity for a multiperspectival world view in today's somewhat xenophobic global climate. At an equal level, this exhibition can afford a context for conversion, commitment, and for seeing the other. I believe that every time we come to a museum we see ourselves in the other and the other in ourselves. The point Murial Rukeyser makes in her poem, *Despisals*, captures what can happen, when she says:

> Never to despise in myself, what I have been taught to despise. Nor to despise the other.
> Not to despise the it. To make this relation with the it: to know that I am it.

Conversion, in religions terms, is a change of heart, a shift in perspective, and while conversion is often considered a divine gift, I believe it is our responsibility to dispose ourselves to conversion, and so viewers or observers in a museum might consider their interaction with the exhibits as disposing themselves to a unique conversion experience that turns on engagement with the other and with the different.

In Judaism, Christianity, and Islam, Moses is honored for his experience with God. I believe that Moses was the first visitor to a museum – in Scriptures anyhow, in the Christian Scriptures. While walking through a desert, he notices a burning bush, and he stops to observe what is going on. And as he draws closer, a voice warns him to take off his shoes, because he is standing on holy ground.

In the mundane activity of removing his shoes, Moses disposes himself to the holy. I suggest that this museum might make a huge sign of that: "Take off your shoes! You're standing on holy ground." And this is certainly what happens when any observer enters and looks at the exhibition that is happening.

Judaism, Christianity, Islam, Hinduism, and Buddhism have teachings on the import of paying attention to the manner of our looking, to what we look at, and in various ways to how we are perceived. And so this faith-based exhibition affords us the opportunity to pay attention to all three of these by drawing near the sacred in various forms. How we look at the displays, which displays capture us, and how the displays encourage us to look at them and beyond them ... these are the key elements, I believe, of the viewer's experience.

Alan Watts, a Zen Buddhist scholar and writer, observed, "We usually don't look, we overlook." This exhibition offers us an opportunity to turn this around. As in the ancient understanding of icons, where it was believed that both icon and viewer were perceiving each other, the Ackland Art Museum invites and encourages viewers to think of the experience as looking and being looked at, observing and being observed, receiving a faith experience and communicating one. This dynamic process mirrors the reality of believers of the major faith traditions as they encounter one another. The exhibition presents a unique forum in which to encourage and model an encounter of religious difference that is marked by coexistence, giving and receiving.

The practical challenge for the museum is to foster the idea of the viewer entering the holy displays in a posture that is open and intentional, about experiencing a circular flow in the encounter, or an encounter that is bi-directional.

In the Christian Scriptures, there is the story of Jesus meeting his first group of disciples, and they say to him, "We want to know where you live." And Jesus' response to them is, "Come and see." I think in the *Five Faiths* exhibition we do just that: we come to see. We come to see what happens in our hearts when we contemplate the divine through images. We come to see how what we see changes our preconceived understandings – and how what we see can change our very lives.

The evocative nature of the artwork – and I am pleased to see that they are multisensory experiences – is strong. But I do wish there were also smells and bells. It would be good to walk into these various things and smell something. But it opens the possibility of the museum becoming a truly transformative space, a space that can lead one to awe, to wisdom, to creative doubt, to affirmation, or to prophetic agency in the world.

Taken as a whole, *Five Artists, Five Faiths* depicts an encounter with the sacred, understood and interpreted through differences, and I believe that is just spectacular. We who observe, we who look at them draw closer to knowing the unknowable which is present in all these religions.

At the same time, we have to admit the danger and limitation of a museum's selection that seeks to be representative of any group of religious believers. Any selection will fall short. Every selection is incomplete, especially in the subjective realm of religious experience. Even for adherents of the same religious faith, what is presented here may seem strange or unfamiliar, and, in some cases, even sacrilegious. Indeed, many challenges must be met in designing the exhibition, so that even the skeptical viewer is engaged in an open-ended, internal and external dialogue.

Here are five questions I think we need to ask ourselves, and then I'll close:

1 How can the museum suggest to viewers that they are on holy ground without hammering them over the head or creating a coercive atmosphere?
2 How can the museum declare that there are limitations that come from the choice of artists, as well as the constraints on space and budget, in terms of what gets included? How can the museum confess the limitations of these displays, owning that when everyone deals with the sacred, a representative is always just a finger pointing to the moon? Not the moon, just a finger pointing to it?
3 How can the museum help the observer to find and to see God, or the Divine, or the sacred in all things? Not just in the museum, but even beyond? I think that has to be the rule, that what you see here you also see on the outside.
4 How can the museum assist the unknowing visitor to avoid leaving with misconceptions about the other?
5 How can the museum be involved in the ongoing work of eliminating hatred, prejudice, misconceptions, and divisive attitudes? Or to say it differently: What more could be done to ensure that these exhibitions both instruct and inspire as agents of change? Maybe there could be a homework assignment attached at every exhibition – You know, go out and do this!

In closing, let me leave you with a Quaker proverb, and I like this proverb because I believe that this display and what this museum does really captures it. It is almost a mission statement of what I have seen so far. "It is the not me in thee that is to me most precious." Let me just repeat that. "It is the not me in thee that is to me most precious." Thank you very much.

David Carr:

Thank you. Mimi Gates?

Mimi Gates:

I am going to speak from the perspective of an art museum director, and I don't presume to speak for the entire profession. These are simply my own thoughts after participating in the first two sessions of the *Five Faiths Project* and I do want to thank the Ackland Art Museum as well as the Luce Foundation for undertaking this *Project*.

How can museums be more thoughtful and risk-taking in the ways we display sacred objects so as to more effectively promote understanding, tolerance, and respect toward world religious faiths and practices?

Why are museum professionals so hesitant to have their museums explicate the richness of world religions? Not only are museums a place for artistic appreciation, where the great creations of human civilization speak, museums are also safe, neutral spaces for learning and dialogue. I firmly believe that meaningful dialogue and rich, multisensory experience – maybe "smells and bells" – is central to museums if they are to be vibrant centers of learning and centers of community. My main point is the need for change, for experimentation and risk-taking by museum professionals, the need to transcend the traditional museum practice. Museums need to go beyond "This is the way we have always done it," and when appropriate, provide visitors with an engaging multisensory experience.

Yes, we must respect constitutional rights to the freedom of religion, and yet we should seek to convey not only factual information, but at the same time empower the sacred object as a living presence.

Let me review some concrete ways to liberate museum practice which have been suggested in earlier sessions of these colloquies, and then I will show a few slides and an excerpt of a video from the Seattle Art Museum.

First, didactic museum labels, CD-ROM random access audio guides, and websites should include multiple voices, including those of the religious community for whom an object was made. The curator steps back in order to empower other voices. This means ceding curatorial authority to others, which many curators do not find easy. Religious communities and religious scholars should play a role and be heard and consulted.

Second, museums need to be clear who is speaking, whose perspective is being presented. Transparency is all too often absent. It is important to visitors' understanding: Who wrote the label? Whose voice is on the audio guide – and hopefully, whose voices?

Third, why not offer snapshots of the worshippers' experience? Last year, Richard Davis provided a powerful approach to sacred objects, recreating the biography of a sacred image of Shiva Nataraja, a biography that elucidates history and ritual context. This and other fresh approaches need to be developed.

What was the ritual setting in which a sacred object was used? What was its function? In-gallery surveys at the Seattle Asian Art Museum indicate that viewers want to know the function of an object. How an object was used is often uppermost in people's minds. Whether through music, live in-gallery performances, or immersive film or video projected on gallery walls, or more conservatively on a small screen, contextualizing sacred objects engages, informs, and brings sacred objects to life.

I will briefly present three examples from the Seattle Asian Art Museum's current installation, *Discovering Buddhism: Seeking the Sublime*, which illustrate how ritual context can be suggested. All of the rituals are incorporated into an in-depth kiosk and a video screen in an adjacent education space, and they are also easily accessible on our website at www.seattleartmuseum.org. (Technology can be a very effective tool. Museums are still exploring how to use technology to advantage.)

In late February, early March 2004, at the Seattle Asian Art Museum, Tibetan monks created a sand mandala. The creation of sand mandalas is common practice at a good number of museums. It is both ritual and art. It creates an ephemeral sacred object, a work of art that is aesthetically inspiring and meaningful within the context of Buddhism.

It also has great appeal to those who explore Buddhism as meditation as well as ritual to a wide range of people as you can see here [referring to slide]. Such ritual ceremonies are often a point of entry, a hook for many visitors to increase their curiosity.

Less common is the performance of a Buddhist ritual of veneration inside the museum. This is a fifteenth-century Japanese painting of Amida descending from the Western paradise accompanied by twenty-four Bodhisattvas that is echoed in the third room of the exhibition, where an altar is composed of a painted triptych, the three paintings behind of twenty-four Bodhisattvas, a sculpture of four guardian kings on the corner and two Bodhisattvas in the central Amida Buddha. This is a generalized recreation of an altar in a Japanese Buddhist Shingon temple. The curators consulted with Shingon priests in its creation.

On February 8, 2004, six Shingon monks chanted the ceremony of veneration in the gallery. Here you see the monks entering in procession [referring to slide], chanting and music echoed throughout the galleries. It brought the exhibition, particularly that room, to life. And there was an appreciative audience that included many families who watched attentively. Curators and educators working with the religious community are extremely constructive, not only inside the museum, but also beyond.

Again in spring 2002, a *Jiso Bosatsu*, a fifteenth-century Japanese Bodhisattva that you see here [referring to slide] was reconsecrated by an opening the eyes ceremony at the Seattle Shingon Buddhist temple. It is one of six Shingon temples in the United States. The image was taken there for the day, and accompanied at all times by museum personnel. The conservator approved the choice of the image and stayed with it throughout the ceremony.

Now for the video, the *Jiso Bosatsu* is up on the altar.

On video: A Buddhist monk kneels and rises before the altar. The monk holds a fan, bows before the altar, and quickly fans the *Jiso Bosatsu*. The monk waves incense over the *Jiso Bosatsu*.

See that the video gives some sense of the richness of the setting. This is one way that we felt was important to feature a Buddhist setting in our own community to which very few people have access. It also makes the historical objects come alive. If you watch the entire video, you can compare the historical object with contemporary objects and counterparts that are also on the altar. In the gallery, this video is shown close to the object. It gives visitors a different sense of the sculpture when seeing it together with the video and, in fact, the Buddhist priests felt it was an ideal way to show the more typical context of Buddhist sculpture that it generally does not have in a museum display.

I leave you with a question that is uppermost in my mind during our discussions: how can we convey not only intellectual knowledge but also the resonant wonder of an object in its original context so we connect emotionally with our visitors?

David Carr:

Mimi, thank you. David Power?

David Power:

I speak to this topic as a museum visitor, without any special background in art or in museums, and indeed, as years pass, feeling more and more as passing through a cloud of unknowing where anything religious is concerned, but it certainly has been a great privilege and a joy to take part in this Colloquy.

In trying to get a handle on the questions ... which the Colloquies and the Ackland are addressing, I do distinguish between three aspects which challenge and present themselves to a visitor. There are the educational purposes, number one; number two, there is the ritual of a museum visit; and number three, there is the aesthetic purpose in presenting the pieces of art and the religious objects.

From our conversations, I do think that the mission of the Ackland puts educational purposes to the fore. Visitors are to be informed. They are to be helped to place objects in their context, so that some understanding and some sense of value are made accessible. In displaying religious objects of five faiths and presenting educational programs that connect up with this, it is hoped to foster some understanding of faith traditions, some mutual understanding between members of these traditions, and indeed it is specifically said that it is hoped to break down some of the prejudice and intolerance which may be inherent to the dominant Christian and specifically Protestant cultural tradition of the region.

And I think that the reactions of the participants in the Colloquies suggest that this objective is attainable. [Our] discussions have often centered on how this goal is to be attained, even down to minutiae of writing labels.

The second aspect is the ritual of a museum visit. I do have the sense that when people say museum visits involve visitors in a ritual it is true. It can of course be a very manipulative ritual, but the hope is to make it a more open-ended ritual, one that invites the visitor to participate in or be sensitive to the world of the religious as presented through objects from the five faiths. But two issues do organize the visit: the distribution of works and the path to be followed in making the visit. Most art galleries in Europe and North America offer a historical approach, so that a visitor walks through art, development, and the history of civilization as seen by the curators. Certain rooms are dedicated to specific periods, perhaps to specific artists, and sometimes to special interests such as folklore or the world of other civilizations.

The Ackland certainly has its abundance of art works from Europe and North America and there is something of the historical approach, certainly, in the layout of the works, so that, indeed, religious representation is simply integrated into the history of art. It is interesting that the visitor's ritual walk in the Ackland, particularly as this applies to religious works and objects, follows something of this pattern and yet tries to challenge it in the layout and in the installations. I do think that encountering Buddhism, Islam, Judaism, and Hinduism for a large number of us and our co-citizens is definitely encountering the world of the Other.

But can we actually, from a Christian perspective, encounter Christianity itself as an Other? For many people, the medieval world is certainly another world to the one in which they live today. And indeed, people live more and more in a secularized world, so that even the religious itself becomes a challenge to an accustomed world view.

But we do have five Others in the Museum's installations. We ask, "Why can't people from the different traditions encounter one another?" But often we are dealing with people of no specific religious tradition and no religious sense – and here we are overpowering them by introducing them to five different religious heritages! Can this indeed be done modestly? Can it be done with humility and yet with authenticity as an invitation, rather than as a coercion?

Then there is the aesthetic purpose of the presentation of works as works of art, representing a world. How much is it possible for an object in a museum to actually speak out of the power of the world to which it belongs? You can enhance the multisensory experience, but it is still another world. The history of museums and galleries shows that there has always been some concern in arranging displays in such a way that the visitor may actually encounter some works of art as art in itself and not as a work that belongs to a history of art, that is, as isolated from the world to which it originally pertains.

I live in Washington, D.C. I am a frequent visitor to the different art galleries on the Mall, and indeed I have heard it said and have had it verified by experience that the National Gallery of Art in Washington, D.C., is the showpiece of the intent of the encounter offered to visitors with individual works, so that one can see them, as it were, unencumbered by what surrounds them. However, in seeking to achieve this purpose there has been a considerable influence of romanticism and an emphasis upon subjective openness and appreciation of art. That seems to work most readily with contemporary art works, which are meant quite often to stand as works in themselves irrespective of any other surroundings or any other world. That can be very deceptive, since the internal references within the work are manifold.

Religious objects present a special issue. They do have their power to communicate, and to put us in touch with the reality and with values from the world to which they belong. Put outside of that world, they may become objects of curiosity. Indeed, if displayed with care, they may readily meet the educational purpose of informing and giving some understanding of a religious tradition. Then, they invite us as it were to open ourselves to the power of the work.

So a question that I'll ask – and I have no answer to it – is whether it is possible to display objects in an exhibition in such a way that certain of them communicate to visitors the power of the religious world to which they belong? In asking this I wonder if it is possible to isolate certain other works, giving them a privileged place where they stand on their own and invite not only a more intent, but now after visitors have seen the other works, a more informed gaze?

There was a recent exhibition of images of the Buddha in the Sackler Gallery in Washington, D.C., which suggested to me a way in which this might be done. The exhibition featured representations of the Buddha from discoveries at Qingzhou in China. The exhibition told the visitor something about the Buddha, something about Buddha representations, and indeed, it also showed how the representations belong within a history of art.

But there was one standing Buddha that was set apart from the others, so that it could become the focus of a more protracted look. And actually it was placed in a very interesting way. It was placed so that one met it, or was met by it, upon entering the exhibition and again on leaving the exhibition.

Some people entering the exhibition stopped in front of it, and it was clear that they knew nothing of the Buddha, nothing of Buddhism. They asked very unfocused questions, expressed likes and dislikes, some of which were amusing. Such as: "Who is this fellow? Where did he live? What country does he belong to?" And, of course, always the question: "Why is he shown that way?"

The interesting thing was to stand there for a while and view the people going in and the people coming out. The people going in had these unfocused questions. But the people coming out, those who had really taken their time in the exhibition, looked at the sculpture for how it might express something of the Noble Truths or how it spoke of the sublime or of compassion. I know that may have been only an intellectual exercise, but at least it could give an incipient appreciation of the religious power of the object.

When you have many different objects to display, it is unreasonable to ask people to truly appreciate each and every one of them. So a good strategy might be to present many of the objects with informative materials to educate visitors, but also to single out a few and to display them in such a way that they may communicate something of their power to a now-informed visitor, who may be from a totally other religious world or of no religious world at all.

David Carr:

David, thank you. Meera, please.

Meera Viswanathan:

First, I should explain that my field is comparative literature. In other words, I have no credentials as far as museums go – and art museums especially. And I have no credentials – except in the fact that I am an individual in my own quest in life in seeking the divine – as someone involved in religious education. But as a comparatist and as someone in literature, I am very interested in how language helps us apprehend the world. And it strikes me that particularly in the context of confronting unknown objects, sacral or otherwise, that we very much depend on language – that it is not enough to have recourse simply to a kind of visceral reaction, that we must think about how language informs our understanding of the world. And similarly that we have no choice but to take a comparatist outlook, that invariably we need to think about things we encounter in terms of the things we have already experienced.

I was struck by Mark's comment about Moses as the first museum visitor. At the first Colloquy two years ago, I told an anecdote about my first visit to an American art museum when I was about seven years old in Los Angeles. We had recently emigrated to this country from India, and it was a dilemma for my mother because we were Orthodox Brahmins in India. Suddenly we were in a place in which there were no structures to support that faith tradition. At that time, there were no Hindu temples. There were no aggregate populations of Hindus, and therefore we were very isolated.

But when we went to the Los Angeles County Museum of Art, which has a fine, fine collection of South and Southeast Asian sculpture, one of the first things that we encountered was a large statue of Nandi. As I noted two years ago, my mother's eyes immediately lit up! Because, we were in this very impressive building which was hushed and clean with muted lighting, and what did she encounter but Nandi, the bull, that is the mount of the god Shiva. Now, our family name is Viswanathan. Viswanathan means in Sanskrit "Lord of the Universe," and that is another name for Shiva.

In many ways, it was a homecoming, and I remember that my mother did just what every museum guard fears. She went up immediately to touch the Nandi as she would have done in India, because the Nandi would, of course, be outside a Shiva temple. You would touch the Nandi as you would begin your circumambulation of the temple. And so, in some ways, I think of my presence here as a kind of nod back to that time, when the museum for me became the first Hindu temple in America.

Now, I am interested in the way we think about museums and, looking at our discussions of the last three years, I am struck as we are confronting the problem of presenting the sacral object in the context of a secular display by our various attempts to name what it is we are doing in this process. And I am struck as well by how often we have recourse to metaphoric allusion.

I am fascinated by the richness and complexity of the mosaic array of metaphor presented here. Of course we all agree on certain issues, the difficulty and need for balance in presentation between those inside the faith community or communities that produced the artifact, and the communities outside, many of whom may be ignorant of the object's function, iconography, and significance. We agree on the importance of consistency in treatment of the various objects, without a kind of homogenization of them between and among these faith traditions. We also seem to agree on the manifold possibilities, as well as the limits, of both verbal and non-verbal communication in contextualizing the artifact and the importance of trying to separate teaching about religion from teaching religion in these exhibitions. And finally, many people commented on the philosophic dilemma of the cosmic and the human, the problem of trying to apprehend the infinite through finite means.

But if you look through you'll see that we varied widely in our specific concerns and approaches. In praxis, some of us inclined more towards cult value, that is, toward the original intent of the object where there is the worshipper's perspective, the insider's perspective, and others were more focused on the display value, that is, the aesthetic value, the museum value, the secularized value. And in talking about our positioning on this spectrum, various metaphors were employed. I want to talk about a few of these.

For some, it was the legalistic notion of discovering truth through witness and judgment; hence, the emphasis on interrogating the artifact and consideration of it as a document, to be read and interpreted. Others saw the museum as a kind of neutral sanctuary, as "a safe place," a friendly and respectful setting for exploration of various faith traditions.

Another person brought up the ethnographer/anthropologist James Clifford's notion of museums as microcosms of society. He uses the term "contact zones," that is, places where traditions, values, belief systems can come into contact – sometimes collision – with one another.

And still others in talking about museums used the metaphor of travel, speaking of a vicarious voyage of exploration, a journey in which we encounter the "alien" and the Other.

The historical Marxist materialist perspective was evident as one person talked about museums as attesting to relations between competing owners and users of material artifacts. Another observer commented that we ourselves, like the objects under consideration, are in fact incomplete artifacts in search of perfection.

The metaphors therefore help position us in terms of our own ideological considerations of this process of the sacral amidst the secular. What is obvious is the incommensurability of these different metaphors of understanding, and yet the importance of the significant partial truth and insight each offers.

One respondent commented with frustration on the limits of language in limning our aspirations and spoke of a need – and I like this phrase – for a "new palette of words." But I wonder, perhaps it is not words themselves that we require, since after all every day neologisms and new idioms emerge. Perhaps what we require are satisfactory metaphors to show us what it is we are after – what it is we are trying to accomplish.

Metaphors, though, are by their very definition failed equivalences. Even as they seek to suggest parallels and similitude, they attest to just the opposite: the fundamental incommensurability of two things. But what they succeed in doing is bringing these two unlike things into a dialogue with each other, a dialogue that otherwise might not have taken place. All of the earlier metaphors to which I alluded spoke of just this sort of dialogue. Perhaps the overarching model for what we are trying to accomplish is the metaphoric process itself, and hence the disjunctures and the dangers implicit in the process are not to be overcome, but function as the very markers of what we are after – and as such, need to be acknowledged explicitly.

Therefore museums are chimerical: they metamorphose into different things – including some things that we cannot control or predict. I think this is very much part of the excitement of a museum. And this is what I think metaphors do for us: they open a universe of possibility.

So, that was my first point about language and our discussions of the last three years. Earlier, I alluded to a story about my mother and the role of Shiva Nandi, and the touching of it. I want to refer again to my mother. A few years back, I took her, as a celebration of her sixty-fifth birthday, on a tour of cathedrals in France and England – something she had never seen before.

One of the cathedrals we visited was York Minster in England, and we went to some wonderful lectures including one by the master glazier, responsible for restoration of the Minster's stained glass windows. And a really charming lecture had to do with one very small piece of glass. Of course the stained glass windows in York Minster are immense, a huge number of panes, marvelous scenes, narratives being depicted, but the piece of glass he focused on, he said, was the piece he liked the very best of all.

This little piece of glass was something like six inches by eight inches, and it was located at the very top in a place that no one in the cathedral could possibly see. It was something of a kind of Japanese minimalist marvel: it showed a small bird, just a few strokes, seemingly about to grab a worm emerging from the grass. There was something of quickness, of life, about it. It had very little color; as I said, it wasn't very dramatic, and most of all, it was so small. What was it doing up there? For whom was this little piece of glass created? Clearly it wasn't one of the biblical scenes or scenes of patrons, or portraits of patrons, that were easily detectable to people standing in the cathedral, nor was it one of those beautiful large-scale designs that we could admire in their glory and their magnificence.

Instead it was a little illustration that could be seen by no one, except perhaps the glazier when he would have to go up every fifty or sixty years or so to make sure that the lead was holding and to reposition it. Actually, there is another answer as well. As every glazier I'm told would have responded, this little pane of glass was for God. So this was a creation that was not necessarily for human eyes, but in some ways underscored the bond between the maker and his or her relationship with the divine.

At last year's Colloquy, Richard Davis narrated a wonderful life history of the Dancing Shiva of Shivapuram, from the moment of its creation and its use (in some ways, imaginative reconstruction) up to the present. It had a long and varied career, which included being smuggled, an elicit reproduction being made of it and being slipped into the temple, unbeknownst to the villagers and so forth – it was quite an exciting tale!

One of the issues that came up was the distinction between the twentieth-century critic Walter Benjamin's use of cult value and display value. The *cult value,* as I said before, has to do with the original intent: the religious ritual function of the object. The *display value* has to do with the aesthetic or secularized museum value, the exhibition value, associated with the object.

One of the questions I want to ask is, while this can be a useful distinction in some respects, aren't we also missing out on something? Are we assuming that the aesthetic function is a universal function? Isn't there an aesthetic implicit in every object? That is, every object brings with it this aesthetic universe in its background. To make a distinction between display value and cult value is, I think, to impoverish our understanding of these artifacts.

To look at that little pane of glass and simply to analyze it without recognizing that it attests to a very private relationship between a maker and the divine, to look at an image of Shiva and ask the question, "Does it really matter if it is a reproduction because it serves the same function?" is to miss the point.

At the beginning, Mark [Bozzuti-Jones] spoke about that relationship in which sacral objects allow us a communion with the divine. That we are able to look at them and in some sense be looked at by them: this is precisely the definition of the Hindu ritual worship known as *darshan,* a term that has come up before in our discussions. It is this two-way street of communion. It is not arbitrary whether an object is real or not, because that object was very much created with the notion of the divine inhabiting it. We would say the same thing in an art museum. It very much does matter whether museums have reproductions or original objects. And I think in the sacral realm it matters as well.

Therefore the aesthetic function in the sacral object is intrinsic to it and not separable. I would like to suggest that when we introduce these objects, it is not enough just to talk about iconography or provenance. I think we need to present the aesthetic universe of the object.

David [Power] was talking about the comments that observers who are unfamiliar with some of these traditions may bring with them. They may ask, for example about Hindu statues, why are they all so plump? I think that is a very sentient observation. The reality is the notion of *prana*, of air, of inspiration, of breath. It is central, I would say, to Hindu theology, as well as to daily life. It is the notion of breath as being a good; thus, a concavity is quite rare in Hindu sculpture and more often than not connotes something negative. What does that plastic convex form convey? I think we need to talk about that. I think we need to educate museum visitors. We need to talk about things like *rasa*, aesthetic relish. We need to talk about *divani*, or resonant undertones, so that the objects are not simply use-function objects within a religion, but that they carry with them their own aesthetic mandate. That was my second point.

My third point is that if we're going to see the art museum as a venue to teach about faith traditions, there is a danger. What does it mean to use the objects alone in the art museum to talk about religion? Mark mentioned the desire for smells and bells, and I think so much of religious experience has to do with ephemeral experience.

Of course, in art museums, we focus on durable goods, particularly old things that have lasted. But I think if we are going to teach about faith traditions, it is important to juxtapose with them ephemeral objects. And I brought a few ephemeral objects just for our own consideration.

One is the issue of smells ... bells ... sound. I brought a tape of the *Hannya Shingo*, which is perhaps the most commonly recited Buddhist *sutra* associated with Mahayana Buddhism. It is a sutra that is chanted many, many times a day in many households and temples. You can find, very often, the Chinese scripture with a Japanese phonetic syllabary associated with it. There are lots of copies of this. And so it seems to me that it would be useful to have some of this available.

In addition, it would be useful to have material objects that are not meant to last. They include, for example a Buddhist amulet from the Kytano-Ten Mongu Shrine in Kyoto. It is a shrine dedicated to a very important figure, a scholar/calligrapher who was accused of sedition and forced into exile and assassinated. Later he was deified and became a patron deity of learning and calligraphy. This amulet was given to me by one of my students to encourage me in my latest book project. This amulet is meant to be kept with you or near your study, but it is also meant to be destroyed at the end of the year.

Similarly, recently there was the Giyong festival in Kyoto. This is a festival that was introduced into Kyoto in the ninth and tenth centuries, because in the summer time, Kyoto, being in a valley and very hot and humid, was a site of repeated epidemics and many, many people would die. This festival was to ward off disease, and one of the artifacts is called a Tihockee and its made out of bamboo grass, called *sa-sa*, and bound together. The purpose of this Tihockee is to function as a talisman in your entryway to ward off disease.

Now you can ask: Is this worthy of being exhibited in an art museum? But it seems to me that, in some ways, this is as important as a Chola bronze – that is, it functions in an important religious fashion. It, too, is destroyed at the end of the year. So much of religious life revolves around calendrical observances and, in many museums we have no notion of the passage of time. Everything is in some ways, almost ironically, atemporal. It is in a kind of moment where it is neither night nor day – in an art museum, you cannot tell if it is night or day. You are in a kind of twilight world. I would like to suggest that we need to pay attention to changes, the changeable, rather than always privileging the constant, the unchanging.

I want to end with the notion of language being hermeneutic, and the reason I use that word is because I wanted to get back to the idea of the Greek God Hermes. Hermes, who is known as Mercury or Quicksilver in Rome, is the messenger God between humans and the Gods, he is the God of Travel and he is the God of Traffic. It seems to me that is precisely what we do in museums. We negotiate traffic, and we need to think about the ways in which this intercourse happens. So the hermeneutic notion of language is one in which language is not about declaring something to be so, but about asking questions, raising possibilities, allowing for a kind of modification and change.

David Carr:

I invite the audience to comment as you will or ask questions of any of us.

Question 1 [from the audience]:

I was thinking about what was just said about the atemporality of museums. It seems to me to be very interesting to bring temporal, or seasonally-situated, religious items into museums, but perhaps we could also look at ways to emphasize the atemporality of the museum. There is a way that museums intimate a kind of "Take off your shoes – You're entering into a different kind of space." We may be served by emphasizing that and emphasizing the museum as a kind of liminal zone, one that it is both outside of time and in time together.

Meera Viswanathan:

I think the key is to make sure that it is acknowledged or explicitly alluded to, so that people can confront the time issue rather than simply pass through without consideration.

Question 1 [continued]:

Right, and I think that in the combination of both sacred time and non-time, or perhaps secular non-time, where you are in this other kind of zone, that we may find a way to take on both of those questions.

Meera Viswanathan:

Well, you used another wonderful metaphor for a museum as a kind of liminal zone and I think it is threshold space, which really is here and there, and allows us to cross that boundary.

Question 2 [Amy Nelson]:

I was really struck by your comment about time, as well, and the use of time in museums, and I think it is such a great suggestion. And as a Muslim, I immediately had five examples that came to the top of my head, just like ritual things that we do that involve time, such as a piece of paper that might be thrown down into the river. And that is very integral to my life as a worshipper, but that is so private that I had never considered that it would be something that would be a part of that space.

Meera Viswanathan:

Well, it is one of our problems. I think as Moderns, too, that we make distinctions between weekdays and the weekend, but days, in some ways, don't have any particular marker; whereas in most faith traditions it matters very much what day of the week it is, what month it is, and how that operates within that liturgical year however we define it.

Question 3 [Vivian Mann]:

I am a little uncomfortable with one of your suggestions that these anthropological items be included in every museum exhibition, or some museum exhibitions. I think that it is very difficult to mix aesthetic values. It is jarring. I myself did a cultural exhibition that had a new development at the end involving a school room. Coming from the high arts to the school room with the children's art – it was jarring. I think that, particularly in the kind of exhibitions that we show, it would just be apples and oranges. We all know that these things exist out there and we might want to do them as ancillary materials, but to put them in a gallery I think would be to denigrate the main exhibition.

Mimi Gates:

I'm not so sure it would. If you had screens of the Giyong festival, and you had in a side case some of these objects from contemporary times that are used in practice ... I could easily see that. I wonder if we shouldn't experiment a bit more? There is a difference between an art museum and an anthropology museum, but at the same time, I often think that we are too delimited in terms of what we do.

Meera Viswanathan:

I think it's a very interesting problem. I am not sure I was suggesting in a kind of monolithic fashion that every art museum run out and obtain the necessary ephemera associated with every faith tradition and exhibit them accordingly side-by-side. But I am suggesting that there is an absence. The danger is that visitors' only access into understanding a faith tradition may be a museum object. My point is to remind people that, in fact, this is not the only thing that is emblematic of that faith tradition or even the central thing, necessarily.

Question 3 [continued]:

One way might be to have a kind of side area, in which the newly made was shown. The notion of sequestering some of the material I think is a possible solution.

Mark Bozutti-Jones:

I guess it is not, as they say, either/or, both/and. I like to jokingly say that we live in a world of multiple personalities, and I do believe that the challenge facing the world is how we can become more and more inclusive. I think quite frequently one display works for one personality and might not work for the other personality, even as appealing as it might be. I think that the more experimental we get, the more risks we are willing to take, the more we view whatever we present as being viewed by people with multiple experiences from different backgrounds, and the more we offer people the range of possibilities and the range of reactions, the more I think we stand to gain. So I can see the place for both, keeping it in one way or keeping it more formal, and at the same time, mixing things up to touch and encourage, shock, appease, or attract different personalities.

Ray Williams:

I'm playing with this idea of things that are jarring. In my experience, maybe aesthetic difference can be particularly jarring to museum-world insiders, but not necessarily jarring to other people. In fact, I think some people find traditional museum displays very jarring in the way that they take things out of the context and present them purely for aesthetic delight.

We have to think about who is being jarred by traditions, too. As you say, this is a time of great multiplicity. The other thought that I had is that people come into the space and make it their own anyway, so I am thinking about some of the things that David Power was suggesting about placement and isolation.

Question 4 [Mimi Gates]:

Ray, what do you think about technology and ways to employ it?

Ray Williams:

I think that technology can provide layers of information, but ... it is not my main thing.

Mimi Gates:

It's a tool!

David Power:

I feel attuned to the general orientation of the conversation, but I think precisely because of the multiplicity there is the danger of a trivialization of experience. In the Catholic Church we often talk about "Cafeteria Catholicism." It is like going into the cafeteria: all the dishes are out there in front of you, and you pick what you want, and you make your own smorgasbord. We are facing an extraordinary reality of the multiplicity and venerability of religious traditions.

But by enhancing the experiential side of it, we could be trivializing it. We offer people things from which to pick and choose, and maybe some breakdown of intolerance occurs, but much of this can be done with very little profundity. And that, I think, is the risk to which we have to be very sensitive.

David Carr:

One of the things that I noticed in our conversation is the idea of incompleteness. The museum ought to make clear to its users that what it offers is incomplete: It lacks context. It lacks, in some cases, time. It lacks the surrounding practices. It lacks expressions of faith. And so, in part, what happens when an individual encounters the object, [is that] he or she completes that object in a way that has meaning or value to him or her.

One of the framing questions that we wanted to introduce this afternoon is, what is it that the museum wants to happen in relation to that completion? How much can the museum affect the completion of the relationship between the user and the object?

In a way, what we have seen today are four different approaches to the completion of that relationship. You have also heard an articulate rendition of the tensions that seem to emerge about ten minutes into any conversation that we have in the *Five Faiths* Colloquy. To do this might be to compromise that, and yet if we do not do that then we surely compromise that ... which I think is just wonderful.

Question 5 [from the audience]:

I wonder if the essence of this is: How do we change people? How do we help them to not slaughter each other? Is it possible from just looking at these objects – even if we included the smells and bells and made it a true experience of each of these five religions – does someone truly become more accepting of us, more accepting of each other? Is there anything else that can be done at a museum with this possibility of thousands and thousands of people going to museums this year, as I understand. More than theater, more than movies ...

David Carr:

Well, it is a question of what we want to have happen. The answer to that question will differ depending on whether you are asking a scholar, a curator, a practitioner of the religion, an artist, an educator, a museum director, perhaps. All of these will be different, and in a way we have heard some of that. Would any of you like to address some of those differences?

Mimi Gates:

I don't know about differences, but I will say that the one thing that I hope is that the museum experience will provoke people to think. Yes, it inspires aesthetically, but it also provokes them to think. It may be thinking about history – I often think of museums as being a history of things. But I hope that it piques their curiosity, and that they will at least search about those traditions, and think about those traditions, and that it would become a part of their thinking. I don't know if that's a step towards tolerance, but I would hope so.

David Power:

I think there is a wisdom in the modesty of the *Five Faiths Project* proposal that is still on the website: The *Five Faiths Project* is founded on the conviction that centering conversations about faith traditions on works of art originally used in worship promotes objective and thoughtful consideration of those traditions, while also inhibiting unproductive ideological debates that impede tolerance, understanding and learning. It evokes a certain thoughtfulness ... It is a modest statement.

Mark Bozutti-Jones:

We have touched on the incompleteness of the work. I mentioned earlier about giving a homework assignment. I think people who go to a museum have to realize that the ultimate mission is to go back outside. That whatever you appreciate on the inside, whatever exists on the inside in harmony or in beauty, that those who observe it now have to commit to going out and living it out. I think that [is] the only way we can prevent people from slaughtering each other. How do we help people to go out, to live out the beauty of whatever they see and experience in their daily lives? That you no longer fear a Jew or a Muslim or a Christian or whatever, that after seeing this exhibition you go out committed to befriending and looking at this human being with the same [appreciation of] beauty with which you looked at the person's objects of faith.

Meera Viswanathan:

I'd like to take a somewhat counter-position, which is I think there is a much more mysterious process between input and output, and I am not sure our principle goal should be – it is laudable, and of course I would like to see that, too – but I'm not sure that our principle goal is promoting tolerance. I think that may be, ideally, one of the outcomes eventually, but I think what happens in these experiences is much more mysterious. It is not as though you read a book and say I am a better person for it? It may provoke you to think, it may produce a kind of chain reaction within you that eventually results in a kind of ennoblement, but I don't think it is so direct.

I think it is possible to go to an exhibition and say, "Wow, I think Hindu worshippers are strange idol worshippers!" and then come out and say, "They are still pretty strange! I know more about them, but they are still strange!" I'm not sure that that's a failure. I think we should allow for the fact that people encounter new things, that they learn things, that they are provoked to think, but it may not be when people emerge outside after that visit that they are changed individuals in necessarily the programmatic way that we'd like to see.

David Carr:

But you know how important it is to introduce the power of that question about what the museum could possibly effect. It reminds me that museum visits are almost always about courage and fear, and the ways in which we can increase one and reduce the other. Ultimately that is what we begin to talk about in our conversations as well.

Question 6 [from the audience]:

I have one comment. I recently spoke to Pat Phelan, who is the abbess of the Chapel Hill Zen Center, and she appreciates this *Project* because anything that engenders understanding and tolerance has got to be of great benefit. I just want to remark on the wisdom of the inclusion of all the different disciplines in this discussion. I don't accept any of the disclaimers from the people on this panel who said that they don't have art or museum backgrounds. I thought everyone said wonderful, pertinent, valuable, and moving things. I think that art has historically been about spiritual experience and that is what art and religion have. That's what they *do*. They tune our minds to higher planes and higher purpose, and I want also to comment on the courage of the Ackland in undertaking this project. I think the prescience of the *Project* in relation to our current world situation is just astounding.

David Carr:

Thank you, thank you very much. And for the panel, I'll thank you all for your conversations tonight – which have not ended, nor will they end this evening. We thank you for your attendance and we thank you for your help and we look forward to more conversations of this kind.

---

i Mimi Gates, Colloquy III, *100 word statement*

ii Anantanand Rambachan, Colloquy III discussion.

iii Mark Bozutti-Jones, Colloquy III, panel discussion

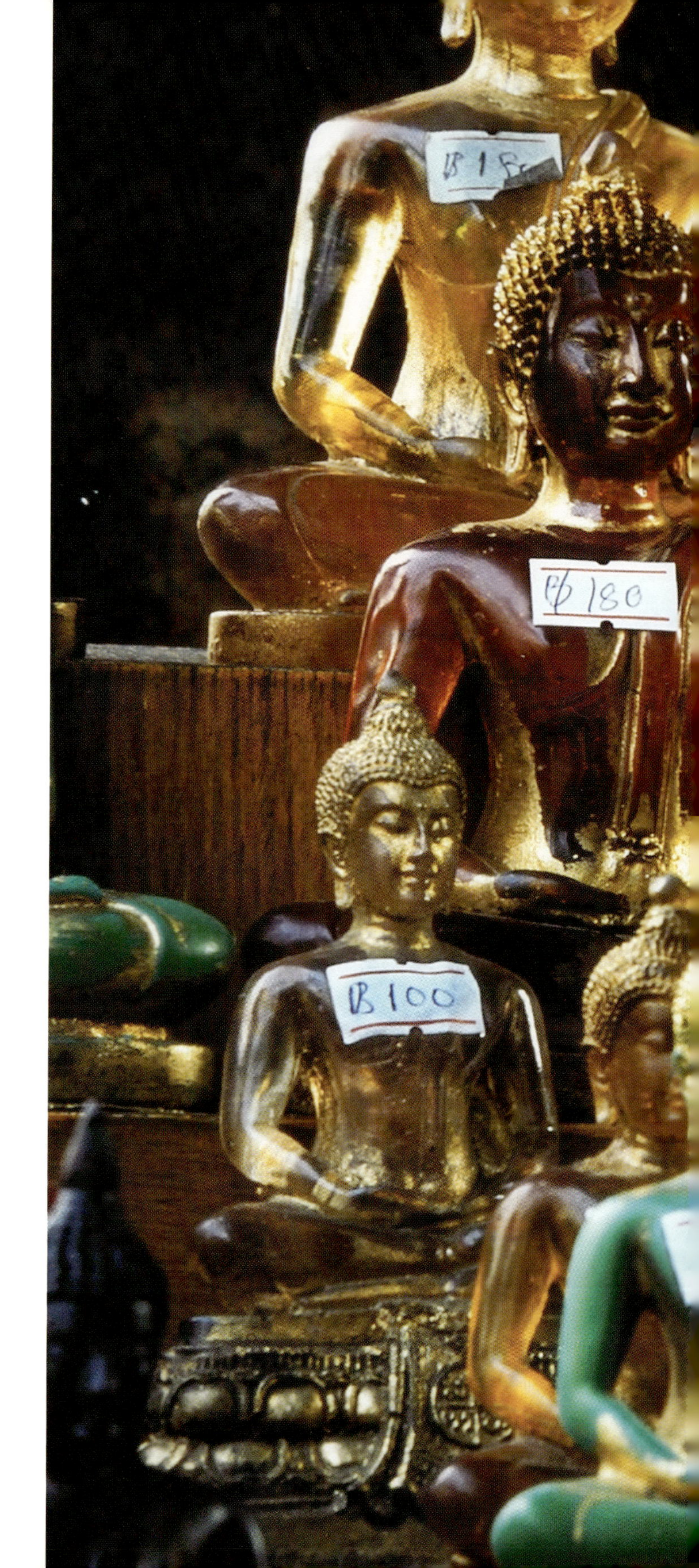
฿180
฿100

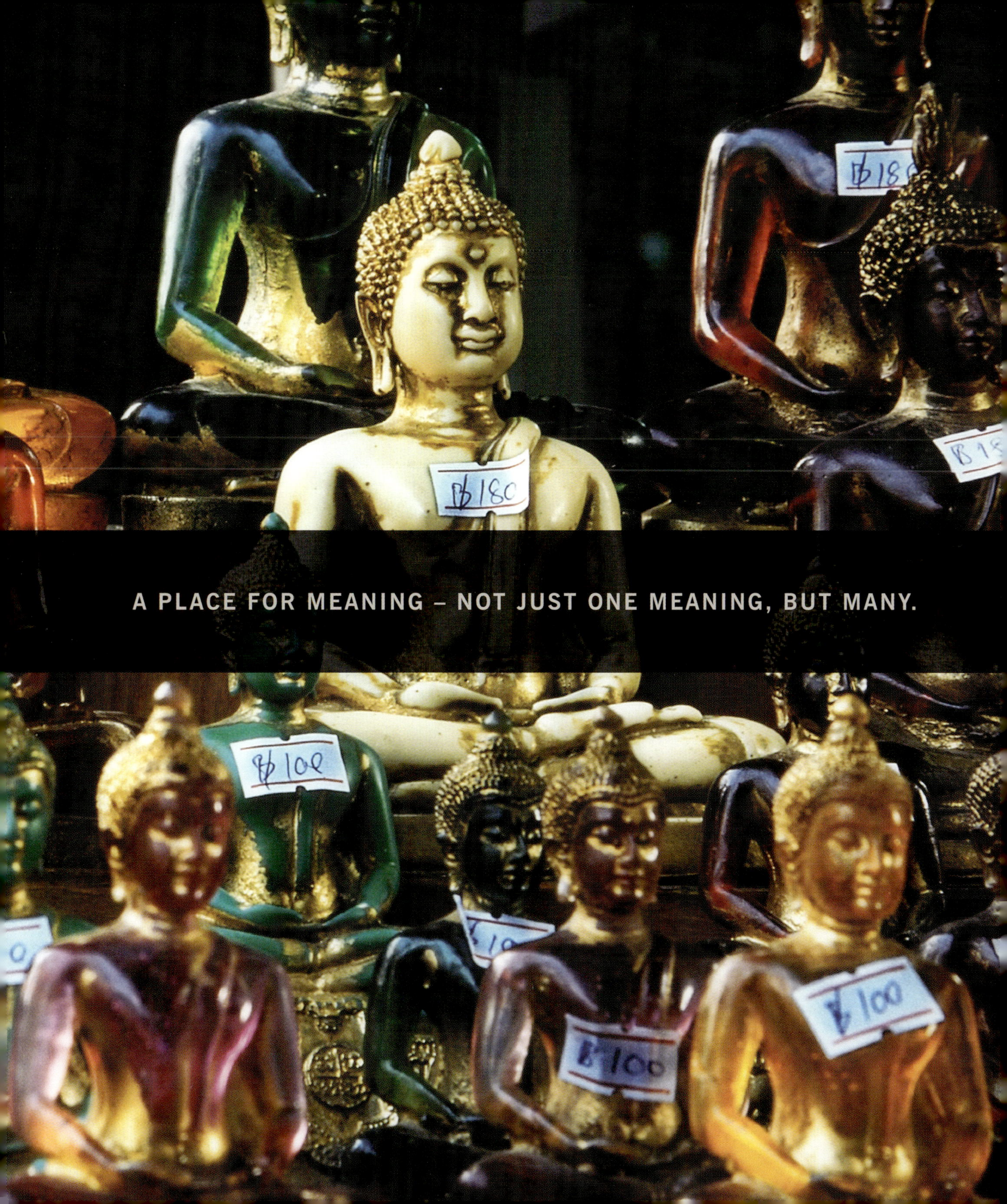

A PLACE FOR MEANING – NOT JUST ONE MEANING, BUT MANY.

FOR SALE, BANGLAMPHU DISTRICT, BANGKOK, THAILAND
Jesse Kalisher
American, 2004, printed 2007; chromogenic print. Gift of Helen and Jesse Kalisher in memory of Ilse Kalisher. © 2004 Jesse Kalisher, 2007.9. (detail)

Conclusions

It has been over four years since the final Colloquy. We have remained in contact with many of the participants and lost touch with others. Most have changed either their position or their institutional affiliation. This is one indication of the difficulty in sustaining any long-term project. Even the authors' roles and responsibilities have changed; neither of us works within the education department any longer and we have each taken on significantly more supervisory and administrative responsibility than when we began the *Five Faiths Project.* Nevertheless, the *Project* continues to resonate for us and we wonder how we will apply all that we learned from our colleagues.

Today at the Ackland, the *Five Faiths Project* has ongoing implications for how this museum will approach works of art (both those with sacred content and without), engage various communities of interest, and sustain institutional support. What follows is a summary of recommendations based on our four years of reflection, trial and error, and internal and external feedback. Every assertion here may be worthy of the same in-depth and sustained investigation that the premise of the *Project* received over the course of three years. Certainly, we are grateful for the ways in which the Ackland has encouraged our consideration and reconsideration of each point. As a full staff, we have argued, wrestled, and wrangled (as Meera Viswanathan suggested) with all this "messy business" for more than a decade in formal and impromptu meetings. What follows are some of the implications of the *Project* for museums and their various communities.

Pay attention to the object

- The individual characteristics of each object help determine what kinds of information are appropriate to present and may suggest how best to install the object. As tempting as it is to elaborate, refrain from saying anything that cannot be demonstrated in the object or other objects around it.
- Museums hold objects in trust for their communities, and therefore museum professionals have an obligation to help these communities understand the limitations of their collections, even as they invite community members to use them.
- Museums should be prepared to support community suggestions for overcoming the limitations of their collections with selected acquisitions. The use of an object is an important consideration in acquisition decisions. Communities can help set fruitful new directions for collection development plans.

Curatorial humility is a virtue

- The object is more important than any single approach to it. The curatorial perspective, no matter how well informed it may be, is not the only valid approach to understanding. Stephen C. Newsome suggests that we reframe our definition of expertise to include "community scholars," because offering visitors "connections to lived experiences and to individual and group expertise" gives new authenticity to exhibitions and programs.
- Guest curators help protect museums from institutional arrogance, complacency, and redundancy, especially when the guest curator comes from a discipline traditionally excluded from the usual curatorial process. As suggested earlier, a degree in art history is not the only credential for selecting, installing, and interpreting works of art.
- Museums benefit when they attend to how they use titles such as "community collaborator," "scholar," even "curator," and how these words suggest hierarchies of meaning to both museum insiders and outsiders.
- Museums must pay close attention to how they articulate expectations

and life expectancy for community partnerships and collaborative projects. Even advisory boards have clearly established terms of appointment and areas of responsibility. The more discrete the tasks and the time lines, the greater the potential for community involvement and museum responsiveness to community interests.

Maintain parity of esteem across traditions and disciplines

- The approaches taken with the objects of one tradition or culture should be offered to all. For example, including honorifics in one tradition compels their use in all traditions. Including references to sacred texts in western traditions compels their inclusion in others as well. By critically examining current installations, new opportunities to create this parity emerge.
- No tradition or time period should be privileged with the presumption of audience understanding. For example, museums cannot assume that contemporary audiences are well versed in any faith tradition and, perhaps, should not even assume that contemporary audiences are well versed in contemporary culture. Particularly as a university art museum, the Ackland continues to see teaching and learning in the gallery as a primary function. This teaching and learning transcends the *Five Faiths Project* and applies to every object in the collection and every temporary exhibition. Of course, resources are finite, but museums can use this priority as a way to approach their exhibition schedules, publications, and interpretive strategies.
- When community members are invited – faith community members or otherwise – to offer informed perspectives about works of art, their perspectives should be integrated into interpretive materials, not ghettoized into study galleries or supplemental materials. Their perspectives should be given the same respect as that of the curator. New technologies increase the opportunities for this kind of inclusion. From labels to cell phone tours, website blogs to streaming videos, the possibilities are virtually endless.
- Parity of esteem requires institutional commitment to transparency because it supersedes the single omniscient voice of the label by layering

many voices. Each voice, even that of the apparently omniscient curator, should be identified.

Choose language carefully

- The words we use to talk about works of art (in labels, gallery talks, audio-tours, etc.) make a difference to visitor experience and provide opportunities to teach. For example: whenever possible use language from the object's original context. The Qur'an does not have chapters; it has *suras.* Hindu practice does not include icons, rather *murtis.* Also use qualifying language: *some* Buddhists believe ... *according to* sacred texts ... *in Renaissance Christian* practice ... in *Zen* Buddhism ... All of these qualifiers promote understanding of the internal diversity of faith traditions and the origins of each tradition's truth claims.
- Sometimes it is best to be flexible in language rules established by the museum. Although we, as insiders to museum culture, do not use honorifics, faith community partners do. As long as their words are attributed to them, honor what they say (the Christ child, Lord Ganesha, etc.). On the other hand, community members may call for a kind of specificity the museum might otherwise never have included. For example, according to our faith community partners, the Ackland does not have a Qur'an, it has a copy of the Qur'an. It is a subtle, but vital distinction. For Muslims, every Qur'an is a copy of the original, which, according to the core belief of Islam, the angel Gabriel dictated directly to Muhammad. Including the word "copy" in a title is problematic in the museum culture that prizes original works of art.

Allow for multiple experiences

- Exhibitions and installations should be designed to allow for different kinds of responses to works of art. Aesthetic appreciation is only one of the many ways that visitors relate to works of art. They arrive with their experiences shaping their expectations, and when they leave, we hope they carry new appreciation for the significance of works of art. For some, this may be the devotional aspect of works of art, for others, the historical. By enriching our installations to reflect various types of response, the Museum encourages community involvement and support.

- Community members assess value with a different set of criteria from curators. Be sensitive to what communities tell you about how they experience objects. For example, a faith practitioner who participated in the Colloquies was more drawn to the small Burmese Buddha because it depicts stories of the Buddha's life, than to the more impressive gilded Thai Buddha head that Ackland curators installed in a privileged location in the gallery. Another faith practitioner expressed discomfort in a small-group discussion because his chair faced a painting of the *Triumph of Christ*, in which King David bows to Jesus. Young people are often the most vocal in their responses to objects. Both authors have led tours in which participants have averted their eyes from *Ganesha* because their Christian beliefs discouraged looking at "idols." Openness to all these responses builds institutional capacity for understanding and responding to this diversity – in labels, programs, and publications.
- Pay attention to the ways that other institutions passively or intentionally promote and restrict different kinds of responses to objects. The Seattle Art Museum, for example, promoted the understanding of a Buddhist altar as a consecrated space by advertising it as such; the Ackland suppressed that information about a similar installation for fear that by creating a sacred space in a public space we might violate the consciences of visitors. The authors are not taking a stand here, but we do wish to assert that avoiding the issue is not a solution. Museums must make a conscious decision and be reflexive in the decision-making process.[1]

Promote risk taking

- Once you engage faith or other communities, they may offer gifts that enrich teaching even if they are not curatorially pleasing. Our experience

1 As Charles Haynes notes, all museums, public or private, have a civic responsibility to take claims of conscience seriously. In his view, claims of conscience from believers and non-believers are best addressed by adhering to the highest standards of scholarship while making room for multiple perspectives.

with the *Five Faiths Project* has been that community members often recommend the acquisition of daily objects as important for assisting with understanding traditional objects in museum collections. The Ackland has been offered everything from a Buddhist prayer wheel to demonstrate ritual activities, a portable plastic prayer mat with which to make the case that prayer can be on any clean surface, and spices, candles, and a *puja* tray with which to honor a Hindu deity. We accepted them all. Some entered the collection, some went to our study collection, and some are in the docent closet for K-12 gallery teachers.

- When institutions invite community members to speak from their own experiences, there are many risks. Faith community members, for example, may make confessional statements or, worse, use the forum to proselytize. They may get well-known facts wrong, mispronounce artists' names, or misidentify subject matter. Nevertheless, their involvement is valuable because, on the one hand, they help museums understand the diversity of their communities and, on the other, they present multiple points of access to audiences.

Measure investment

- A project of this scope is extraordinarily time consuming. While there is no simple formula for calculating the resource investment this level of engagement with objects and communities requires, it will inevitably take more time than originally expected.
- Given the transitions and changes within institutions, an external advisory board of committed community partners is important for continuity and responsiveness to changing communities, funding, staffing, and all the other factors that affect an original vision.
- Keep in mind your institution's mission. The Ackland's mission is to animate, inspire, and transform people's lives with works of art. One way to measure wise investment is to examine the ways in which our activities focus visitors' attention on the object.

We believe that the *Five Faiths Project* has profound implications for any type of museum, its various communities, and its collections: it maps a future for museum practice. In our view, the *Project* demonstrates that collections built in part in response to the needs of museum educators, local communities, and public school teachers and students offer a promising new prospect for museums. By inviting communities into conversations about collections and honoring their responses and perceptions, museums will connect with the contemporary cultures that support them.

The *Five Faiths Project* did not begin as a case study for community outreach or for innovations in collection development. The Colloquy series turned our attention to the *Project*'s "limits and potential" as a model for both. We believe that the core ideas presented in this manuscript can be broadly applied to prospective museum initiatives, for example: an education project to help health care professionals, both caregivers and researchers, to approach clients from different cultures with appropriate regard; an outreach program to engage immigrant communities directly, providing them with an environment in which to gain insight into American culture *and* to affirm their own cultures of origin; or an exhibition installation to juxtapose traditional objects with contemporary works in order to explore the impact of American freedoms on religious and cultural expression. Of course, there will likely be institutional resistance to the most innovative applications. Nevertheless, with the benefit of hindsight, we identify three reasons why the *Five Faiths Project* flourished: visionary leadership of the director and head of education, persistence and flexibility in the scope and application of the core ideas, and unyielding devotion to objects and their power to transform.

In the end, it is all about the objects and the communities that surround them. When museums engage in conversations with their fellow communities, they establish themselves as places for meaning – not just one meaning, but many.

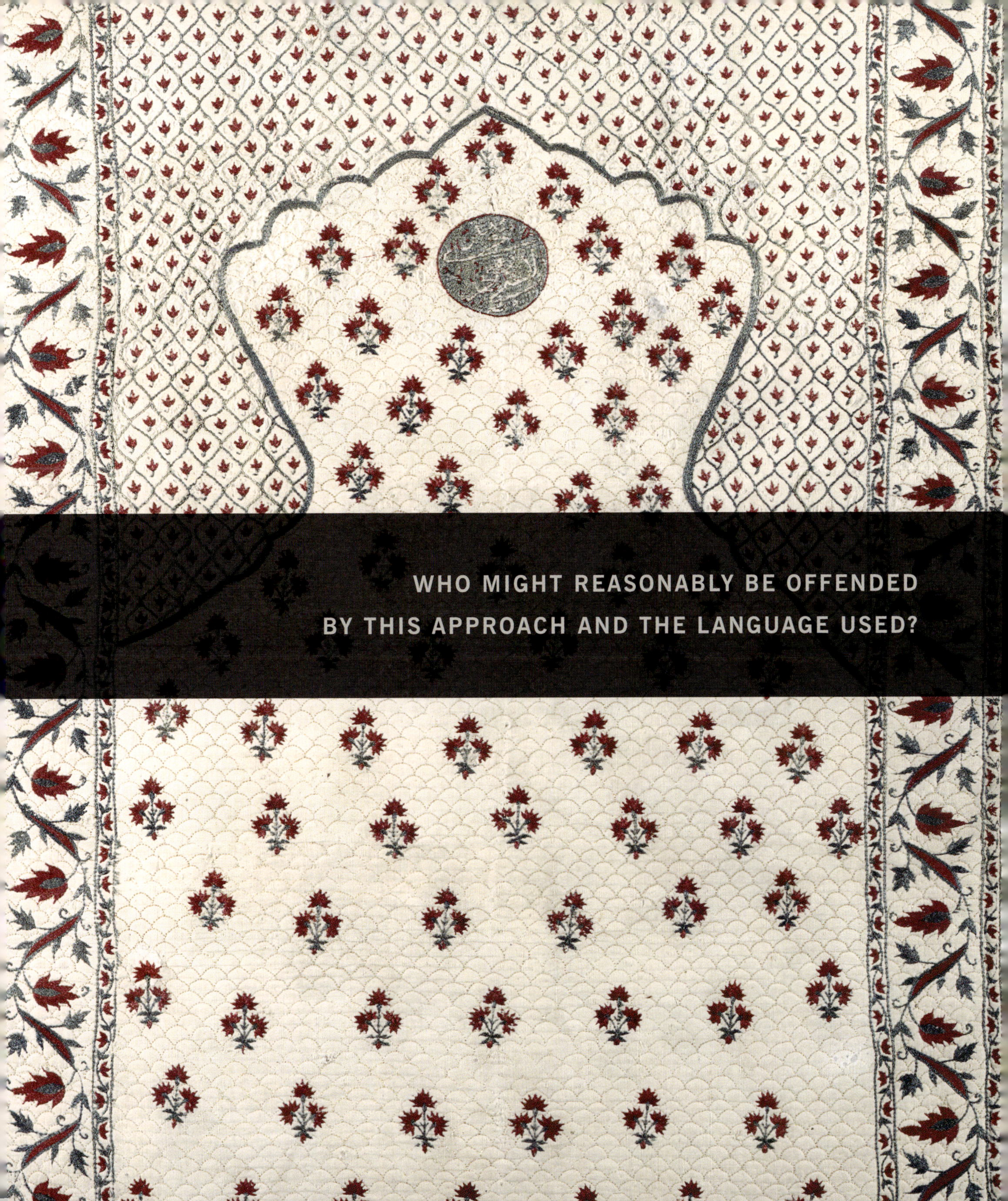
WHO MIGHT REASONABLY BE OFFENDED
BY THIS APPROACH AND THE LANGUAGE USED?

PRAYER MAT
Unknown
North Indian, Mughal, 18th century; silk embroidery on quilted cotton. Ackland Fund, selected by The Ackland Associates, 96.5. (detail)

Tools for Teaching & Learning

Throughout the course of the *Five Faiths Project*, the Ackland developed tools for use with teachers and students, gallery teachers, and other programs that engaged objects within the Ackland collection with sacred histories.

We include the following as templates that may be useful to other museum professionals as they develop new programs related to this work. These templates, except where noted, were developed in collaborative processes by Ackland staff members.

Consider Your Responses

Submitted by:
Ray Williams

> A kind and experienced middle-school teacher has a new Cambodian student in her math class, one of a small-group of refugees who have recently settled in her small community. A devout Christian, the teacher gives the student a small Bible during lunch one day. The student accepts the gift, saying only, "Thank you."

Analyze the interpersonal and cultural dynamics at play in this situation, trying to imagine the motivations of the teacher and the student.

1. "Africans believed that by creating a sculpture of a twin child who died – and by caring for it with offerings of food and adornment – the spirit of the child would bring favor to the family."
2. "Europeans believed that when the priest said the appropriate words in front of a painting like this, bread and wine could be turned into the body and blood of Jesus and eaten by worshippers to strengthen their spiritual life."

Compare the preceding statements. Which would you be more likely to say on a tour? What aspects of the statements might be problematic?

The Hindus had a lot of myths – stories about their gods and goddesses and various impossible creatures. This is a statue of Ganesha; he is part human, part elephant. Now use these art materials to create your own picture of a god or goddess that combines human and animal body parts. Back at school you can even write a myth about your god's adventures.

Why does this gallery teacher suggest these activities? Who might reasonably be offended by this approach and the language used?

A female Muslim student, following cultural dictates about modesty in dress, comes to school every day with her hair completely covered, wearing long sleeves and a long skirt. One day, when the sophomores are gathering for English class, one of the rowdier boys sneaks up behind the girl and yanks off her scarf. The girl's hair is exposed to all, and she angrily grabs for the scarf before bursting into tears.

Analyze the interpersonal and cultural dynamics at play here. How should the English teacher deal with this situation? How might your own cultural background influence your understanding of this event?

The parents of a student in your world history class telephone to state emphatically that they do not wish their child to be exposed to information about religious traditions other than their own. They are concerned that, as you begin the unit on India, information about Hindu and Buddhist beliefs will be discussed in class.

Analyze the dynamics of this conflict and identify a range of options available to you in this situation. Which of the options would you choose?

Hindu people are required to remove their shoes in sacred spaces, as shoes are considered unclean. Some Hindu museum visitors try to remove their shoes as they enter a gallery that features bronze processional images of gods and goddesses, but the security officer prevents this based on museum rules. The visitors, shocked and upset, write a letter to the museum director, who responds by citing concerns about sanitation and safety. She also reminds the visitors that the statues are deconsecrated at this point and, according to Hindu ritual texts, no longer imbued with the divine presence.

Describe the conflict here, trying to imagine the various points of view. How would you have handled this situation as the Hindu visitor ... ? the security officer ... ? the museum director ... ? Think about how you would present your perspective to the others. Can you propose a reasonable compromise to resolve this conflict?

Five Object Exercises

Submitted by:
David Carr

Restoring Missing Contexts

The museum's possession of an object removes it from original, functional, cultural and worldly contexts. The presentation of an object, however, can suggest or restore some of these contexts.

Select any two faith objects in the museum:

- What contexts* are most important to restore to these objects?
- How might this restoration happen best?

*Possible contexts:

- Aesthetic qualities
- Cultural or ethnic origins
- Imaginative origins
- Place in an historical era
- Practice in the faith community
- Processes of craft
- Responses of the faithful
- Scholarly observations

What other contexts occur to you?[1]

Likenesses and Differences

The museum places an object among many other objects, and so creates a problem for the user's attention. We might encounter museum objects in isolation, or in a series or a set; they may be linked by a theme, a structural similarity, their history, geography, or

---

1 Among other considerations, Carr reminded us to allow for other, and unanticipated responses. By asking this open-ended questions, participants are encouraged to resist understanding yes and no as the right or the only responses.

maker. Despite the museum's efforts to shape our attention, however, we tend to juxtapose and compare similar objects in our desire to think critically about their differences.

Select any two faith objects in the museum:

- What grounds for comparing these objects appear to be most promising?
- What might such comparisons suggest?

The Incomplete Object

The museum's presentation of an object or a text does not assume that the object or the text is complete; only our attention, mindfulness, and individual observations and expressions can complete our experiences of the object. In this way we construct a bridge from the artifact to the human being.

Select any two faith objects in the museum:

- What do you not know that you need to know in order to complete the objects in your mind and connect them to other experiences?
- What are your questions about these objects? If there is a pattern in your questions, try to articulate it.

The Moving Object

In the museum, in every object, we might assume that something powerful and compelling continues to move. We might say that certain pieces impress themselves upon us, resonate and stay with us, remaining powerful to us long after we have been in their presence.

Select any two faith objects in the museum:

- What moves in each of these things?
- You may wish to use metaphors, analogies, and other figurative language to enrich your discussion.

Set the Table

When similar objects are juxtaposed, their proximity may create a feeling of connection and resonance, illuminate a common quality, or create an unanticipated tension and uncertainty.

Select any five of the museum's faith objects, each from a different tradition:

- If we were to place them on a table together before our group, how would we speak about them? How would we interrogate them?
- What might their differences in material, size, style, form, or image (for example) imply or suggest?

Process Observations

After these exercises, the following questions were used to discuss the process:

- How would you describe the conversations you had?
- How did the questions change when you moved closer to the objects themselves?
- How would you revise the questions?
- How would you describe your thinking, individually and collectively?
- What lessons does this process offer for our understanding of questions in museums?
- What lessons does this process offer for our understanding of the experiences of museum users?

The actual outcomes of the conversations are far less important than the conversations themselves, but discussing how the individual exercises worked is likely to lead to further insights about processes.

The information on the following pages been compiled to help you consider neutral language to use in your gallery teaching about the five faiths. A glossary and pronunciation guide are also included for each faith. Many of the terms in the glossary refer specifically to objects in the Ackland Art Museum's collection; others are general terms that help provide contextual information about each faith.

Talking about Hinduism

Some Terms to Avoid	Why?	Suggested Substitutions
church synagogue sangha	These terms refer to places of worship specific to followers of other faiths, therefore inappropriate terms to denote places of worship for people who are Hindu.	temple bhavan
Bible Torah Dhammapada Sutras	Each tradition has its own sacred texts, even when certain narratives are held in common with other traditions. Reference to the specific sacred text helps direct visitors to additional resources for further study.	Vedas Rig Veda Upanishads Bhagavad Gita
idol	Although this term is sometimes used to describe large- and small-scale religious sculptures seen in Hindu temples and festivals, this term is a European convention that does not accurately describe the relationship between devotee and deity that exists in Hinduism. Hindu people believe that, after receiving the essence of a deity through ritual, a sculpture possesses that essence, which devotees can perceive and receive. The word "idol" can mean an object of worship or a false god; because these two definitions differ significantly in meaning and "false god" is most often associated with the word idol, it is best to avoid using the word at all.	murti: *body of the deity* utsava murti: *festival body* deity sculpture of a god or goddess religious sculpture sacred sculpture

Glossary

arati (AHR-tee) A form of puja in which the devotee offers lights with prayers, rotating the light(s) evenly at specific points.

avatar (AH-vuh-TAR) A physical manifestation (human or animal) assumed by a Hindu deity when making a visit to earth. Varaha and Krishna are avatars of Vishnu.

bhavan (buh-VAHN) "House" or "community," therefore the term used for a Hindu temple, which is primarily a community meeting place.

Brahma (BRUH-muh, BRAH-muh) The creative aspect of Brahman. Brahma, who is often depicted with four heads, is the creator in the three-part cycle of each creation of the world, along with Vishnu the preserver and Shiva the destroyer.

Brahman (BRUH-muhn, BRAH-muhn) (Sanskrit: "a swelling, expansion, growth") Brahman is the term used to describe the supreme principal of the universe. Brahman is often described in two ways – with attributes (saguna) and without attributes (niguna). In either case, Brahman retains an unknowable aspect of power and holiness, and is present in all things.*

Brahmin (BRAH-mihn) A member of one of four Hindu classes. Brahmins are responsible for officiating at religious rites and studying and teaching the Vedas.

cakra, chakra (CHA-kruh)

1 Disc-shaped weapon. Symbol of the sun and the mind. The cakra can represent the Universal Mind, the limitless power which invents and destroys all spheres and forms of the universe, the nature of which is to revolve. Used as an attribute of Ganesha and Vishnu.

2 In Hindu thought, the centers of force and consciousness located within the inner bodies of people; the seven principal cakras are often depicted as colorful, multipetaled wheels or lotuses. Aligned along the spine, the seven upper cakras progress as follows: base of spine (memory, time, and space); below navel (reason); solar plexus (willpower); heart center (direct cognition); throat (divine love); third eye (divine sight); and crown of head (illumination). The seven lower cakras relate to fear and lust, anger, jealousy, prolonged mental confusion, selfishness, absence of conscience, and murder and malice.

darshan (dar-shahn) Literally, "seeing(?)" (Sanskrit). Seeing the essence of the deity in a murti or utsava murti in the context of puja or a festival dedicated to a deity/deities. After visiting a temple and returning home, a person may be asked, "Did you have darshan today?" or "Did you have good darshan today?" suggesting that contemplation of the deity is valued, and unimpeded contemplation even more so.

dharma (DAR-muh) The orderly fulfillment of an inherent nature or destiny, or, as it relates to the soul, the mode of conduct most conducive to spiritual advancement. A complex and all-inclusive term with many meanings, including: divine law, law of being, way of righteousness, religion, duty, responsibility, virtue, justice, goodness, and truth.

Diwali (dee-VAH-lee) One of several Hindu holidays in the calendar, sometimes called "The Festival of Lights." This lunar holiday celebrates the return of Rama after his exile, as described in the *Ramayana*. Also a holiday associated with inviting Lakshmi, the goddess of good luck, to one's home with cleanliness and lights.

Ganesha, Ganesh (GUH-nesh-uh, GUH-nesh) A Hindu god with the head of an elephant and the body of a man. Known as the remover of obstacles, Ganesha is important to many Hindu people because acknowledging him before worshipping your primary deity (even if it's not Ganesha) helps prepare you for clearer and more focused devotion. Images of Ganesha are often featured on banks and wedding invitations. Attributes include four or six arms, a double-headed axe, a conch shell, and a noose. Son of Shiva and Parvati.

karma (KAR-muh) "Act, deed(s), works or, in particular, sacrifice." A principle which ensures that good actions have positive consequences, and bad actions have negative consequences." In Hinduism, the actions of previous lives influence the lives that follow, and the actions taken by someone in the current life may make positive or negative impact on future lives.

linga/lingam (lin-guh/lin-gum) Abstract form of the Hindu deity or god Shiva; sometimes plain or with very little decoration. Other forms may have a different face on each of four sides, representing different manifestations of the deity, each manifestation relating to one of the cardinal directions. In its original context, the linga emerges from its feminine counterpart, a yoni.

moksha (MOCK-shuh) (Sanskrit: "release, liberation") the most commonly used term applied to the release of the human soul from the cycles of birth, death and rebirth. Moksha is the goal of many Hindu practices.

mudra (MOO-druh) Hand gesture that expresses a specific energy or power, used in Hindu sculpture, worship, dance, and yoga. Mudras are also used in Buddhist sculpture. One of the best known mudras used in images of Vishnu and Buddha is the *abhaya mudra*, or gesture of fearlessness, in which the hand is extended with the palm facing forward, fingers together, and the thumb to the side.

murti (MUR-tee or MOOR-tee) "Form; manifestation, embodiment, personification." An image of a deity used during worship; may be a permanent image for installation in a temple, or a smaller, portable image that is housed in the temple and transported into the streets during special festivals. After a distinct ceremony in which priests awaken the deity that resides within it (not just one small part, but a small part representing the Universal Mind, murti are the means for making the essence of a deity manifest to the viewer, and help facilitate *darshan*.

Murtis range from aniconic (*avyakta*, "nonmanifest") such as an unornamented Shiva Linga, to *vyakta* "fully manifest," such as anthropomorphic images like the Ackland's *Goddess Parvati, Krishna,* or *Standing Vishnu*. The Ackland's Linga or Shiva Linga, or multifaced *mukha linga*, is considered partially manifest.

Parvati (PAR-vuh-tee) Goddess, also called "Daughter of the Mountain;" consort of Shiva; mother of Ganesha.

prasad (pra-SAHD) Food that is distributed among devotees after it is offered to a deity during puja; one form of receiving a god or goddess's blessing.

puja, pūjā (POO-zha) Worship in the form of an offering given to, or a ritual performed for, the veneration of a Hindu deity, god or goddess. *Pūjā* may include *arati*, chanting or singing, ringing bells, lighting incense, or presenting food, water, dyes, or flowers to a deity.

samsara (sahm-SAH-ruh) The cycle of a soul's birth, death, and rebirth.

Sanskrit The language of Aryan tribes who entered India in the second millennium BCE. Sanskrit is also applied as the name of the literature as a whole generated by the Aryans. Sanskrit is the ritual language of Hinduism, containing the laws of Brahman, in much the way a textbook might be said to hold the laws of physics.

shakti/śakti (SHAHK-tee) "Power," energy, or creative force of a deity, especially Shiva, personified as his wife and semi-independent of him.

Shiva, Siva, Shiv (shee-vuh, shih-vuh, shiv) Shiva is "the destroyer," the name and form of God who accomplishes endings in order that new beginnings may occur.

Upanishads (Uh-PAH-nish-ahds) (Sanskrit: lit. meaning: "to sit down near to") Meaning secret, mystical teaching, the term Upanishad is generally applied to the sacred texts of Hinduism which contain the culmination of what is called Vedic wisdom.

utsava murti (oot-sah-vuh mur-tee) The "form; manifestation, embodiment, personification" of a deity used to make the deity available to the public in a smaller, but much decorated and beautiful form. Some *utsava murti* have their own niches within a temple, and are attended to in the same way as a murti because they have been awakened or "consecrated" and hold the essence of that particular deity. At other times, the utsava murti is invested with the essence of the deity in a ceremony involving fire and water performed by priests from (in conjunction with) a murti of the same deity in the same temple. *Parvati* and *Dancing Krishna* in the Asian gallery are example of *utsava murti*.

Varaha (vuh-rah-huh) One of the first avatars or incarnations of Vishnu, the god known as the Preserver. Distinguished from other avatars by having the head of a boar and the body of a man. As an avatar of Vishnu, the *cakra*, club, and discus are his attributes. See Varaha in the Asian gallery.

Vishnu (vish-noo) Vishnu is the creator and protector, appearing on earth at intervals to rescue, restore order, and protect life.* *Krishna* and *Varaha* are two of the many avatars of Vishnu. Attributes include the abhaya mudra, four arms, discus, and cakra.

yakshi (yahk-shee) Dravidian (pre-Hindu faith) female nature deity existing before Hinduism later incorporated into Hindu art, particularly in sculpture.

Sources cited or used to prepare this glossary:

American Heritage Dictionary of the English Language, Third Edition. Houghton Mifflin Company, Boston, New York, 1996.

Five Faiths Project Curricular Resources Materials by Amanda Hughes. Ackland Art Museum, Chapel Hill, North Carolina, 2001.

Indian Mythology: An Encyclopedia of Myth and Legend by Jan Knappert. Diamond Books, Hammersmith, London, 1995.

Loving Gaṇeśa: Hinduism's Endearing Elephant-faced God by Satguru Sivaya Subramuniyaswami. Himalayan Academy, India, USA, 1996.

The Myths and Gods of India by Alain Danielou. Inner Traditions International, Ltd., Rochester, Vermont, 1991.

Talking about Judaism

Some Terms to Avoid	Why?	Suggested Substitutions
church	Refers to a building used for Christian worship, therefore an inappropriate term to denote places of worship for people of other faiths.	synagogue
Holy Bible	Refers specifically to Christian sacred texts. When used in the context of discussing other faiths, may too easily imply that other sacred texts are not considered holy. Use of specific names provides more accurate and neutral information: Bible (Christianity), Qur'an/Koran (Islam), Torah (Judaism), Dhammapada (Buddhism), Upanishads (Hinduism), etc.	Torah (Old) Testament Five Books of Moses Pentateuch
Names for G-d	In monotheistic religions, different names often reference specific attributes of G-d. "Judaism does not prohibit writing the Name of God per se; it prohibits only erasing or defacing a Name of God. However, observant Jews avoid writing any Name of God casually because of the risk that the written Name might later be defaced, obliterated or destroyed accidentally or by one who does not know better … Normally, [observant Jews] avoid writing the Name by substituting letters or syllables, for example, writing "G-d" instead of "God." www.Judaism-101.org, "Writing the name of G-d"	G-d [Some Jewish people say Hashem (hah-SHEM), which means "the Name"]

Some Terms to Avoid	Why?	Suggested Substitutions
priest minister imam	In Judaism, "priest" or "priesthood" refers to the hereditary class established during the lifetime of Moses. Priests were responsible for performing particular services and sacrifices in the first and second temple periods in Jerusalem. One high priest was given extra responsibilities. Although members of this priestly class still exist, there has been no high priest since the destruction of the second temple (70 CE). Many observant Jews believe that the next high priest will be identified when the Messiah comes and the third and final temple is built in Jerusalem.	None A congregational leader is called Rabbi (literally: teacher)

Glossary

In Hebrew, "ch" has a guttural sound (as in da*ch*sund), rather than a "tsh" sound (as in *ch*op).

ark A cupboard or chest in the front of the synagogue which holds the Torah scroll(s) and indicates the direction of prayer (toward Jerusalem, where the holy temples stood)

bar mitzvah (bahr MITTS-vuh) Literally: "son of the commandments;" the moment at which boys are publicly recognized as adults within the Jewish community, usually by taking a specific role during a prayer service that they couldn't take before now; their thirteenth birthday.

bat mitzvah (baht MITTS-vuh) Literally: "daughter of the commandments;" usually acknowledged at the age of twelve, sometimes thirteen, not necessarily publicly.

breastplate A metal pendant sometimes hung over the front of the covered Torah scroll; reminiscent of the breastplate traditionally worn by the high priest (see above) until the destruction of the second Jerusalem temple in 70 CE.

challah (CHAH-luh) Braided egg bread, traditionally eaten on Shabbat and holidays

Hanukkah or Chanukah (HAH-noo-kuh or CHAH-noo-kuh) The eight-day "Festival of Lights" called Hanukkah; celebrated to commemorate the successful revolt (c. 165 BCE), against foreign rulers who had invaded the land of Israel, occupied it, and destroyed the holy Jewish temple there. This victory was called a miracle for a couple of reasons. First, a small band of Jewish rebels was greatly outnumbered by the enemy, yet they won. More important, however, the victors were able to clean, repair, and rededicate the Temple because they found one small container of olive oil.

In order to rededicate their Temple to G-d, the Jews needed to re-light the menorah, a seven-branched candelabrum that was always kept burning in the Temple (as a sign of the eternal connection between G-d and the Jewish people). They found enough oil to burn for one day, and they knew it would take eight days to make more. The legend of the miracle of Hanukkah says that the one-day supply of oil burned for eight days and nights until more oil was ready.

hanukkiah (hah-noo-KEE-uh or chah-noo-KEE-uh) The eight-branch candelabrum used during the eight-day holiday of Hanukkah. A ninth branch stands higher than the rest and serves to light the other candles on successive nights of the holiday (one candle the first night, two the second, etc.)

havdalah (hahv-DUH-luh) Literally: "separation;" blessings that signify the end of Shabbat and holidays, separating the sacred (Shabbat) from the mundane (weekday). The blessings are said over a cup of wine (which marks the onset and end of every Sabbath and festival), a multiwicked candle (the strength of which symbolizes the strong fire associated with work, as opposed to the separate candles used on Shabbat for pleasure) and sweet smelling spices (which symbolize the sweetness of Shabbat, now departing).

hidur mitzvah (hih-DOOR mitts-VAH or HIH-door MITTS-vuh) Literally: "glorify the commandment;" refers to using beautiful objects to celebrate the beauty of Shabbat, a holiday or festival, or any other commandment (a mezuzah case or charity box, etc.)

kiddush (kih-DOOSH or KID-ush) Literally: "sanctification;" the blessing said over a cup of wine to sanctify the onset of Shabbat and festivals.

kosher (KO-shur) Literally: "fit;" conforming to or prepared in accordance with Jewish dietary laws.

Judaism A monotheistic religion in which there are three main streams – orthodox, conservative and reform – which vary in their organizational structure, tenets and practice.

menorah (meh-NOR-uh) Literally "from light;" the seven-branch candlestick that has been a symbol of Jewish identity since antiquity (symbolizing the seven days of creation); originally made for the tabernacle and ultimately for the temple in Jerusalem (not to be confused with hanukkiah, the nine-branch candelabrum used during the holiday of Chanukah which, just to confuse matters, is frequently called a menorah!).

mezuzah (meh-ZOOH-zuh) (oo as in poor) Literally: "doorpost;" a parchment scroll, containing a passage from the Torah and often placed in a container; affixed to the door post(s) of a home in order to fulfill the commandment to place the words of G-d on the door posts of one's house.

mitzvah (mits-VAH or MITS-vuh) Literally: "commandment;" in Judaism there are 613 which legislate legal, social, ethical, and ritual issues.

rabbi (RAB-eye) A learned man (or sometimes woman) who has received ordination; commonly denotes the spiritual leader of a congregation.

rimmonim (rih-mo-NIM) Literally: "pomegranates;" although they can take any shape, they are the finials that adorn the tops of the wooden Torah staves.

Shabbat (Shah-BAHT or SHAH-bus) Sabbath; the seventh day of the week – Saturday – on which no work is performed. It begins at sundown Friday evening and ends after sunset on Saturday.

siddur (see-DOOR or SID-ur) (door as in poor) Literally: "order;" prayer book.

synagogue Place of communal worship, study, and some social events; often called a temple in reform Jewish congregations.

tabernacle Temporary tent of meeting used by Jews from the time they left Egypt until the construction of the first temple in Jerusalem (c. 970 BCE).

tallis (tah-LEET or TAH-liss) Fringed prayer shawl worn by men (and, in some conservative and reform congregations, women) for morning prayers.

Torah Literally "teacher;" the fundamental teachings of Judaism; the parchment scroll on which these teachings are written.

yad (yahd) Literally: "hand;" a pointer used to help the Torah reader keep track of the place when reading from the scroll (which, because of its holiness to Jews, cannot be touched with the human hand).

kippah / yarmulke (kee-PAH / YAHR-ml-kuh) Skullcap; worn by men and boys (and some women) as a sign of humility before G-d. Some wear it always; others wear it only during prayer.

Sources cited or used to prepare this glossary:

American Heritage Dictionary, second edition, Houghton-Mifflin, 1985.

And I Shall Dwell Among Them: Historic Synagogues of the World by Neil Folberg. Aperture, 1995.

The Oxford Dictionary of World Religions, Oxford University Press, 1997.

Jewish Literacy by Rabbi Joseph Telushkin. William Morrow and Company, Inc., 1991.

Talking About Buddhism

Some Terms to Avoid	Why?	Suggested Substitutions
church synagogue Hindu temple	Places of worship specific to followers of non-Buddhist religions; therefore, inaccurate terms to denote places of worship and religious communities for Buddhists.	(Buddhist) temple sangha center
Bible Torah Vedas Upanishads Qur'an	The religious texts for Buddhism are distinct from those listed on the left because they reflect the words and/or teachings of Buddha instead of God, or the narratives of Gods or Goddesses, which the other texts do.	Pali Canon Sutras Great Treasury of Sutras (also called Taisho) Dhammapada
God god deity	In Buddhism, Buddha is an enlightened being. Buddhists believe that all sentient or thinking beings have the potential to become enlightened, so using these terms would not be accurate.	Buddha enlightened being; sacred being
minister imam rabbi priest	The terms on the left are specific to other faiths: minister (Christianity), imam (Islam), priest (Catholicism or Hinduism, depending upon context) and rabbi (Judaism).	monk lama Buddhist priest
Hinayana	The term "Hinayana" means "lesser vehicle" and was generated in relation to the term "Mahayana," which means "greater vehicle." As teachers, the idea of lesser and greater does not support objectivity among religions, which the term Theravada does suggest.	Theravada – *Literally, "the teachings of the elders"*

Glossary

Amitabha Buddha (ah-mee-tah-bah BOO-duh) In Mahayana Buddhism, the Buddha of the Western Paradise.

abhaya mudra (ab-HI-yuh MOO-druh) Hand gesture with palm facing toward viewer, meaning "fear not."

Bodhi Day (BOH-dee day) December 8, the day that Mahayana Buddhists commemorate the Buddha's enlightenment.

bodhisattva (boh-dee-saht-vuh) Literally, "bodhi" or wisdom, and "sattva" or essence. An enlightened being who, out of compassion, forgoes nirvana in order to save all sentient (conscious or feeling) beings. Particularly important in Mahayana Buddhism.

Buddha (BOO-duh or BOOH-duh) (booh as in book) Enlightened being; one who has achieved a state of perfect spiritual enlightenment. The historical Buddha (the one Buddha acknowledged by Theravada Buddhists) was born Siddhartha Gautama, an Indian prince, who later founded Buddhism. One of the three refuges/jewels. According to Mahayana tradition, Buddha was born on April 8 in 563 BCE in Lumbini Gardens (present-day Nepal) in the midst of flower blossoms (S.A. Nigosian, p. 324).

Buddhism Buddhism, like other religions, has many distinct streams that reflect distinct beliefs and/or practices, some of which include: Theravada and Mahayana (which includes Pure Land, Zen, and Vajrayana Buddhism)

dhamma, dharma (DAHM-muh, DAR-muh) Doctrine, or law; religion; particularly the teachings of the Buddha; also, virtue, or realization of the law; the universal truth; duty, goodness, rules, and truth (truth about the state and function of the world, truth about how to eliminate its evil tendencies, truth about its immutable spiritual potentiality). One of the three refuges/jewels.

Dhammapada (DAHM-muh-pah-duh) One of several sacred texts in Buddhism. Belongs to the second of the Three Baskets or Tripitaka (Tipitaka). Means "sayings of dhamma" or support "pada" of the literary corpus of canonical teaching "dhamma."

enlightenment State of total awareness (of dharma) that leads to entering nirvana.

karma (CAR-muh) A spiritual law that every cause has an effect.

lama (lah-mah) Acknowledged master, teacher, and leader of a given stream or school of Buddhism. A term used in the Tibetan tradition.

Mahayana (mah-hah-yah-nuh) Stream of Buddhism that accepts the existence of multiple Buddhas in the world, and multiple boddhisattvas who serve as intermediaries for practitioners. This form of Buddhism emerged somewhere between 150 BCE and 100 CE. Its distinctive features include the new emphasis given to compassion and the Bodhisattva ideal, the three-bodies of the Buddha doctrine, emptiness (or sunyata), and skill in means.

Mantra Repetition of a word or phrase that has spiritual significance. This can be a simple word such as "Buddha" or a whole phrase. One of the most widely known is the Tibetan *Om Mani Padme Hum* ("Hail to the Jewel of the Lotus").

Monk Person who renounces earthly goods and life to study Buddhist texts.

mudra (MOO-druh) Specific hand gesture(s) with a specific meaning in a given context; often used in the context of Hindu and Buddhist art.

nirvana (neer-vah-nuh) Literally "blowing out, extinguishing" (Sanskrit). The state of being that comes with enlightenment.

"This is peace, this is exquisite – the resolution of all fabrications, the relinquishment of all acquisitions, the ending of craving; dispassion; cessation ..." AN III.32

Nirvana Day Mahayana Buddhists commemorate Buddha's death and entry into nirvana on February 15. Some Buddhists also reserve this day for a memorial service for the deceased members of the family. Theravada Buddhists celebrate Nirvana Day based on a lunar calendar.

Pali Canon (pah-lee can-non) Buddhist sacred text that consists of three divisions, the *Tripitaka* (in Sanskrit) which literally means the "three baskets." Each of these baskets has different concerns. The first is the *Vinaya Pitaka*, the Book of Discipline, which includes the rules of monastic discipline given by the Buddha during his lifetime. The second division is the *Sutta Pitaka*, a collection of the Buddha's discourses. This has particular significance as it contains the essential teachings of the Buddha, accounts of his own enlightenment experience, and instructions on morality and meditation. The third division is the *Abhidhamma Pitaka* or Higher Teachings, which offers an intricate analysis of the nature of mental and physical existence.

Paranirvana (pair-uh-neer-vah-nuh) The transformation into nirvana at death for one who has attained enlightenment in this life. For this individual, there are no further rebirths, and a freeing from samsara.

Pure Land This stream of Buddhism emerged in China in about 400 CE and later spread to Japan. This school venerates the Buddha Amitabha who is said to reside in the Western Paradise (*Sukhavati*), or Pure Land.

samsara (sahm-SAH-ruh) The cycle of birth and death; Buddhists believe that this cycle is broken through enlightenment, resulting in nirvana.

sangha (SAN-guh) The Buddhist community of monks and nuns. The third of the three refuges/jewels.

Siddhartha Gautama (sih-DAR-tuh GOH-tah-mah) The birth name of the founder of Buddhism, later to be known as Buddha.

Sutras (SOO-truhs) Buddhist sacred texts that include three commonly used in Mahayana Buddhism: the Lotus Sutra, the Heart Sutra, and the Diamond Sutra.

Theravada (TAIR-uh-VAH-duh) "Thera" means "old" and "vada" means school; the word is sometimes translated as "The Teaching of the Elders." Its main scriptures are contained in the Pali canon, which was written down in the first century BCE. The emphasis in Theravada Buddhism is on perfecting one's life and thereby reaching enlightenment, often referred to as the "arhant ideal." There are Theravada communities throughout the world but this form of Buddhism is culturally dominant in Burma, Sri Lanka, and Thailand.

Three Jewels The Buddha, the Dharma, and the Sangha. Jewels, as precious stones, signify the extent to which these three essentials of Buddhism are valued.

urna (ER-nuh) Symbolic mark of Buddha located above and between his eyes. Sometimes, as in the image of Guan Yin in the Ackland, the urna is indicated by a depression in which a semi-precious stone would have been placed. In other works of art, it suggests a lone curl of hair.

ushnisha (oosh-neesh-uh) Symbolic mark of Buddha; a pronounced protuberance on his head that indicates the additional knowledge he gained in his enlightenment.

Wheel of the Law or Dharmacakra (DAR-muh CHA-kruh) The Buddha's first sermon at the deer park in Benares, which set the wheel of the law (dharmacakra) in motion

Other resources:

www.buddhanet.net/e-learning/5minbud.htm

Books related to Buddhism in the docent closet or on docent bookshelves at the Ackland:

Symbols of Tibetan Buddhism by Claude B. Levenson. Editions Assouline, 1996.

The Atlas of Sacred Places: Meeting Points of Heaven and Earth by James Harpur. Konecky and Konecky, 1994.

Childrens' books:

Buddha Stories by Demi. Henry and Co., 1997.

The Golden Goose King: A Tale Told by the Buddha, retold and illustrated by Judith Ernst. Parvardigan Press, 1995.

Silent Lotus by Jeanne M. Lee. Farrar, Strauss and Giroux, 1994.

Talking about Christianity

Some Terms to Avoid	Why?	Suggested Substitutions
Christ Lord	In Hebrew, "Messiah" or savior and deliverer of the Jews; a title derived from a Greek meaning "the Anointed One;" this term confirms belief in Jesus, the historical figure, as the Messiah – a belief not all visitors possess.	Jesus (the personal name given to the historical figure)
Savior	Title given to Jesus by Christians because they believe he brought salvation to humanity.	Jesus
Holy Bible	Implies that the sacred texts of other faiths (Qur'an/Koran (Islam), Torah (Judaism), Upanishads, Dhammapada, etc.) are not considered holy.	Bible Christian sacred text/book
The Trinity	Reference to "The Trinity" implies that the Christian idea of the Father (Mother), Son, and Holy Ghost is the only trinity that exists. Other faiths have different trinities that may be equally important in the context of those faiths.	The Christian Trinity the Trinity in Christianity
Holy Communion	"Holy Communion" suggests a level of sacredness that not all visitors may ascribe to or agree with; the terms "communion" and "eucharist" are religious terms, but do not imply a hierarchy in the way that the word "holy" does.	Communion Eucharist
Virgin Mary the Virgin Queen of Heaven Madonna	"Virgin Mary" is an honorific title for Mary, Jesus' mother. Many Christians believe in the virgin birth, but not all Christians. Using Mary's given, or personal, name is more neutral and does not impose belief in the virgin birth on non-Christians.	Mary – *Carefully consider your use of **Madonna**; include a definition of the term as you talk about a work of art, and clearly place the term in a Christian context*

Glossary

Annunciation — According to the birth narratives in the Bible, the angel Gabriel announced to the Mary the coming of Jesus. Many Christians celebrate this story on March 25.

Ascension — According to the sacred narratives of Jesus' life, death, and resurrection, forty days after his resurrection from the dead, he was taken up to heaven in a cloud.

Assumption — The Assumption is described in *The Golden Legend*, a popular sourcebook for artists, which was created from the apocryphal texts of the Bible. "And anon the soul came again to the body of Mary, and issued gloriously out of the tomb, and thus was received in the heavenly chamber, and a great company of angels with her."

attribute — An object(s) associated with and serving to identify a figure, often a saint. (In Jacopo Sellaio's *Madonna and Child with Saints Lucy, Sebastian, John the Baptist, and Catherine*, each saint may be recognized by their relative attributes: Lucy with her eyes and the knife in her throat, Sebastian with his arrows, John the Baptist with his staff and coat of fur/feathers, and Catherine with her crown and wheel of spikes.)

communion/Eucharist — A sacrament and the central act of worship in many Christian churches. During this ritual, bread and wine or grape juice are consecrated and consumed in remembrance of Jesus' death. Communion also refers to the consecrated elements of the Eucharist (bread and wine/grape juice), or the part of the mass or a liturgy in which the Eucharist is received. In the Ackland's collection, *The Mass of St. Gregory* and Sellaio's *Madonna and Child with Saints Lucy, Sebastian, John the Baptist, and Catherine*.

Crucifixion — In Roman times, a widely used form of capital punishment, reserved for baser criminals and slaves. In the Ackland's collection, see *The Repentant Thief*. In Christianity, the punishment of Jesus and eventual cause of his death, as prescribed by Pilate, the ruler of Jerusalem and judge of Jesus on earth. The Crucifixion of Jesus is a central image in Christian art and the visual focus of Christian contemplation. Many Christians believe that by sacrificing himself on the cross, Jesus brought about the possibility of humanity's redemption, or delivery from the original sin of Adam, which all humanity inherited. The image of the cross paired with Jesus' body was first used in the sixth century; prior to that the cross was more often used alone or was represented symbolically with a lamb juxtaposed with a cross. In the Ackland's collection, see *The Crucifixion of Christ*.

Dormition — From *dormir*, French for "to sleep." According to one tradition, prior to the Counter-Reformation Mary was not considered dead but only sleeping during the three days until her Assumption, in which she was carried body and soul directly to heaven. *The Golden Legend*, an apocryphal Christian text, tells how an angel caused the twelve apostles of Jesus, who were scattered over the world, to be caught up in a cloud and borne to Mary's door. Many scenes show Mary's body on a couch, or bier, or on a canopied bed in a typical domestic interior. She may be still living and holding a lighted candle, in accordance with an old custom of putting a candle in the hands of a dying person, its light a symbol of the Christian faith. The apostles stand round. The Counter-Reformation taught that Mary died without pain, death taking her unaware. In the Ackland's collection, the German sculpture *The Dormition of the Virgin* depicts Mary in a bed surrounded by the Apostles with their respective attributes.

IHS These letters are the first three letters *Ihsus*, *Ihcuc*, the name of Jesus in Greek. Often misinterpreted as an abbreviation of the Latin phrase *Iesus Hominum Salvator* (Jesus Savior of Men)

INRI These represent the four initial letters of the Latin words *"Iesus Nazarenus Rex Iudaeorum."* In John 19:19-20 of the Bible, the inscription Pilate wrote to be fastened to the cross, meaning "Jesus of Nazareth King of the Jews."

Instruments of the Passion Tools used by soldiers to inflict pain upon Jesus during the Passion, including a crown of thorns, nails, lance, a whip, a spear, a staff with a sponge soaked in vinegar. In the Ackland's collection, see the sculpture *Angel with Instruments of the Passion* by Roccatigliata.

Jesus The historical name for the prophet acknowledged as such by some faiths, and considered the Messiah and Savior by Christians.

Madonna Obsolete Italian expression, technically meaning "lady of the house." Historically and currently used as another term for Mary, mother of Jesus, in her maternal role.

Mary Personal name for Jesus' mother; several honorific names were given to Mary, including Queen of Heaven, the Virgin, Virgin Mary, and Madonna.

Passion Term used to refer to the final events in the life and death of Jesus as recorded in the Gospels of the New Testament. The full series of scenes generally begins with the "Entry into Jerusalem" and may end with the "Descent of the Holy Ghost" at Pentecost; the number of episodes varies considerably and sometimes ends with the Entombment or Ascension. In the Ackland's collection, the Spanish sculpture *Mater Dolarosa* or *Sorrowing Virgin*, was most likely carried in the streets during the week before Easter, during which plays reenacting the Passion and parades of sculptures acknowledged the different religious figures associated with the Passion.

Queen of Heaven Honorific title given to Mary, most often in the Catholic Church.

Resurrection The Christian belief that Jesus rose from the dead on the third day after his death; considered one of the fundamental tenets of the Christian faith.

sacrament — A visible form of invisible grace. In the Eastern, Roman Catholic, and some other Eastern Christian churches, any of the traditional seven rites that were instituted by Jesus and recorded in the New Testament and that confer sanctifying grace. In most other Western Christian churches, the two rites, Baptism and the Eucharist, that were instituted by Jesus to confer sanctifying grace. Also refers to the Eucharist and the consecrated elements of the Eucharist, especially the bread or the host.

stigmata — Marks or sores corresponding to or resembling the crucifixion wounds of Jesus; in the Ackland's collection, *St. Francis Receiving the Stigmata* by Vincente Carducho (see page 28).

transubstantiation — The belief held by some Christians that when partaking of bread and wine during communion or the Eucharist, that one is partaking of the actual body and blood of Christ.

Sources cited or used to prepare this glossary:

Dictionary of Subjects and Symbols in Art by James Hall. Waterview Press, second edition, 2007.

Signs & Symbols in Christian Art by George Ferguson. Oxford University Press, London, Oxford, New York; 1954.

The Golden Legend of Jacobus de Voragine by Granger Ryan and Helmut Ripperger. Longmans, Green and Co., Inc.; 1941; renewed 1969.

The American Heritage Dictionary of the English Language, third edition, Houghton Mifflin Company, Boston and New York; 1996.

Talking about Islam

Some Terms to Avoid	Why?	Suggested Substitutions
church synagogue temple	Places of communal worship, study, and some social events specific to followers of other religions, therefore an inaccurate term to denote a place of communal worship, study, and some social events for Muslims.	mosque masjid
Holy Bible	This term applies exclusively to the sacred texts of the Christian tradition.	Qur'an
priest minister pastor rabbi	These terms refer to spiritual leaders in other faiths who have received ordination; there is no parallel in Islam.	A congregational leader is called an Imam, but only such when leading prayer (any upstanding member of the community can serve as an Imam)

Glossary

Allah (ah-LAH) The Arabic word for "god;" when capitalized, it is the name of the one true God in Islam.

Eid (eed) Literally: "festival;" two major festivals are Eid al Fitr (the feast of fast-breaking at the end of Ramadan) and Eid al Adha (the feast of sacrifice, commemorating Ibrahim's [Abraham's] sacrifice of his son).

Five Pillars of Islam The basic tenets of Islam, comprised of:

- Confession of faith in the one true God and in his prophet, Muhammad
- Prayer five times each day, at prescribed times (salaat)
- Pilgrimage to Makkah (hajj)
- Observance of Ramadan including fasting and prayer
- Charity (zakat)

Hadith (hah-DEET) Literally: "report" or "account;" these are considered to be reliable transmitted reports of the sayings and acts of the Prophet Muhammad; a sacred text for Muslims.

hilya (HILL-yuh) A calligraphic portrait of the Prophet Muhammad based on first-hand accounts of both his physical traits and personal qualities.

Hajj (hah-dj) The pilgrimage to Makkah, to be undertaken by all Muslims (if at all possible) once during their lifetime; one of the Five Pillars of Islam.

Hijra (HIDJ-ruh) Muhammad's journey from Makkah to Medina; also the year from which the Islamic calendar is counted.

imam (ee-MOM) A religious leader or mosque official.

Islam (iss-LAHM) A monotheistic religion (from the Arabic, meaning "surrender" or "submission" to Allah); in Islam there are three main streams or traditions – Shiite, Sunni, and Sufi – which vary in organizational structure, tenets, and practice.

Kaaba (KAH-buh) The black stone cube-like structure in Makkah (in present-day Saudi Arabia) which Muslims face during prayer, and which is the destination of hajj; in Islam, considered the spiritual and geographical center of the world.

Khadija (kah-DEE-juh) Wife of Muhammad, considered to be the first Muslim.

Makkah (also Mecca) Birthplace of Muhammad and location of the Kaaba.

masjid (MAHS-jid) Arabic word for mosque.

Medina (meh-DEE-nuh) A sacred site for Muslims because it was a refuge for the Prophet after he fled (from Makkah) and where he established the first community of Islam.

mihrab (MIH-rob) The niche in a mosque that indicates the direction for prayer (toward Makkah); its form may also be discerned as decoration on prayer rugs.

mosque A building used by Muslims for communal prayer, instruction, and some social events; also called a masjid.

Muhammad (moo-HAH-mud) For Muslims, the last or final of Allah's prophets; referred to by Muslims as the Prophet or the Prophet Muhammad.

Muslim (MOOS-lim) Literally: "submitter." A Muslim is one who has surrendered to Allah.

Qur'an (koor-ON) Literally: "recitation;" the sacred text of Islam, which Muslims believe to be the literal word of Allah as revealed to the Prophet by the angel Gabriel and written down by his followers.

Ramadan (RAH-mah-dahn) The annual month of fasting in the Muslim calendar (daily, from sunrise to sunset) that commemorates the time during which the Qur'an was revealed to Muhammad by the angel Gabriel (Because Muslims, like Jews, follow a lunar calendar, the month of Ramadan may occur on different dates each year according to the Julian calendar.); one of the Five Pillars of Islam.

salaat (sah-LOT) The act of prayer or worship performed five times each day, and at other prescribed times; one of the Five Pillars of Islam.

Shiism (SHEE-ism) Tenets, organizational structure, and practice followed by about 10-15% of all Muslims (see Islam); followers are called Shiite.

Sufism (SOO-fism) A general term for the mystical path in Islam; one who follows this path is called a Sufi.

Sunna (SOON-uh) Tenets, organizational structure, and practice followed by the majority of Muslims (see Islam); followers are called Sunni; another sacred text for many Muslims.

zakat (zah-KAHT) Literally: "growth, purification;" extends to mean setting aside a portion of one's income for charity; one of the Five Pillars of Islam.

Sources cited or used to prepare this glossary:

The Oxford Dictionary of World Religions, Oxford University Press; 1997.

The World's Religions, Our Great Wisdom Traditions by Huston Smith. HarperOne Publishers; 1991 (revised).

FIVE FAITHS CHART

	Hinduism	Judaism	
Central Figures depicted in art	Shiva Vishnu Parvati others	None (human images are prohibited in ritual art)	
Sacred Text(s)	Vedas Upanishads	Torah Five Books of Moses	
Original Language of Sacred Text(s)	Sanskrit	Hebrew Aramaic	
Communal Worship:			
Where	Temple	Synagogue	
When	Holidays (and other times)	Sabbath (Saturdays), Holidays (and other times)	

TIMELINE

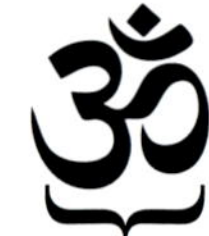

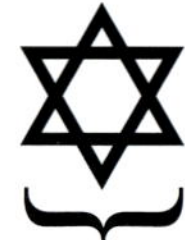

5000 BCE — 4000 BCE — 3000 BCE — 2000 BCE

	Buddhism	Christianity	Islam
	The Buddha Bodhisattvas	God Mary Jesus Saints	None (human images are prohibited in ritual art)
	Canons (written records of the Buddha's teachings)	Bible (Old and New Testaments)	Qur'an Hadith
	Pali Sanskrit	Latin (Catholic Church translated texts from Hebrew, Aramaic, and Greek)	Arabic
	Temple	Church Cathedral	Masjid Mosque
	Holidays (usually related to events in the Buddha's life, and other times)	Sundays, Holidays (and other times)	Fridays, Holidays (and other times)

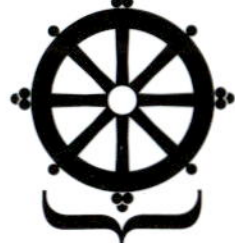
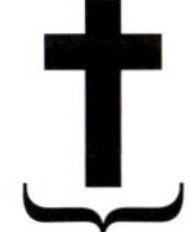
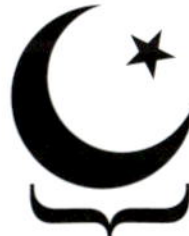

1000 BCE 0 1000 CE 2000 CE

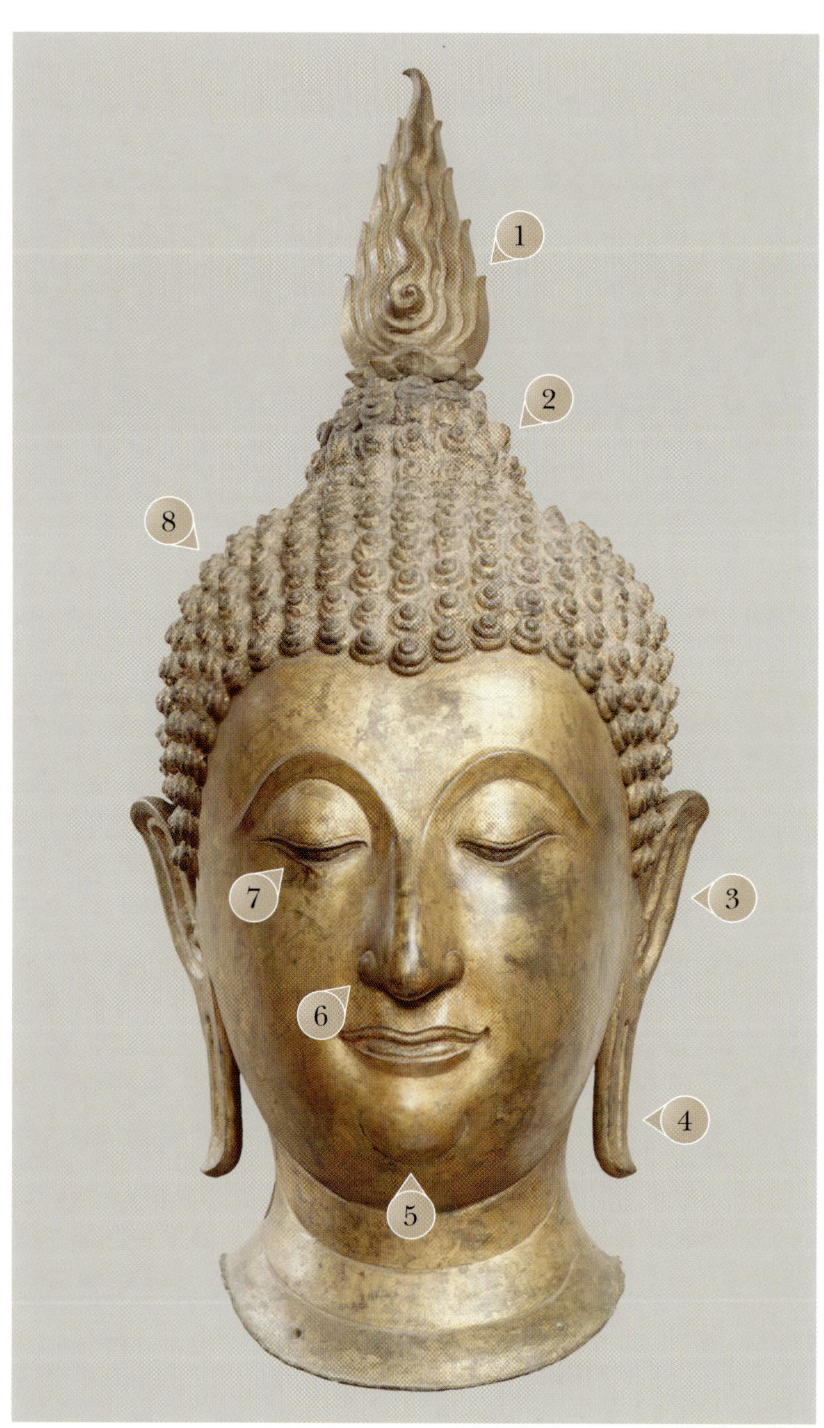

HEAD OF THE BUDDHA
Unknown
Thai, 13-15th century; gilt bronze.
Ackland Fund, 91.2. (detail)

OBJECT STUDY 1
HEAD OF THE BUDDHA

This head of the Buddha was originally part of a large seated or standing Buddha. Thai artists pay close attention to human proportion, which helps to explain the realistic and lively appearance of this piece. When the Buddha is represented in his human body, he is depicted carefully, with attention paid to the auspicious signs listed in the *Pali Canon*, but also with an eye to showing that he was not a god, but a man.

The Buddha is also represented symbolically, by an eight-spoken wheel in some art objects. Many of the same attributes surround the wheel as surround the image of the man. He is often seen with lotus flowers nearby. His followers are often in attendance, particularly in relief sculptures.

How does the artist convey the Buddha's compassion in this piece? Carefully consider the facial expression of the Buddha. What might such an image suggest about the nature of meditation?

The *Pali Canon* lists 32 auspicious signs of the Buddha. Several can be seen in this piece.

1 *The flame:* his enlightenment
2 *The bulge on his head:* a sign of extra knowledge
3 *Large ears:* a sign of his listening well to the concerns of life
4 *Long earlobes:* a sign of his royal lineage
5 *A chin like a lime,* and *golden skin*
6 *A parrot nose*
7 The Buddha's eyes are not closed. He is aware of his surroundings. The general expression on his face is one of kindness and compassion.
8 There are differing accounts as to the covering of the Buddha's head. In India, tradition says that when the Buddha shaved his head as a sign of his renunciation, the hair grew back in tight curls. In Japan, the story says that while he was seated in meditation, the sun beat down upon his shaved head. First the fish and then frogs tried to offer him covering from the sun. They could not. But snails came and lined up on his head to keep it covered from the sun during the day and the cold at night.

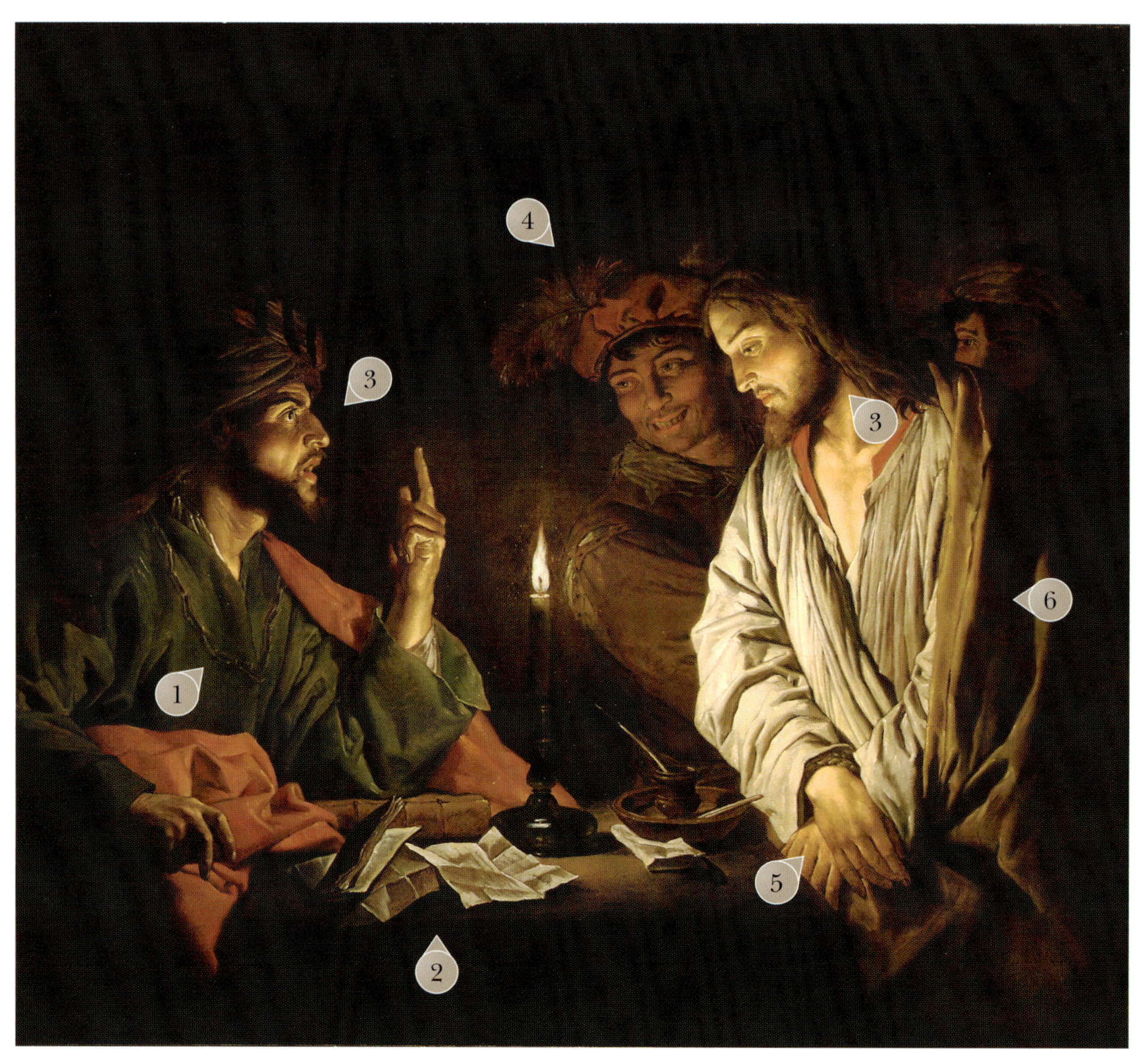

CHRIST BEFORE CAIAPHAS
Follower of Matthias Stom
Dutch, active in Italy, 1600-after 1652, early 1630s; oil on canvas. Ackland Fund. 79.58.1.

OBJECT STUDY 2
CHRIST BEFORE CAIAPHAS

Not all works of art from the Christian tradition were intended for use in religious settings. In the 17th century, it was common for wealthy individuals to commission artists to create large paintings for display in their homes. The pieces were far more dramatic, hyperbolic, and emotional than those created in previous centuries. Individuals used these pieces as a way of expressing their own faith, and also as a way of reminding themselves and their families of the stories of the Bible, with a particular focus on the life of Jesus.

These paintings were intended to draw the viewer into the drama and mystery of the life of Jesus. By focusing on his unique life, Christians deepened their commitment to the church and their faith. The artist depicts the characters in this story in a naturalistic world and in what the artist believed to be the dress of the time and culture in which Jesus lived.

1 Note how Caiaphas is dressed. He is wearing far more elaborate clothing, indicating a higher rank in society.
2 He leans on a book and has papers around him. These objects indicate that he is educated, and understands the rules and regulations of his culture.
3 Note the different facial expressions of the characters in this painting. What emotions are represented? How might Christians see this painting as inspirational? What does Jesus' expression suggest about faith in the face of difficulty?
4 The artist is showing a moment within the story, rather than telling it symbolically. The story is recorded in Matthew 26:57-67. Using this text, who might the man in the back might be?
5 Jesus' hands are bound, but relaxed. He appears to be looking directly at the candle. The candle is central to the image; fire, a natural phenomenon, is used to suggest the spiritual light of the world.
6 The artist establishes Jesus as the central character of this image by dressing him in nearly white garments and by casting the greatest amount of light on his face and body.

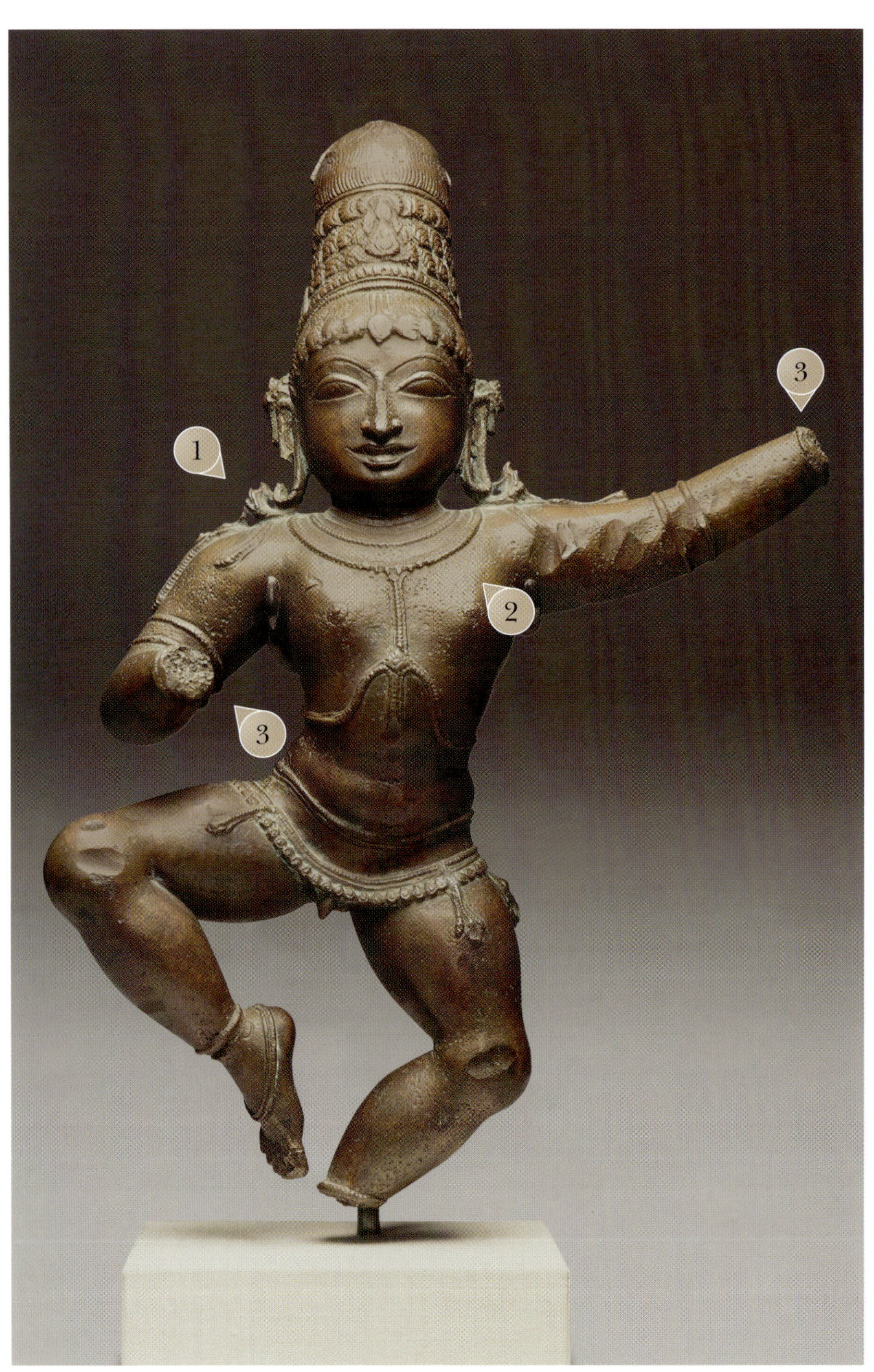

DANCING KRISHNA
Unknown
South Indian, Vijayanagar, late 12th or early 13th century; bronze. Gift of Clara T. and Gilbert J. Yager in honor of Charles Millard (Museum Director 1986-1993), 97.8.

OBJECT STUDY 3
DANCING KRISHNA

Krishna has attracted many devotees within Hinduism. He is one of the avatars of Vishnu. Krishna's stories focus on love. He was a loved infant, a loved child, a loved man, and a beloved God. He exemplified ideals of parental, familial, erotic, and devotional love.

The artist's name does not appear anywhere on the piece (as is common in Hindu art) because the creation of the sculpture was seen as an act of devotion and no attention should be called to its manufacture.

Within the Hindu tradition, devotees and the spiritual leaders of the community must offer true *puja*, or acts of devotion, to the sculpture, in order that the sculpture may become a true vessel for divinity. They offer prayers, clothing, light, and food to the God. There is an exchange of spiritual energy between the God and the devotee through the sculpture. When these ritual offerings are complete, the artist opens the eyes of the god and the spiritual leader aids in the first breath.

Krishna and The Butter Pot

Thousands of years ago in India, villagers of Gokul would nap in the afternoon because of the heat. One boy, Krishna, loved butter and while everyone slept he crept up to their butter pots and ate his fill. When his mother discovered this, she tied him to a fence post. As the villagers watched, the more she tightened the rope, the more it loosened, and a golden glow appeared around his head. When his mother heard the gasps of the people, she looked the boy in the eye, and saw a halo of light around his head. Everyone realized that Krishna was blessed, and from that day on set out crocks of butter just for him.

1. As a freestanding sculpture, this dancing Krishna would have been found within a Hindu temple. On holy days, it would have been dressed and carried through the streets in procession. This is done to remind followers that the Gods and Goddesses are available to people and willing to come to their aid.
2. The bronze reflects light, suggesting the glow of divinity.
3. Both hands on this sculpture are broken off. A damaged sculpture cannot be used in rituals.

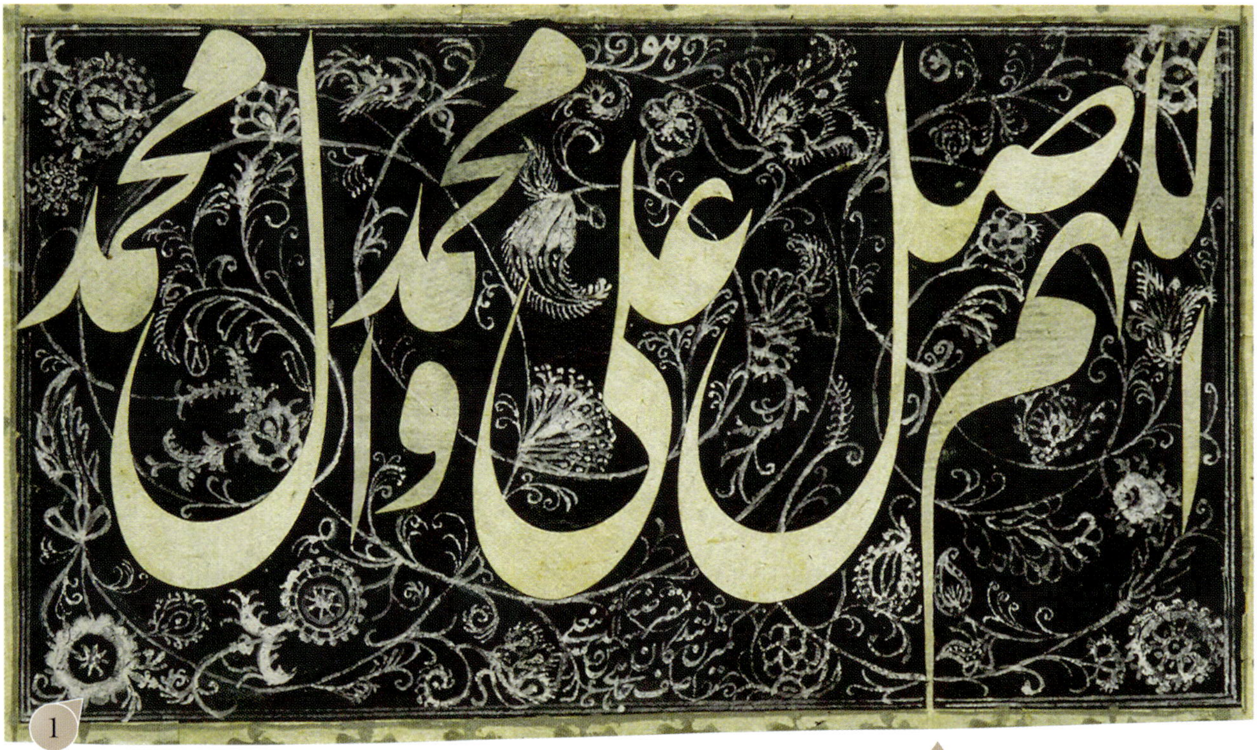

PANEL OF CALLIGRAPHY
Attributed to Shamsuddin Asaf Jahi
Indian, Deccan, Hyderabad; paper appliqué and white opaque watercolor on dark blue paper. Gift of Charles Millard. 91.75.

OBJECT STUDY 4
PANEL OF CALLIGRAPHY

According to the Qur'an Arabic is the language in which the angel Gabriel spoke to Muhammad, revealing the message of Allah. The letterforms of Arabic play a significant role in Islamic art. The letterforms themselves are considered to be uniquely able to contain Allah's teachings, and have the capacity to communicate sacred truths.

For Muslims, merely looking at the forms is an act of devotion. Speaking the words, even without full understanding, may also be employed as a religious practice and discipline.

1 In this piece, the letterforms have been placed on a background of flowers and vines. The garden imagery is considered to be a symbol of paradise.
2 While Islamic art does not contain images of God or of the prophet Muhammad, because idolatry is forbidden, it is common to see the name of God and the name of the prophet. The calligraphy says: "God bless Muhammad, and the family of Muhammad."

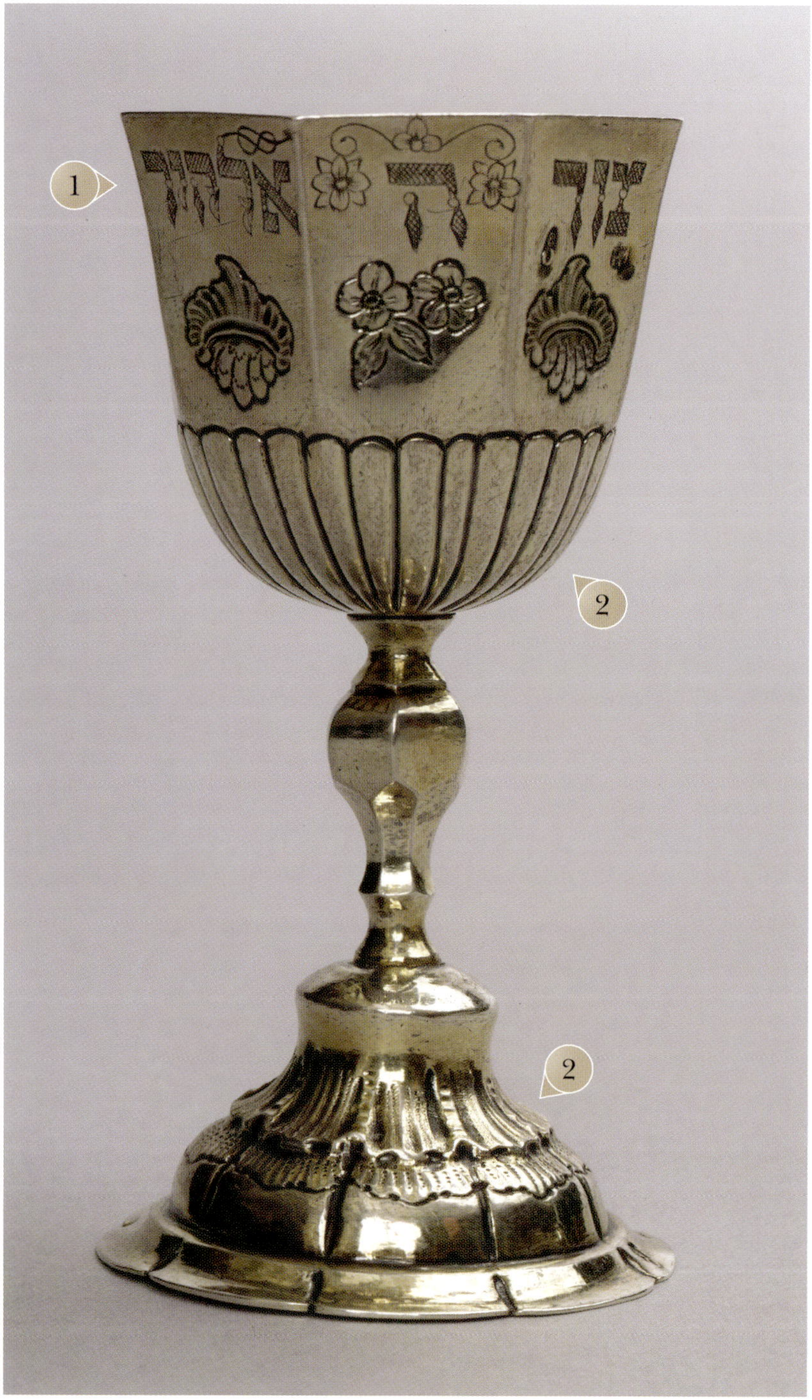

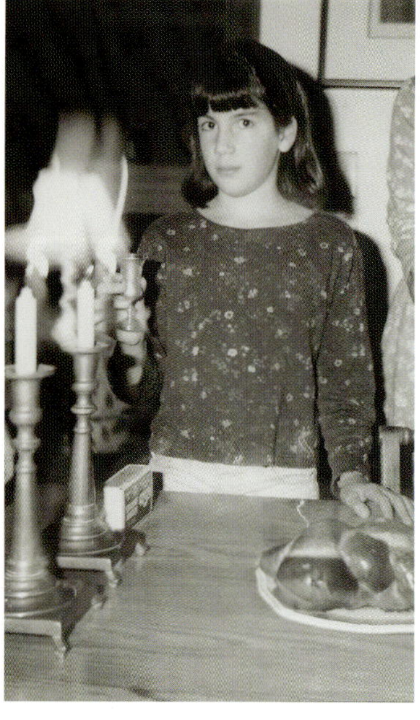

Visions of Faith brought images of private rituals and religious practices into our consideration of works in the Ackland Collection.

Here one can see a daughter holding a kiddush cup during the Shabbat meal.

KIDDUSH CUP
Hieronymus Mittnacht
German (active in Augsburg), died 1769: 1759-1761; silver-gilt, engraved and chased. The William A. Whitaker Foundation Art Fund, 99.21.

OBJECT STUDY 5
KIDDUSH CUP

The *Kiddush Cup* is used in the family ritual of the Shabbat (or Sabbath) meal. Kiddush literally means "blessing." Wine is poured into the cup and a prayer of blessing is spoken. The Shabbat meal is the central ritual within Jewish life. The meal is shared in the home on Friday evening and is considered to be as holy a ritual as those celebrated in the temple or synagogue. During the meal, many prayers are spoken and stories told which recount aspects of Jewish history in order to remind practicing Jews of the interventions of God in their common history. It is also considered to be a time of instruction, when children may learn about their faith and heritage. By refraining from activities which can be defined as "work" from sundown on Friday to sunset on Saturday, many Jews use the time to be with their families, to read the Torah or other Jewish texts, and to celebrate Jewish life. Shabbat is considered a joyous time in the life of a Jewish family.

1 On each side of the cup the artist engraved words in Hebrew. The text reads from right to left and says: "Guard the Sabbath day and keep it holy as the Lord your God has commanded you." This text comes from the Torah, Exodus 20:8. As part of their religious training, many Jewish young people learn to read, write, and speak Hebrew.
2 The cup is decorated with a floral motif with symmetrical lines in the cup and base.

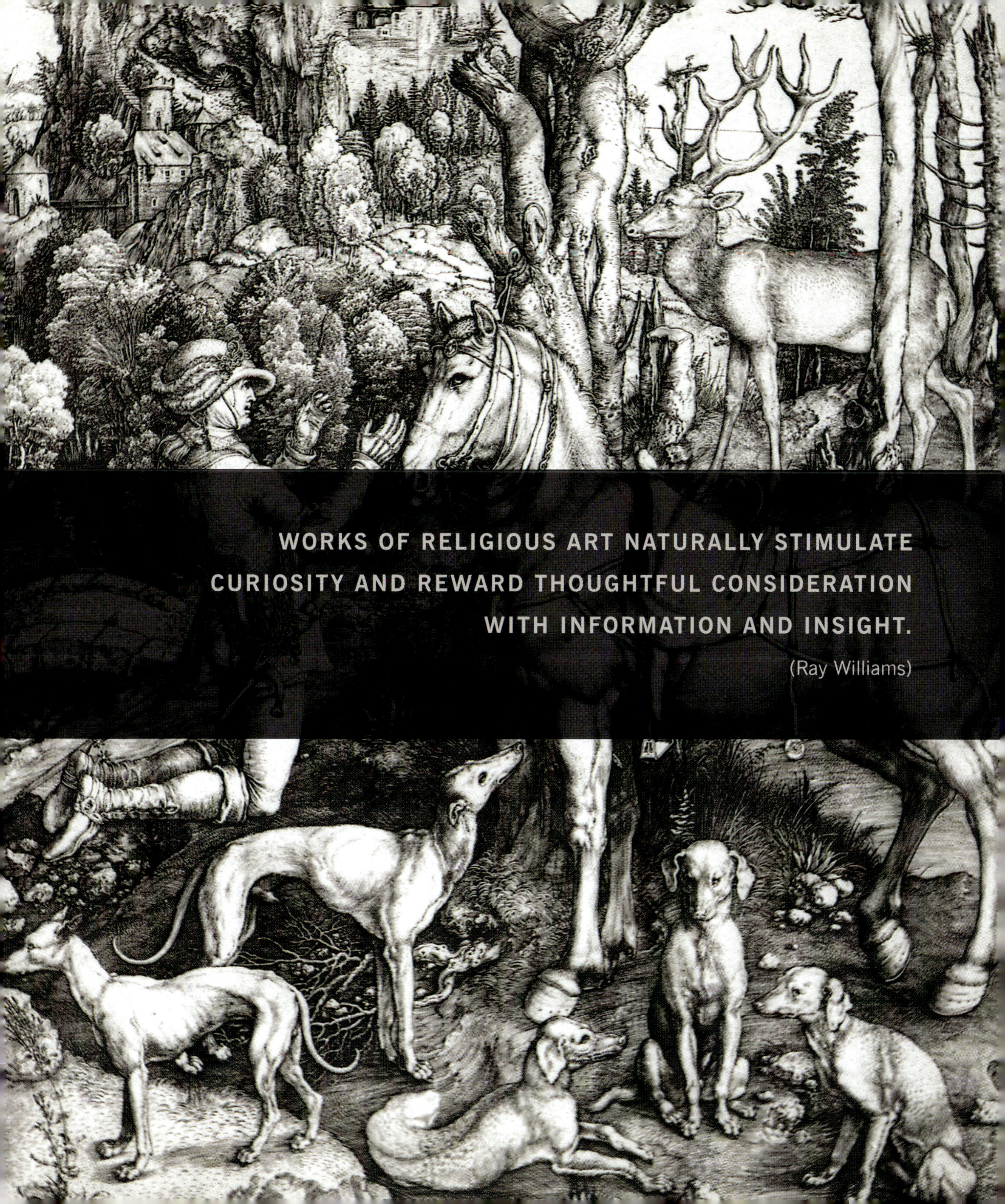

WORKS OF RELIGIOUS ART NATURALLY STIMULATE CURIOSITY AND REWARD THOUGHTFUL CONSIDERATION WITH INFORMATION AND INSIGHT.

(Ray Williams)

ST. EUSTACE
Albrecht Dürer
German, born 1471-1528, about 1501; engraving. Gift of Commander and Mrs. L.E. Stahl in memory of Charles Kistler. (detail)

One Hundred Words or More

As a final exercise, we asked participants to offer us a summary of their thoughts. Having worked on labels with a two hundred word limit, we invited them to the challenge of only one hundred words. Most found it impossible to comply. The following are the participants' contributions. We include them because they offer one last glimpse of the perspectives these participants brought to each conversation.

Submitted by Carolyn Allmendinger

Objects with sacred content have the greatest potential to increase understanding about faith practices when they are used as starting points for discussion. As concrete, physical things they can function as historical or cultural products that when interrogated yield information about the people who made and used them. As documents, they can provide evidence to support or interrupt assumptions or lines of questioning about beliefs, practices, and practitioners.

As objects that communicate principally through visual means, they provide the best, most reliable interpretations when paired with other tools: people or labels that sensitively frame questions, written references to additional resources, and an overt acknowledgment that no object will answer all relevant questions.

Submitted by Yaakov Ariel

Having participated in the Five Faiths Colloquia, and having read the transcripts and notes, and reflected on the ideas expressed by the participants, my main conclusion is that museums can play a major role in promoting an atmosphere of tolerance towards religious faiths and practices. The very act of presenting the symbols, art, and religious objects of the various faiths in a museum setting in a manner that allows the audience to learn and interact, promotes interest, respect, and tolerance towards those traditions. Visitors then see the religious traditions as legitimate, if not compelling, and feel closer to them, as they have observed and studied them in a friendly and respectful setting.

Submitted by Leslie Balkany

Why use religious objects to promote tolerance and understanding of different faiths?

- Objects themselves are effective discussion starters. By their very nature, they raise questions both within and between faith traditions.
- Contextual information about objects (visual, written, and tactile if possible) can guide viewers' looking, and increase understanding, by anticipating questions and answering them.
- Objects provide opportunities to consider different voices, as well as to layer visual and verbal information.

But using, or trying to use, ritual objects also carries limitations.

- Religious traditions are richer than what a small selection of works can show.
- Deciding what to include and what to leave out – in installations, written material, discussion in the galleries – is self-limiting.
- Galleries too often lack sufficient space to exhibit objects, and interpretive material, to best advantage.
- Finally, in a guided group experience, visitors' previous knowledge and experience that can enrich the discussion aren't always present.

Discovery:

It is possible, often preferable, to create meaningful display and interpretive material by committee; it just takes a lot of time and investment!

Submitted by Jerry Bolas

The potential to convey both personal and collective religious experience through visual expression to those conversant with the sacred language is unlimited; art can lead to enlightenment (sacred experience). For "foreigners" outside the sacred language, two intertwined paths may lead to appreciation, and beyond, to enlightenment. One path: study the beliefs, values, and rules of a faith tradition and open the heart and mind to the wisdom of the vast "other" outside one's immediate experience. The other path proceeds by analogies – usually imperfect and often wrong – to appreciate broader patterns of human experience conveyed through sacred artistic forms.

Submitted by Mark Bozzuti-Jones

From the dawn of human consciousness human beings have sought to express, verbally and artistically, their experience of the Infinite and Unknowable Reality. Verbal and visual representations of the sacred serve as means of meaning-making for both the artist/speaker and the observer/hearer. However, the task of meaning-making for each involves intrinsic limitations that need to be owned and acknowledged. Mutual understanding and openness to other religious traditions happen when we recognize the limitations of all our representations/interpretations of the Divine. The present day challenge, for followers of all religious traditions, is to guard against believing that what is created or interpreted represents conclusive and ultimate meaning.

Submitted by Patrice Brodeur

The "sacred" is always eminently relational, that is, in relation to a particular power dynamic resulting from the intersection of five particulars: the nature of the sacred object; its history; its spatial location (which delimits its possible functions); its multiple stakeholders (those who claim some form of ownership); and its multiple interpretations. The relationality of any sacred object is not only between its different forms/contents and functions; it exists also between "owners" and "users" who compete over whose privileged modes and reasons for relating to the sacred object must be the dominant interpretation presented in a museum.

Submitted by David Carr

Every human being is an incomplete, impermanent artifact of faith and experience, sustaining in one life the cumulative traces of reflection and challenge over time. Each of us is unfinished differently from all others, and continuously capable of new questions, new lessons, and new experiences. Every artifact similarly shows the traces of a human engagement with skill, passion, and mystery, intended to fill the incompleteness of the world and overcome human impermanence in it. But these artifacts never yield fully to our presence. Among faith objects, we want to feel continuous with the traces that mark other lives, while confirming the solitary uniqueness of our own. We want to understand the sources and consequences of believing. We hope for a journey beyond the usual dimensions of experience. We reflect on the meanings of possible but unproven relationships with an invisible divinity.

Submitted by Terrence E. Dempsey, S.J.

A Safe Place

Our discussions at the Ackland Art Museum over these past three years could not have been more timely. At no other period in our history, both national and international, have the conversations and often the arguments about the various religious traditions been so pervasive and intense. Out of these verbal exchanges have come both light and a great deal of heat. The museums can play a crucial role now of offering an understanding of many faith traditions in a "safe place," as Shabbir Mansuri stated in 2002.

This museum "safe place," while showing an informed and respectful understanding of both the artifacts and the faith traditions they represent, will remain a "safe place" only if it stays free of any form of advocacy. Few other institutions are so strategically situated to be "safe places." Because of its traditional status within communities, the museum has the authority to provide a respected forum to gather artists, theologians, art historians, museum professionals, and others whose voices can make significant contributions to the present conversation. Museums with affiliations to institutions of higher education are particularly well positioned as they already have a strong educational component already built into their *raison d'être.*

Submitted by Mimi G. Gates

The Power of the Sacred

In our age of global conflict, how can museums empower sacred images to offer not only aesthetic delight and wonder but also cultural reconciliation and interfaith dialogue? Museums have unexplored potential as places to experience the other in a non-proselytizing way that respects Americans' right to freedom of religion. When sacred images are removed from their ritual settings and transported to museums, they require innovative approaches to communicate to the uninitiated visitor the profound emotional power they possess in their original context. Words convey knowledge; dynamic visual experience (video, audio, etc.) contextualizes sacred images, engaging the emotions as well as the mind.

Submitted by Charles Haynes

Taking Religion Seriously in Museums

As educational institutions, museums have an academic and civic responsibility to take religion seriously when displaying (and teaching about) sacred objects and images. This means, first and foremost, allowing faith traditions to speak for themselves in the descriptions of the object or image and, to the extent feasible, creating settings that reflect sensitivity to the religious meaning and significance of the object or image. Including voices from within faith communities is vital for helping the viewer to understand religions from the inside.

The museum itself, however, should remain neutral and fair toward religion. Voices from within should be balanced by careful attention to voices from without – particularly the best available scholarship – in order to provide linguistic, historical, and cultural contexts for interpreting religious objects and images.

Submitted by Amanda Millay Hughes

In a recent edition of the Phi Beta Kappa newsletter, a letter to the editor included the following benefits of a liberal arts education:

- Breadth of perspective with concomitant depth of focus
- Celebration of diversity with appreciation for shared humanity

- Commitment to clarity and precision, with tolerance for uncertainty and ambiguity.

These may help establish standards for the potential of works of art with sacred content to communicate in the galleries. The inclusion of multiple voices and perspectives (scholars, faith leaders, practitioners, and artists) ensures both perspective and depth of focus – literally, encouraging visitors to look closely and to look again. By implementing parallel interpretive practices, we encourage a celebration of the diversity within and across the traditions. Thematic approaches to religious practices suggested by works of art may also suggest our shared humanity. Finally, by upholding the rigorous standards of the museum culture – principally artistic excellence and curatorial accuracy, we encourage visitors to strive for clarity and precision as well. The real challenge lies in developing means to express the limits of our visual and verbal representations. Our own tolerance of uncertainty and ambiguity could be expressed in open-ended questioning strategies and the presentation of what we don't know about particular works of art, as well as what we do.

Submitted by Eugene Korn

Expression of religious intuitions, ideas, and experiences entails paradox: The Divine is Infinite, but human expression is trapped in finitude; the object of religious awareness is cosmic, yet sacred experience is private and subjective. Religious expression is condemned to inadequacy.

How much more complex is exhibiting religion via human artifacts and representation. Exhibitors (curators?) face yet another central dilemma: Should an exhibit intimate spiritual experience and draw the visitor into the devotional life of the believer, or only present sacred objects, qua objects, i.e., the focus of analysis for an outside observer? Can a museum achieve both via dialectical balance? The answers will influence the ambience, choice, and placement of objects, and signing of religious exhibitions.

Submitted by Vivian Mann

The Five Faiths Project: Summing Up

In our meetings over the last three years, we have learned not to generalize about all five faiths. The concepts of belief and the sacred may be so different as to elude equivalency, although it is probably easier to find common ground between Judaism and the two religions that developed from it, Christianity and Islam.

The museum presentation of faith-based objects must demonstrate both cognizance of their relationship to the artistic tradition in which they were created, and their meaning within the religion. If a religious context is stresses – to the extent that the ensemble requires ceremonies of sanctification – then viewers who are believers and others may adopt a worshipful, rather than an aesthetic response. An exhibition of religious art within an art museum can become too literal, turning into an anthropological exercise, which may not have been the intent of the curators.

Submitted by Shabbir Mansuri

The colloquy has provided an excellent model for collaboration among a diverse range of advisors, prompting rich conversations and exchanges, and facilitating sustained engagement with the issues of visual and verbal communication through museum displays. The project demonstrates that museums can truly educate the public, not only about the distant past, but also about the living traditions that inform our lives today. By combining professional museum curatorial practices with a constitutionally appropriate framework for teaching about religion, the project has the potential to set new precedents in promoting civic conversations about the role of the sacred in our society.

Submitted by Barbara Matilsky

The potential of visual expression in objects with sacred content is limitless. It is an expression of the artist's personal interpretation of sacred content filtered through his/her assimilation (or at times, rejection) of traditional beliefs and conventions of representation. The only limits are those that reside within the viewer him/herself, i.e., lack of understanding/empathy for the work's sacred content or the way that it is represented. Verbal representation of objects with a sacred content is a different story. Language can potentially describe or explain sacred content in a way that deepens our experience of an object. However, unless we invent a new palette of words, we are limited and often unable to convey the essence of spiritual content.

Submitted by Amy Nelson

Religious art, for the devoted, often serves a function. The object may have been used in a ceremony or a daily ritual. Or perhaps it was used to foster reflection and contemplation. In a museum setting, the religious object should somehow tell a story about the relationship between it and the worshipper or the worshipper and the beloved, via the object – whatever the case may be. People can relate to human emotions and relationships. Talking about objects as objects only may limit the discussion and maintain a barrier between the visitor and the "unfamiliar" piece of work. It's important to emphasize the function of the object in as accessible and un-alienating terms as possible.

When writing cards, we need to put ourselves in the minds of the visitor, remembering the questions, "what? why? when? where? and how?" Why does this Hindu sculpture have four faces, each looking in a different direction? Where was it used? How was it used and how often? Would a family have this object in their home? Would it be this big or smaller?

While it's not easy to replicate a "sacred space" within the walls of an art museum, we can still offer the visitor snapshots of the worshippers' experience. We can use the museum space in new ways. For example, how might a subtle audio component help "fill out" the experience and make it more "real" for the visitor? What about placing a prayer rug in the direction of Mecca – on the floor? Or providing a sampling of some of the spices that would be used in a spice box?

Submitted by Charles Orzech

> When museums are seen as contact zones their organizational structure as a collection becomes an ongoing historical, political, moral relationship – a power charged set of exchanges.
> – James Clifford, *Routes* (1997: 192)

Museums are worlds in miniature, and like the world, they are the product of cultural and religious interaction. If museums are places of cultural and religious contact, and if we wish to promote a pluralistic encounter of religious voices in them, then we must strive to foreground this social interaction.

This effort can be pursued in several ways. First, great care should be taken to structure the museum to foreground historical and contemporary religious interaction. In doing so we can push to the background everything that encourages use of the museum as a catalogue to be browsed randomly in social isolation. Second, we can encourage religious communities to take a role in the display and use of objects in the collection. Third, we can provide "thick" descriptive and illustrative material for key objects in the collection, being especially careful to unpack the metaphoric worlds of certain objects and their role in religious practice and cultural interaction.

Submitted by David Power

In our discussions the last three years, there has been a strong focus on how galleries and museums can give the right information about objects displayed: what information, how to present it. This is surely vital and promotes understanding between people of different faiths, or speaks of religion to visitors who do not have a religious faith.

A second focus has been on the questions viewers ask/may ask and on how to respond to these.

We have not talked much about how people may grasp the artistic value of objects displayed or of how the aesthetic may address viewers. While each object has its proper setting in its own faith tradition and information tells viewers of this, may the object in its form speak to viewers and raise "meaning" issues? It seems that for all their particularity, religious objects (like texts) may say something beyond the limits of a people of a particular faith. For a genuine dialogue, we may ask how to let objects address the viewer by what they express of the holy. From the particular of each representation, can anyone be called, invited, challenged, to a sense of the holy?

At present in the Sackler Asian Gallery in Washington, D.C., there is a display of statues of the Buddha from a Buddhist shrine in China. The gallery displays them well and provides historical information, as well as information on how artistic forms changed over time in presenting the figure of the Buddha. Whether by design or not, there is however one statue that stands apart, in its own corner, and before which one can stand, a little apart from the melee of museum visitors. It is the face that is striking, with that peculiar mixture of a sense of the sublime and a welcoming compassion which can catch anyone's attention, whatever one may know or not know about Buddhism.

I was also thinking of the display of the Hindu linga in the Ackland, with the problem that it is totally outside its worship setting. Westerners tend to see only the male genitals. Does one have to come upon such a symbol in the dark centre of a Hindu Temple or washed by the waves on the seashore outside Madras, to be moved by its call to an appreciative awareness of a flow of world energies? Or what of the Adult/Child figure addressing a viewer in the painting we looked at last year? Whatever faith one brings, does the giving of this form to an emanation of Word, of address, coming from "elsewhere" have significance?

The issue then is perhaps how to combine information about objects to promote understanding of the faith traditions to which they belong, and letting them stand forth as "art" objects that can address even when distanced from a specific religious setting.

Submitted by Pat Phelan

The task of presenting art from another culture requires that we find the means to present it from its context rather than from our perspective. This requires a commitment by the museum staff to lay aside their values in order to learn something of the culture, language, significance, and use of the piece.

In describing religious art, I feel it is important to use terms from the language in which the art is/was practiced and to define them in order to help the viewer get beyond the cultural assumptions so heavily reinforced by our common language.

The museum also has the potential, and perhaps the responsibility, to create a space in which to present its art that encourages the viewer to go beyond any language, words and understanding about the work, no matter how accurate, so he may enter its living presence.

Submitted by Anantanand Rambachan

Murti: Challenge and Opportunity

The display of Hindu *murtis* (icons) in a museum setting offers both opportunity and challenge. These icons continue to be a part of the living Hindu tradition and the visual apprehension of an icon (*darshan*) constitutes an act of worship. The challenge here is one of presenting the object in a non-traditional setting, but doing so in a manner that is faithful to Hindu practice and self-understanding. At the same time, the museum needs to be cognizant of the fact that murtis are displayed in a religio/cultural context that is deeply suspicious of imaging the absolute and is prone to equating murti with idol. This offers an opportunity for the museum to educate the visitor by making him conscious of his assumptions and facilitating the possibility of experiencing the murti through Hindu eyes. In creatively responding to the balance of challenge and opportunity, the museum can meaningfully cater to the needs of the faithful and the inquisitive.

Submitted by Beth Shaw McGuire

Objects with sacred content in museums are limited in their inherent effectiveness to teach about religion, even when presented with ample interpretive materials and other primary resources near them. A museum cannot ensure visitors' conceptual understanding of the abstract religious and aesthetic concepts related to objects, or the faith that informs them. Such understanding comes from repeated experiences with art, information, and people that are interdisciplinary and multisensory. Developing this understanding requires repeated periods of interaction in front of and with the objects themselves that include the voices of a faith's practitioners. Just as it takes learning, practice, and experience to become an active practitioner of a faith, it takes those same processes to become a thoughtful viewer who can articulate the relationship between the visual and verbal elements of a faith and the objects that were created for it.

That being said, objects with sacred content do have the unique ability to attract and intrigue individuals who are not practitioners of a given faith to examine and consider images from that faith. This is particularly important in a museum environment – one often perceived as a more objective and egalitarian than other social spaces in American society.

The museum environment can also encourage visitors to consider the meaning and value that objects with sacred content may have for them from a variety of perspectives – [their value] religiously, technologically, aesthetically, culturally, and socially. It can be designed and created to address viewers and readers at different cognitive and emotional stages of development, and has the capacity to acknowledge that viewers and readers have different religious, educational, and cultural perspectives, beliefs, and practices that inform their approach to information about others' faith or their own, if they have one.

Submitted by Ruth Slavin

Museums matter when they provide the motivation and opportunity for questioning what we think we know and invite us to become curious, both inside ourselves and out loud. Museum professionals must make a commitment to fostering the deepest, best, and most important conversations we can, otherwise we are cultural sideshows awash in trivia. While conventional practices may be useful guideposts for visitors, "the way we have always done it" should not be used to block new modes or subjects for conversation.

Submitted by Tom Tweed

Religious Mediation, Variable Muteness, and Museum Display:
Visual Communication and Verbal Representation in Exhibitions

My reflections on this project, which has explored the limits and potential of visual communication and verbal representation in exhibitions of art with religious content, have led me to three inter-related hypotheses about the importance, interpretation, and display of religious artifacts:

1 *Religion.* Religious artifacts matter. Artifacts mediate religion, so noting how visual culture negotiates meaning and power for devotees is a central task for those who want to understand religion. Religion's meaning-making function entails more than doctrinal assertions about the nature of things. Religions are not just beliefs, or even the expression of beliefs. Religions provide orienting tropes – including metaphors, similes, myths, and symbols – that function as the figurative tools for constructing imagined worlds. Those tropes are anchored in artifacts and enacted in ritual, and they are passed on to future generations by institutions like the family, the school, the monastery, the church, and the temple. It is in this sense that visual culture is central to religion.[1]

1 When I suggest here that artifacts "anchor" symbols I am following the suggestion of the archeologist Steven Mithen. He has talked about artifacts as "anchors" of religious symbols that cross cognitive domains and argued that "religious ideas that are presented in material form gain survival value for the process of cultural transmission." Steven Mithen, "Symbolism and the Supernatural," in Robin Dunbar, Chris Knight, and Camilla Power, eds., *The Evolution of Culture: An Interdisciplinary View* (New Brunswick, New Jersey: Rutgers University Press, 1999), 162, 164.

2 *Interpretation.* Religious visual culture is more or less mute. It is less mute either when the artifact includes verbal elements that prescribe a meaning for viewers who know the vernacular or when an object without verbal content includes polyvalent symbolic referents that limit the range of meanings for viewers with cultural fluency – even if they do not unambiguously identify a single referent. So, for example, the late-nineteenth century watch and compass in the Ackland's collection might say little to most contemporary American viewers. They might be able to identify it as a pocket watch, but for the most part the object will remain mute. However, for a North Indian Shi'a Muslim it might overflow with meanings. That culturally fluent viewer might notice that concentric circles of calligraphy decorate the polychromatic exterior of the brass pocket watch, which was made in Switzerland in the late-nineteenth century for a North Indian Muslim. That viewer might note the Urdu inscription and Arabic prayers and verses addressed to the five holy persons of Shiism. The interior includes a clock to determine the time for daily worship (*salat*), which Islamic ritual prescriptions suggest should be performed at dawn, noon, mid-afternoon, sunset, and night. The compass in the stem also helps to discern the direction toward Mecca. Muslims face toward the *Kaaba* in Mecca during daily worship, and so the compass orients the devotee in space. All of this would have been available to that Muslim viewer. For the culturally fluent observer, then, the artifact might say a great deal not only about that form of Islam but about the ways that religions orient devotees in time and space. Other viewers would miss most of those meanings.[2]

3 *Display.* Since artifacts mediate religion by anchoring tropes, it can be very helpful to employ art exhibitions to communicate the meanings of objects – from paintings and sculptures to domestic furnishings and ritual implements. However, since those objects will be more or less mute,

2 On the Muslim pocket watch see Carl Ernst, *Following Muhammad: Rethinking Islam in the Contemporary World* (Chapel Hill and London: University of North Carolina Press, 2003), 154.

depending on the nature of the artifact and the cultural fluency of the viewer, the public display of religious artifacts in an officially secular and religiously diverse culture should not assume that objects speak as loudly or clearly to all viewers. Rather, museum officials should accommodate a wide range of observers with varying levels of cultural fluency. That means layering written and oral interpretations that accompany objects, so that viewers can choose the sort of experience they want or need – from a more unscripted encounter with a culturally familiar artifact to a more enriched introduction to an object that remains mostly mute at the first viewing.

Submitted by Meera Viswanathan

What has become increasingly clear to me in the *Five Faiths* Colloquies is that we are no longer concerned merely with the aesthetic, cognitive, or even spiritual functions of museums that exhibit sacral works as art, but rather increasingly with their civic function in shaping the thinking of a heterogeneous population in order to ready them to accept their roles as members of a pluralistic and predominantly secular culture that is, at least putatively, the United States today.

What does it mean not only to place objects from different faith traditions side by side, but also sacral objects amidst secular ones, as well as those that may be perceived to bridge or oppose the two domains (i.e., secular works invoking sacral topics ranging from those of Pamela Singh to Andres Serrano)? The role of language in all of this must be hermeneutic: to juxtapose meaningfully, to mediate, and to uncover possibilities between and among. The goal is not identity but delineation. Rather than relying on its assertive function, language in this context serves to call attention to the provisional, contingent, and experimental nature of understanding itself.

Submitted by Ray Williams

America's recent immigration patterns have resulted in the most religiously diverse nation on earth. Art museums with collections of ritual objects can play an important role in creating a tolerant, vibrant, multifaith society. Museums must put our collections to work in new ways. Works of religious art naturally stimulate curiosity and reward thoughtful consideration with information and insight into related beliefs and practices. The relative safety of the museum environment and its social authority make it an ideal setting for exploring unfamiliar, even challenging, territory. To make the vital social contribution for which they are so well suited, museums must provide opportunities for people of faith to contribute their perspectives to a rich interpretive program, to participate as volunteers and advisors, and to build relationships across cultural boundaries.

Submitted by Christopher Wilson

Making Room for Religious Interpretation in the Museum and Classroom

Though the *Five Faiths Project* concentrates on museum exhibitions, I have found that it has important implications for teaching as well. To take one example: a Puerto Rican student in one of my classes recently embarked on a research project dealing with the Virgin of Guadalupe. Though the image is believed by many Hispanic Catholics to be of divine origin, the student encountered research that discounts such claims and offers instead the name of a possible artist and earthly artistic prototypes for the image. Not surprisingly, the student wondered whether serious academic work requires that she override her religious beliefs with a "scholarly" tone of skepticism. In the classroom and in academic research, as well as in the museum setting, we must work to make room for religious ways of seeing in the presentation of religious ideas and images.

Submitted by Carolyn H. Wood

In *Resonance and Wonder*, Stephen Greenblatt suggests that museums find a balance between two exhibition models. One evokes and, ideally, explains "the complex, dynamic cultural forces from which art emerged." The other isolates art so that it retains its power to command "intense, enchanted looking." I think we will be successful if we can prompt what he calls "resonant wonder," but I also know that Greenblatt's goal raises issues for museums exhibiting works with sacred content. By accepting his challenge, museum professionals must overcome any reluctance they might have to create the conditions that enhance such works' potential to elicit feelings of awe, devotion, veneration, wonder. But those professionals must also, in collaboration with scholars and faith practitioners, provide what I call "affirmative actions" that enable works of art not just to elicit awe but to engage visitors in a thoughtful, empathic understanding of cultural and ritual contexts. The question is: how can we have religious art promote greater appreciation for confessional experiences without destroying a desirable balance between explaining and inspiring, that is, without having the art become confessional?